# A Shakespearean Actor Prepares

# A Shakespearean Actor Prepares

Adrian Brine

and

Michael York

A Smith and Kraus Book

Published by
Smith and Kraus, Inc.
177 Lyme Road, Hanover, NH 03755
www.SmithKraus.com

Copyright © 2000 by Adrian Brine and Michael York

*Cover and Text Design by Julia Hill Gignoux, Freedom Hill Design*
*Cover Photo by Paul Ronald:* Lucentio (Michael York) disguised as a schoolteacher
waits in the garden to give Bianca (Natasha Pyne) her lessons. Scene from
*The Taming of the Shrew,* starring Elizabeth Taylor and Richard Burton as Katherine
and Petruchio. Directed by Franco Zeffirelli for Columbia Pictures, 1967.

First edition: May 2000
8 7 6 5 4 3 2 1

Brine, Adrian.
A Shakespearean actor prepares / by Adrian Brine and Michael York. — 1st ed.
p. cm.
Includes bibliographical references.
ISBN 1-57525-059-4 (cloth)  ISBN 1-57525-189-2 (pbk.)
1. Shakespeare, William, 1564–1616—Dramatic production.
2. Acting. I. York, Michael. II. Title.
PR3091 .B75  1999
792'.028—dc21    99-048900

# CONTENTS

# ACKNOWLEDGMENT

I would like to thank the Collège de la Commission communautaire française, Brussels, for a subsidy that helped toward the writing of this book.

A.B.

The publication of this book resulted from the happy alphabetical accident of *W* being close to *Y*. A letter from Marisa Smith to that great Shakespearean actress, Irene Worth, was inadvertently addressed to me. This initiated a correspondence with Marisa, then a conversation, and, ultimately, this collaboration.

Both Adrian and I would like to thank Marisa for her enlightened seven-year stewardship of our book, and for her words of encouragement made all the sweeter by annual gifts of local maple syrup.

We would also like to thank Richard Brestoff for his editorial assistance and Julia Hill Gignoux for coping so generously with reams of rewrites and for her elegant book design.

We are indebted to all three for coordinating our bihemispherical efforts. For, as Hamlet observed,

> O 'tis sweet
> When in one line two crafts directly meet.

M.Y.

# NOTE

This is not a how-to-do-it manual. It contains no systems, rules, or instructions, and it prescribes no special technique or style. How could it, since Shakespeare created nearly a thousand roles, and each is a case apart. Besides, we are dealing with a playwright who learned his job at the workplace, and who quickly overtook his contemporaries who were held back by their too great respect for theories and traditions.

Shakespeare knew more about the art of acting and the art of the theater than any playwright before or since, and so while he gave his actors seemingly impossible tasks to fulfill, creating often superhuman characters and setting them in situations that stretch the imagination to its limits, at the same time he provided them with keys to how this can be achieved. Nearly all the questions about how he can best be played find their answers within the lines themselves, if only we can decode them. But often this demands that players jettison some preconceived ideas about what acting is, and approach him with an open mind.

He was himself a distinguished actor (we find his name heading the list of "Principal Actors in all the Plays") in the first collected edition—though he was not a star; and unlike Molière, who *was* a star and who was most inspired in the roles he wrote for himself, he spread his talent generously, giving even the small parts something challenging to do, something to *act*.

Many of the problems actors have with Shakespeare arise from their not drawing a clear line between his writings themselves, and what they have dreamed up about him, or read and seen elsewhere. Traditions, theories, other players' performances, only get in the way. We believe in taking a good, hard look at what he actually wrote. This will entail watching him at work, at a time when the English theater was being reinvented, and the English language was being formed. The plays abound with wells of energy, which, when tapped, will galvanize an actor's fantasy and liberate his talent. In this book we locate those wells.

N.B.

Most of the examples quoted in the text are from Shakespeare's best-known plays—notably *Hamlet* (with which, it can be assumed, most people are familiar). Further, a working knowledge of *Macbeth, Othello, As You Like It,* and *Henry IV* will be helpful, and a certain familiarity with *Henry V*—especially the Chorus' speeches. Besides, it is useful to have a copy of his Sonnets on hand...

"THE GLORY OF THE BANK."
Shakespeare's Globe Theatre on Bankside in his own day.
An engraving from about 1612.

*Courtesy of the Guildhall Library.*

Exterior of Shakespeare's Globe Theatre.
Sam Wanamaker's reconstruction on London's South Bank.
First performance June 12, 1997.

*Photo by Richard Kalina.*

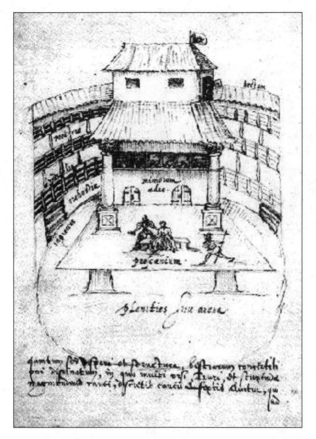

The Swan Theatre.
A Dutch university student drew this neighboring theater in 1596,
probably from memory.

Foreword by Michael York

# KEEP THY FRIEND UNDER THINE OWN LIFE'S KEY

drian Brine, like me, was born in England and grew up in the suburbs of London. Our schools, which nurtured an early enthusiasm for theater, were separated by mere miles. We both now dwell many leagues apart—I, by the California Pacific, he, by the boisterous North Sea in Holland where he continues to practice and perfect his craft as a director, actor, and teacher. Thus we tend to share an internationalist view of Shakespeare, having been conditioned to see him, not as exclusively English, but as a potent commentator on the fine points and foibles of all mankind.

Like me, too, Adrian has acted on screen as well as stage, but, in general, has focused his passions on the latter. His work in his adopted Low Countries has been recently acknowledged with many honors that crown a career in which cultural cross-fertilization has produced extraordinary results.

We met forty years ago—appropriately on stage in a theater—and, ever since, have been adding to those "hoops of steel" that bind a friendship. A correspondence began soon after that first encounter. I was about to go up to Oxford University from which

Adrian was a recent graduate and where he had made a considerable name for himself in the student theater. Now a professional actor and director, Adrian's epistolary skills were, paradoxically, usually most active at that stressful and demanding time, the dress rehearsal. Whether writing from "digs" or dressing room, the heightened creativity seemed to infuse his pen, rendering insights and observations especially acute: "I wonder why Westmoreland and Prince John *both* come in and tell York (Archbishop) how his role should be played. Certainly necessary in this production (of *Henry IV*)! I'm wondering, too, what Shakespeare had against the clergy that he always made them such boring old windbags. Perhaps it was personal enmity against the actors who played the parts?"

Though recently they have tended to metamorphose into faxes—"a fine volley of words, gentlemen, and quickly shot off"—most of these letters have somehow survived to "call back yesterday and bid time return."

## "SALAD DAYS, GREEN IN JUDGMENT"

As with countless other shining, morning-faced schoolboys before us, my initiation into the Shakespearean mysteries came in the classroom. There his texts seemed as exotic and foreign as those describing the Gallic War of one of his own dramatic heroes, Julius Caesar, which, with my same "small Latin and less Greek," also challenged comprehension. In this I resembled the twelve-year-old California schoolgirl that the late Professor G.E. Bentley recalled contacting him thus: "As I have an essay on Shakespeare to write next Thursday, I should be grateful if you would tell me *every thing* you know about him. I enclose a postcard for your convenience."

In my prep school, however, Shakespeare was fortunately prevented from being turned into the kind of boring old windbag that he himself seemed to anticipate and deplore: "small have continual plodders ever won / Save base authority from others' books." He was also presented where he rightfully belonged: on the stage as Bard, not Bookworm, giving full, thrilling voice to his verse. I had my first whiff of his heady allure, spellbound by a senior school production of *Cymbeline,* replete with that delightful conceit of boys dressed as girls dressed as boys, as in Elizabethan times. There were also Romans here too, as well as ancient Britons, magic potions, and even headless bodies to rivet attention when the meaning of the words became opaque.

I had just become aware of the muscular power and quaint beauty of this language—and also of incipient thespian ambitions—by being asked to read the King James Bible aloud in the school chapel. "In the beginning was the word," I piped in my childish treble, little realizing that I had hit upon its primacy as the building block of a performance by Shakespeare, that other principal architect of our language, who employed at least five times as many words as those found in the good book.

It is salutary to be reminded in the ensuing pages that, like the Bible, Shakespeare's plays were intended to be spoken aloud, not mumbled with the windy suspirations of forced academic breath. As will be demonstrated, it was the demands of rhetoric that shaped the very pattern of the verse. I am constantly astonished at Shakespeare's resilience: how he not only survives unspeakable vocal affronts and the vagaries and fads of passing time, but also the continual attempts to weigh down his buoyant lines with an over-accumulation of weighty commentaries and leaden annotations. Used judiciously, however, these same footnotes and appendices can anchor the text and prevent it from drifting off into obscurity.

I came to grips with this in my first attempt to perform Shakespeare—donning doublet and hose and my father's leather slippers as Bassanio in a school production of *The Merchant of Venice.* Chin now "rough and razorable" and voice newly broken, with lines of greasepaint aging to confirm this recent maturity, I was still innocent enough to be surprised that so many classical allusions, as well as complex phrases, had to be digested before the text became intelligible enough to be properly communicated. I felt kinship with Portia's overmodest confession: "The full sum of me / Is an unlesson'd girl, unschool'd, unpractised, / Happy in this, she is not yet so old / But she may learn."

As indeed I did, for Shakespeare provided an ongoing education for the mind and soul alike, imparting his own special brand of all-encompassing knowledge. The revelation was that this philosophy was not remote or intellectual. Even though his language could be complex and old-fashioned, he was often speaking in modern, relevant terms. The play dealt with issues of mercy and anti-Semitism, themes made even more relevant in the shadow of the recent Holocaust. "The oldest hath borne most; we that are young / Shall never see so much nor live so long."

The B.B.C. enhanced this educative process with frequent radio broadcasts of the plays, giving "To airy nothing / A local habitation and a name," and creating a potent theater of, and in, the mind. In a postwar age of limited travel, this also presented a literally wonderful way to venture abroad. The Chorus in Laurence Olivier's astonishing film of *Henry V* that, more than anything, had won me over to the Shakespearean cause, urged me to exercise those natural gifts of childhood, the "imaginary forces": "And thence to France shall we convey you safe, / And bring you back: charming the narrow seas / To give you gentle pass." As Bassanio, I made a further mental voyage to Italy, where Shakespeare's own muse travelled with such obvious delight.

But this textual tourism required some effort. As the Preface to the First Folio advises: "Reade him, therefore; and again, and againe." It seems almost too obvious to point out that unless the actor has mined the glossary, scrutinized the footnotes, and combed through the dictionary, becoming totally aware of the meaning of his lines, he will remain resolutely earthbound, his words perhaps full of sound and fury, but potentially signifying nothing. Particularly obscure words to be elucidated were those associated with practices that have fallen out of fashion—like falconry. However, even though "jesses" and "haggard" may now present problems, "hoodwinked" is as current as another neologism, "gloomy," describing Shakespeare's most famous character. They are representative of the two thousand vivid coinings that he poured into the language, forcing it into a new and often fantastic mold.

Even the seemingly straightforward can often assume an unexpected, illuminating subtlety. Take the simple word *Queen,* as in the celebrated "Queen Mab" immortalized by Mercutio in *Romeo and Juliet.* When working on his own production, Adrian noted, "I don't think it is 'Queen' (Majesty) but 'quean,' meaning 'old woman.' (Mrs. Capulet calls her husband an 'old cot-quean' when he's interfering in household matters.) 'Quean Mab' makes more sense—look at the second line: 'She is the fairies' midwife,' so she can't be Queen of the Fairies!"

## "THE PLAY'S THE THING"

Fortunately, I lived close enough to Shakespeare's real creative birthplace, the center of London, for frequent visits to its many theaters, so my early amateur, schoolbound discoveries were augmented by those made amidst the profession itself. The Old Vic—like Will's old theater, on the "wrong" side of the river Thames—presented a repertory of his plays. In fact it had been the first theater in the world to perform all of his works contained in the First Folio. True to the Vic's music hall origins, the fare was still varied, popular, and inexpensive. The Olympian heights of the upper balcony, or "the Gods," were eminently affordable and provided divine revelations.

"Behold, the heavens do ope, the Gods look down…" And

so we did to observe many a multifaceted lesson on "what a piece of work is man."

This theater was in strong contrast to its gilded West End cousins. Here the custom for matinee tea trays, chocolate chomping, and applauding the decor persisted—as did, fortunately, a continuing tradition of presenting Shakespeare, one that extended from David Garrick, to Edmund Kean, Henry Irving, Herbert Beerbohm Tree, Harley Granville Barker and up to Laurence Olivier and John Gielgud. I remember Gielgud's noble and mellifluous Prospero, whose calm authority impressed as much as did the wild tempest on stage, and demonstrated how a voice, properly used, could transfigure the spoken words.

I witnessed further verbal idiosyncrasies from Robert Atkins, at the "lean and slippered pantaloon" stage of his long career as an actor manager, playing Polonius in the suburbs in a rather creaky version of *Hamlet*. He, too, impressed with his authority, that took the obvious managerial form of audible stage directions to his cast, and also with his actor's ingenuity. Frequently losing his way in the text he would intone, "Couch we awhile and mark" and retire to the prompt corner to be re-acquainted with his lines and set on his faltering way again.

And yet, what lines these were! Some made "each particular hair to stand on end / Like quills upon the fretful porpentine." I can still remember the shock of delighted recognition at hearing for the first time such wisdom as:

"This above all, to thine own self be true / And it must follow, as the night the day, / Thou canst not then be false to any man."


## "FLAMING YOUTH"

*Hamlet* inundated my sixteen-year-old soul shortly afterwards when I successfully auditioned for a company called The Youth Theatre, that had been newly formed by a visionary and enterprizing schoolteacher named Michael Croft. His idea was to mount Shakespeare productions with large schoolboy casts, giving straightforward and unpretentious readings of the text made vivid by a superabundance of the raw energy and enthusiasm elsewhere manifest on school playing fields—and often in short supply in professional productions.

The Youth Theatre's purpose then—as now, having become a respected national and coeducational institution—was to give young people a sense of discipline and adventure, as well as academic and performance skills. We were like those famous troupes of boy actors, the little eyases, that so captivated Elizabethan audiences and Rosencrantz's censure. At the same time, we tried manfully to be as unlike as possible the "squeaking Cleopatra" that the great queen had so presciently predicted would "Boy my greatness."

Having youths interpret the women's roles seemed quite natural, especially as Shakespeare brilliantly and tastefully exploited this very limitation imposed on him. In the comedies, the lovers tend to trade bon mots not kisses, and even in the tragedies they join together, not so much in passion but, like Hamlet in Ophelia's grave, as a prelude to parting in death. Mark Rylance, the artistic director of the rebuilt Globe Theatre in London, recently vindicated this time-honored convention by playing the Egyptian Queen  himself in an acclaimed all-male staging of *Antony and Cleopatra*.

The Youth Theatre was immediately successful, performing *Hamlet* in the West End. Shakespeare headed the bill, as did Sir John Gielgud once more, for he preceded us into the Queen's Theatre, the scene of so many of his own youthful triumphs, this time with his celebrated one-man recital, *The Ages of Man*. Moreover, our company  patron happened to be Gielgud's great contemporary and partner, Sir Ralph Richardson. Their work was as legendary as it was inspirational. A serious, if subliminal, standard was thereby set, as well as a gentle reminder that our play was great poetry. Sir Ralph both encouraged and dismayed me by stating, in his kindly, avuncular tones, that I had "a face for Horatio" at a time when I was playing the faceless Voltemand, a man of few words and little importance, and was longing to unpack my heart with more words, words, words.

We took *Hamlet* on tour in Europe and were agreeably surprised to discover that our enthusiasm for Shakespeare was matched by that of our audience. After crossing "the main, that water-walled bulwark," and triumphing in Paris, we were fêted at each stage door in Holland by a gaggle of jiggling, ambling, and lisping Ophelias, all seemingly grateful for the rich gifts of our master poet dramatist and disconcertingly familiar with his lines.

*Hamlet,* however, was a play with which all adolescents—and certainly those, like me, infatuated with the theater—could easily identify. The prince loved actors and valued their work, making the emotional kinship with him even more conspiratorially daring, and providing joyful justification for my spending so much of my school vacation in thespian pursuits. On the practical side, moreover, his advice to the players was still one of the best acting lessons available, with its plea for a new kind of naturalism or "modesty of nature" to match the newfangled drama.

Temporarily reprieved from the drafty rigors of Tudor apparel with its constant mystery of wearing a cloak convincingly, we also performed a modern dress *Julius Caesar* in Italy in which I played Messala, and understudied Brutus. I was also Aumerle, another friend to the hero, in a more traditional *Richard II,* memorable for some clog-wearing courtiers in Amsterdam. The parallels between the two plays were striking: just as Brutus' idealistic honor conflicted with Antony's pragmatic strength, so self-righteous ineptitude was set against ruthless opportunism in the characters of Richard and Bolingbroke.

Brutus—not to mention Aumerle—was cautious, sober, and discreet, and one longed for a taste of Marc Antony's flamboyant vocal passion. In the same way, given his relative youth and neurasthenic self-regard as well as his exquisite language, one tended to identify with Richard and his cause and to despise Bolingbroke and his colorless authoritarianism. It was only later, with perhaps more practical experience of the world, that one began to see the characters in a more complex Shakespearean synthesis—that they were different sides of the same coin.

Writing several decades later during the dress rehearsal of one of his own francophone productions of *Richard II,* Adrian confirmed that indeed the play concerned "*les frères ennemis.*" "Richard and Bolingbroke are cousins, but since J. Gaunt was formerly Regent when Richard was a child, we can assume they were brought up together: brothers, they've now become the mighty opposites. Bol. is everything that Richard is not (prosaic, practical, calculating); Bol. is a leader (active, decisive, demagogic) but R is a *king*.

"I used to think the play was a concerto for soloist and orchestra: but it's a *double* concerto—for two men who hate each other because they used to love each other ('I hate the murderer, love him murdered.') Yes, maybe Elizabeth and Essex are somewhere behind it all! (We end with Bolingbroke alone on stage hugging Richard's corpse.)"

Later, involved in another version of the play, Adrian confided: "In the last two years I've read lots of professors' books on the play (garden imagery, sun imagery, Christ references, etc.) but no professor can *know* the play from the inside like a director who is working with *living* material in *space*. I appreciate those Oxford dons (in my day) who say, 'Just read Granville Barker' (though I've never unearthed what he wrote about Richard)."

## "SUCKING THE SWEETS OF SWEET PHILOSOPHY"

In 1961, this donnish world became mine as a student at Oxford University. Fortunately Shakespeare was experienced here both on the clamorous stage as well as in the hushed library and lecture hall, so I was able to give intellectual and acting skills a welcome polish. In a creative mix of town and gown, the university even shared a professional theater with a resident company. "Ignorance is the curse of God, / Knowledge the wing wherewith we fly to Heaven" and this multiplicity of opportunities to perform as well as learn seemed indeed paradisaical.

The various colleges also vied with each other in a profusion of productions in halls, cellars, quadrangles, and gardens. These last could provide an extravagant summertime setting for so many of the plays in the best florid Beerbohm Tree tradition. They reflected Shakespeare's abiding love for the garden imagery that Adrian mentioned: "Here's a marvelous convenient place for our rehearsal. This green plot shall be our stage, this hawthorn-brake our tiring-house." The pastoral comedies, with their Ardens and woodlands naturally benefited from this rus-in-urbis landscape. In such plays as *Twelfth Night* and *A Midsummer Night's Dream* especially, it served to point up the intended contrast between court and country. There was even a *Tempest,* where, by means of submerged runways, Ariel raced across a lake, "thorough flood, thorough fire," making quite plausible his boast that "Jove's lightning, the precursors / O' th' dreadful thunder-claps more momentary / And sight-outrunning were not."

It became quite apparent that, though Shakespeare could be acted with energy and enthusiastic instinctiveness, this was not always in his best interest. So, as if attending an unofficial drama school, the acting fraternity took itself very seriously, arranging voice and movement classes, and searching out books with similar intentions as this one. Adrian wrote helpfully about a production of *Othello* in which he was acting: "I suspect that Shakespeare should be played *very fast*, the emotions not acted phrase by phrase like a modern play but chunk by chunk. The days we tear through to catch a train, or to save overlapping with the second house, it takes on a new life. The Russian-Germanic way is *all wrong*. Lightly and gracefully: even the heaviest of plays."

His letters continued to inspire and confirm my own discoveries. Learning how to read the punctuation of a Shakespearean text like a musical score, and where best to breathe and emphasize, was vital research. Granville Barker indeed proved to be invaluable, especially his insight that Shakespeare had created, not just a new theatrical language that was strictly contained "within the framework of the verse," but a whole new style of acting that deplored grandiloquence and encouraged subtlety. All this enquiry was a useful counterweight to the ambient academic environment exemplified by the wag who punned that there were "footnotes at the bottom of his Arden!"

I was fortunate to be studying English language and literature, with easy access to different editions of Shakespeare's texts. The Bodleian Library alone contained two First Folios and forty-three Quartos. It was a revelation to see how these original publications, with their spare punctuation and compacted lines were so much more charged and vigorous than later editions that had been cleaned up and "corrected" in order to fit into a strict iambic pentameter scheme and to look good on the page.

The earlier linear density, one found was often deliberate, usually occurring at moments of maximum pressure both on the character speaking and on the situation described. Over time, the most widespread editorial offense was to ignore this and increase the number of printed lines, as well as punctuate in the middle of sentences. This academic aeration flew in the face of the original rhetorical intention, prompting Peter Hall's inflexible rule about Shakespearean acting: "Never, ever breathe in the middle of the line."

Sir Peter, incidentally, had been responsible for a memorable production of *Coriolanus* with Laurence Olivier and Edith Evans at the Shakespeare Memorial Theatre in nearby Stratford-on-Avon, and it was with some considerable anticipation that I had earlier gone on a schoolboy pilgrimage to see my screen idol playing the title role. "All places yield to him ere he sits down." Rarely sedentary, however, Olivier had injured himself performing a spectacular backwards death fall and was "off." "On" was his understudy, Albert Finney, so disappointment was minimized, but the episode illustrated both the fragility and ephemeral nature of stage performance and its inextricable connection with fate, and with fitness.

When I later became a member of his company, Olivier would set an example of regular workouts at the gym. Being "fat and scant of breath" was hardly compatible with eight performances a week, especially as so many plays demanded a dance or a duel at the end of the evening. No wonder that, in 1835, writing about Edmund Kean's Othello, John Forster reported: "Of late years Mr. Kean had always so much exhausted himself in the previous acts that he was obliged to rest on a sofa during his fearful dialogue with Desdemona to gather strength for the murder." Being an actor himself transformed Shakespeare into the most practical of playwrights. He addresses this very real problem of fatigue by giving his major protagonists "time out" in the penultimate act to "bend up every spirit to it's full height" for the emotional catharsis of the final one.

*King Lear* was one of the set texts of the Oxford English course. By a fortunate coincidence it also happened to be the subject of another great production at Stratford. Its director, Peter Brook, and his Lear, a still youthful Paul Scofield—reminiscent of the young man, Burbage, who had first fleshed out the wizened despot—combined to give a mesmerizing immediacy to the "vicious mole of nature" that afflicted Lear and precipitated his tragedy.

Brook's cutting of a crucial scene, where the servant offers to tend Gloucester's blinded eyes, set the play in unmistakable—and then fashionable—Beckettian territory. I still find it impossible to erase the image of Alan Webb—with whom I later acted in happier circumstances in my first Shakespeare film—staggering sightlessly around the stage as the appalled audience filed out for their uneasy intermission. It was performances like these that put the very nature of humanity in a mercilessly revealing spotlight, making the theater seem not just important, but essential.

As if to compensate for the universities' indifference to Shakespeare in his own day, there was now a long tradition of academic performance of his work, exemplified in my day by those duel dons of drama, Nevill Coghill at Oxford and George Rylands at Cambridge. Their productions maintained an equally traditional rivalry between the two institutions, one upheld by such progeny as Peter Brook, Peter Hall, Trevor Nunn, Ian McKellen, and, with respect, the humble authors of this little treatise.

Fortunately, both places encouraged a co-mingling of professional and amateur resources. Undergraduate casts would be bolstered with the addition of established actors, and professional directors would be invited not only to lecture but "produce" as it was still called. John Gielgud produced *Romeo and Juliet* for the Oxford University Dramatic Society with Peggy Ashcroft guest-starring as Juliet, and later, also for the O.U.D.S., a young Maggie Smith was recruited into *Twelfth Night.* Among other legends, I did see Sir Donald Wolfit, an actor-manager seemingly still gaslit in modern times, who was rounding off a celebrated, if controversial, career with recitals in the provinces. Or, as another wag put it: "Olivier is a tour de force and Wolfit is forced to tour."

However "Sir" (for, indeed, he was the prototype for Ronald Harwood's *The Dresser)* still had a great deal to offer. He had studied Shakespearean text under William Poel, with his back-to-basics approach after the fussy, visual literalness of most turn-of-the-century directors. Voice darkly orotund but diction exemplary, Wolfit's theatrical wisdom was grounded in practical reality— such as his advice to a fellow actor about to play Lear to "Get a small Cordelia."

Like most great actors he was a showman to the core; even

in less demanding roles than "The Dane," "The Thane," "The Moor," and "The Jew," he was the master of the "all passions spent" curtain call. Despite his threadbare and egocentric productions, Wolfit was nevertheless a keeper of the flame when it had guttered in postwar austerity a long time before the government came to its senses and nationalized the resources for Shakespearean production.

In 1962 Adrian wrote to me from Paris, where Sarah Bernhardt had once played Hamlet, and where, in the Théâtre Sarah Bernhardt, the Youth Theatre had presented *Hamlet*, reminding me that Wolfit's kind of one-man-band eccentricity was not exclusive to English actors. "Wish you could have been at (Jean-Louis) Barrault's *Hamlet*. The French would say bizarre. He'd borrowed a couple of tombstones with seats, which did for the throne and which he himself (being small I suppose) always sat on the back of with his feet on the seat. The costumes he'd got from a pageant about England. The King was dressed as Thomas à Becket; Ophelia was Titania, Polonius had a wizard's hat, so I suppose was Merlin, and Reynaldo came on as Robin Hood.

"M. Barrault marches about and plays Hamlet *with his fingers*. Yes he has his trouvailles all right. What will he get up to next one wonders. Ros. and Guild. catch him stroking one hand, held up high, with another, and making dove noises. He skewers Polonius and wipes the sword on Mother's red velvet bedspread. He marches out after the ghost with his sword over his shoulders like a rifle, and pinching his nose, as though he'd been wearing tight pince-nez. And he puts his hand up Yorick's skull and does glove-puppet acting; ending up by putting it on his own face to talk to Horatio. Actually I shouldn't mock this. That bit's never been so clear to me—Hamlet and death."

Joining the O.U.D.S., I played Prince John, complete with a neck-chilling Plantagenet pudding-basin haircut, in both parts of *Henry IV,* that epic panorama of feudal life. With regard to these English history plays, I had recently been enormously impressed with yet another extraordinary production by the recently renamed, in echo of earlier Elizabethan noble patronage, Royal Shakespeare Company.

An era of distinguished presentations, both at Stratford and in London, had just been inaugurated, *The Wars of the Roses* being Peter Hall's reworking of the *Henry VI* tetralogy with *Richard III*. Combined, they constituted one vast Marlovian morality play demonstrating how the sins of the fathers are inexorably visited on their hapless children. I saw the whole cycle in one day and it remains unforgettable. And relevant. The recent assassination of President Kennedy had confirmed how easy it still was to destabilize a nation with murder.

Pablo Picasso who, incidentally, has provided one of the most delightful portraits of Shakespeare in, quite appropriately, flowing pen and ink, noted that, "Art is a lie which tells the truth." In the same way, Shakespeare's English history plays are primarily imaginative recreations of the past where truth lies in the artistry rather than the factuality. Ben Jonson may have mocked his friend's ambition in recreating wars with little more than "three trusty swords and some few foot-and-a-half words." In doing so, however, Shakespeare demonstrated how the past was a guide to the present, shedding especially vivid light on that vexed question of how mankind is best governed.

There is a sense of his fusing together not just different words, but disparate worlds, as he merged the medieval with the modern. All human life is there, centered around, as it still is today, the royal court and the public tavern. Mouldy rubs plebeian shoulders with aristocratic Mowbray, Wart with Westmoreland. As in real life, the sublime coexists with the banal, and is even reflected in the verse: "The latest news is: I have to London sent/ The heads of Salisbury, Spenser, Blunt and Kent."

"Sounds like someone's unhappy translation of an opera libretto," Adrian commented, "There's nothing like this in Racine!" The concept of Shakespeare as a barbarian, though, seems to me one of the dimmest of the so-called Enlightenment whose philologists hobbled him in a grammatical stranglehold, reducing his roar of wild rhetoric to the murmur of polite poetics. Others blithely rewrote his tragedies with happy endings, Nahum Tate presuming to transform England's *Richard II* into *The Sicilian Usurper!* Even Charles Lamb, who did so much to promote interest in Shakespeare, claimed that *King Lear* was unactable and that the Bard was best read, thereby bowdlerizing these mammoth works into tasteful tales.

In more recent times Henry James saw Shakespeare as "the monster and magician of a thousand masks." Indeed, his fascination for theatrical camouflage and sleight of hand is used constantly to dramatic advantage, notably in *Henry IV* in the pivotal banishment scene. Just as Hamlet uses the actor's art to unmask reality, so Hal and Falstaff resort to role playing to cover the pronouncement of unpalatable truths. Elsewhere, and especially in the comedies, cross-dressing provides disguises that, at the same time profound and amusing, reveal as much as they conceal.

## "IN FAITH, HE IS A WORTHY GENTLEMAN, EXCEEDINGLY WELL READ..."

In 1963 Adrian was invited back to Oxford to direct "the wealthy curled darlings of our nation" in an O.U.D.S. production of *Othello.* By now a semi-seasoned professional, he was able to identify and resolve many of the problems facing a young cast that, I'm delighted to say, included myself playing Roderigo, "a gull'd gentleman," who was Desdemona's thwarted suitor and Iago's pathetic plaything.

"Professionals are like a machine; you start them acting and then you have to slow the machine down, put the brake on," Adrian confided to a student magazine. "Here you have to wind the machine up to get it going. Very few Oxford actors have the freedom to go through a scene and just let it happen to them. They're all the time stopping in the middle and accusing themselves of doing something wrong. On the other hand, the enormous amount of work and thought they put into a production makes them very valuable to work with."

I am still uncertain whether the university-trained actor has an advantage over his drama-schooled colleague, as the profession recruits from both sources. The essential requirement, it seemed, was not so much stage theory, but practical experience and personality. With this regard, Adrian also observed that, "The best way of working with an actor is to find his individuality and see how that works in the part. When you have to bring in things from the outside that the actor doesn't appear to have, then you have to see whether he hasn't got them buried somewhere. Often you find that he has."

Buried within me, I discovered a puzzled pugnaciousness that seemed well suited to Roderigo. The first line of the play was mine, an aggressive and aggrieved: "Tush, never tell me!" Like the "Who's there?" that opens *Hamlet,* it gave an explosive, high-energy start to the play, compelling attention.

I also had an energetic finale—a duel, the first in a long career of staged swordsmanship patiently, and often, painfully, acquired. One thought enviously of the Elizabethan actor for whom dueling, dancing, and music making were second nature: an integral part of the job and not an exotic addendum to the rehearsal process. My most memorable moment was arriving in Cyprus rolled up in a carpet, one of many directorial felicities that graced this production. I celebrated my twenty-first birthday touring France with the play—a rite of passage that seemed to accurately presage the ensuing years of maturity spent so happily in similar circumstances, certain that "it is the cause, my soul!"

"I'm still convinced that Roderigo is a better part than Cassio," Adrian wrote a quarter of a century later. "Sh. evidently had a pretty juv. lead in the company who couldn't act, and gave him roles like Cassio and Paris." Adrian acknowledged how the more one tackled Shakespeare, the more it seemed there was to learn and to be revealed: "(I've) discovered how much the play owes to the Faust legend: in Act 5 Othello goes on to the murder because he's somehow programmed by Iago—he must do it, to obey Iago, though his better nature tries to fight against it. (As Macbeth is somehow programmed by Mrs. Macbeth.)

"Discovered also that Emilia is really a comic role, more akin to the nurse *(R & J)*: W.S., keeping his feet on the ground in high tragic moments and channeling off irreverent laughter (as Pandarus does when Cressida's heart is breaking.) And Iago thinks he's *won* at the end—proved that the "Noble Moor" is really an animal at heart ("what you see, you see.") Finale, with Iago looking down mockingly at "the tragic loading of this bed."

At the end of my stay at Oxford I had graduated to playing leading roles, including a Romeo in a production that, after being performed in England, in Cornwall's romantic, open-air Minack Theatre, was taken on tour in Israel. The response was gratifying, confirming my growing awareness that Shakespeare's influence was truly international. Our costumes were those very ones used in a famous mold-shattering Old Vic *Romeo and Juliet* that had inflamed my youthful imagination, directed by Franco Zeffirelli—someone who would later immeasurably affect my own life and professional career. In it, he had banished languid English *sangfroid*, transforming the proceedings into a passionate *verismo* drama.

Somehow our splendid garments were lost en route in Venice, that center of so much Shakespearean intrigue, obliging us to perform in Israel in our own improvised modern dress, like refugees from the latest Shakespeare-based hit show, *West Side Story.* "So may the outward shows be least themselves." We were thus thrown back to Elizabethan basics, to the "unworthy scaffold" where the words themselves both dressed the characters and conjured up the dog-day Italian heat and the torch-lit nights. This, added to the exotic setting of this star-crossed story told under starry skies, gave a surreal quality to the piece.

"Dreams are *so* important in this play," Adrian noted. "Queen Mab isn't an exterior aria, as Granville Barker says. It's purely functional I discover. Romeo won't go to the ball because he's had a dream: Mercutio sets out to prove that dreams are all nonsense—"the children of an idle brain / Begot of nothing but vain fantasy." And Queen Mab is so small as to be insignificant. The fantasy of the speech is *against* Mercutio's natural character, which is earthy, materialistic and reality-loving: he switches it on just to show how easy it is to dream—anybody can do it—watch!"

Playing Romeo, I noticed that you could get away with a certain obscurity of diction, especially if the key words were boldly and persuasively spoken and the audience was lulled into a sort of benign trance by the accumulation of verbal felicities. Also, perhaps, by a certain lack of fresh air. Indeed it was John Gielgud who later assured me that during one hot matinee of *Hamlet,* he had intoned "Angels and ministers of grace defend me, get me a cup of tea," without the slightest untoward reaction from either his audience or stage manager!

I was forced into a similar absurdity by a fellow actor incarnating the Old Apothecary, who insisted on spoonerizing a key line, "My poverty, but not my will, consents." My enforced, earnest rejoinder, "I pay thy woverty and not thy pill" raised nary a murmur, pills and apothecaries presumably making some sort of acceptable sense!

Israel was then in a state of war with its Arab neighbors, giving further edge to the timelessness of this story of foes that "from ancient grudge break to new mutiny." The play appealed for a typically Shakespearean restraint and harmony. The Montagues and the Capulets reflected the tragic enmity that had also divided the houses of York and Lancaster, disharmonizing the nation from the ideal expressed in *Henry V,* where "high and low and lower, put into parts, doth keep in one consent, congreeing in a full and natural close, like music."

Performing without a set as well as without costumes seemed to liberate the production. It reminded me of the occasion when Laurence Olivier, acting Hamlet "on location" in the open air at Elsinore Castle, had also been forced to restage the play. Moved indoors by inclement weather, perhaps it was here that he discovered the freedom that a thrust stage provided—experience that he later put to good use in his Chichester Festival Theatre, the first open-stage theater built in England since Shakespeare's time, and in the auditorium that bears his name at the National Theatre in London.

Simplifying the decor also brought into sharp focus the visual irony that the undefined space provided. Juliet's balcony, for example, became her tomb. The ballroom gave way to a duelling ground. Adrian had noted the subliminal potency of this effect in his Belgian production of *Troilus and Cressida:*

"Diomedes and Cressida have their scene in exactly the same place that Troilus and she had their last scene; Hector is harangued by Andromache about the dangers of war in the same place that he is finally killed by the Myrmidons."

The single, resounding steel set for the entire sequence of Peter Hall's *Wars of the Roses*, further confirmed and brilliantly exploited this quality. Similarly Peter Brook's memorable *A Midsummer Night's Dream*, for the same company, was entirely contained in a plain white box full of fascinating stage tricks. Later, I would play a Hamlet in which a huge Nordic cross dominated the stage, serving with symbolic reverberations as altar, throne, and bed.

Realistic scenery was the stepchild of modern editing practices with their arbitrary inventions of specific—and restrictive—"locations." Even so brilliant and reformist a practioner as Stanislavski came to grief with some of his early Shakespeare productions by making them *too* realistic. There are reports of a

Chekovian cherry orchard in his *Julius Caesar*—perhaps in unconcious genuflection to that master of realism.

My final Oxford outing in Shakespeare was a *Twelfth Night* that commemorated the 400th anniversary of its author's birth. It was gratifying to learn that the time-honored mixture of high poetry, low comedy, mistaken identity, and sexual reversal still had the power to draw the town. I played Orsino, a typical melancholy lover in love with love, rather as Romeo had been with Rosaline before Juliet gave him a fateful taste of real passion. This time, our costumes had been updated to the eighteenth century as if in quaint genuflection to the play's subtitle, *What You Will.*

"Is it a world to hide virtues in?" In my case, it was not, for I used my performance as a shop window for future theatrical career representation. Appearing in at least three productions a term, I was by now an experienced amateur actor, and even on vacations had worked backstage with professional companies. My love for the drama was like Orsino's for Olivia: "As hungry as the sea / And can digest as much." I was reluctant to compromise this passion, as I felt so many of my own teachers had, by staying in relatively safe circles and vicariously pursuing the actor's life. The theater beckoned as a career as irresistibly as the ghost waving on Hamlet.

And so in 1964, I exchanged tutor for agent and Oxford's hallowed groves for the uncharted wastes of "The Business," becoming that longed-for "brief chronicler," a professional actor. "This above all, to thine own self be true," Polonius' advice to Laertes, a youth in similar change of circumstances, echoed urgently, and I felt that unless I heeded the calling, I could not happily live with myself. Certainly Hamlet's soul-searing search to find the proper course gave further strong example.

I took a traditional, well-trodden and in this case, far-flung path by joining a repertory theater company in Dundee, Scotland. Here, modern farce was presented cheek-by-jowl with Shakespearean tragedy, ensuring that, in this weekly celebration of Jacque's "seven ages of man," you were the "juv." one week and a whiskery old dodderer the next. I was pleased that Adrian came north to direct several productions; he even gave his Friar Francis and Second Watchman in *Much Ado*. As the phrase in *The Merchant of Venice* has it, "we turned over many books together," as well as many ideas and, inevitably among actors, endless stories about our theatrical forbears and contemporaries. As another phrase from the same play put it, our world became both literally and figuratively "a stage where every man must play a part."

With one production swiftly following another in repertory, our theater seemed "like a fashionable host, / That slightly shakes his parting guest by the hand, / And with his arms outstretched as he would fly, / Grasps in the comer." The dearth of rehearsal time seemed to concentrate the mind and focus energies. However, one was often catching the nearest way. Playing the callow Claudio in *Much Ado,* I was puzzled by the extravagant length of time allotted to our exits and entrances. All was made clear, however, when it was revealed that our director had borrowed not just the costumes, but the prompt copy from a recent production at London's Regent's Park Open Air Theatre, where actors were required to make their entrances via lengthy promenades over the grass!

Robert Atkins had founded this theater and, with each of my own entrances, I could hear echoes of a famous story in which he had rebuked another young actor as inexperienced as myself: "Scenery by the Almighty, words by our Master Poet Dramatist, direction by—someone not bad—and then *you* bloody well come on!" The great David Garrick—himself a notable Benedick—had similarly upbraided the same kind of ambitious tyro: "No. No. You may humbug the town some time longer as a tragedian, but comedy is a serious thing."

But it was Garrick himself who, in turn, had been chided by his old schoolmaster, Dr. Samuel Johnson, over that vexed question of the emotional involvement appropriate to a Shakespearean performance—an essential issue addressed in the ensuing pages. Garrick insisted that Shakespeare had "dipped his pen in his own heart," but the cooler, more logical Johnson argued that if Garrick really shared the same feelings as some of his more iniquitous heros, then he too should suffer their same violent fate at the end of the performance!

It was absorbing work and I relished its variety. Despite finding it hard to accept that one was actually being paid to play Shakespeare, I felt a new freedom—and a new responsibility. The Bard's reputation—the immortal part of himself—was in my eager novice's hands that, like his Dyer's hand, were now irrevocably steeped in my newfound trade. That torch that had flamed over the centuries, illuminating the most obscure details of the human personality with a time-defying truth, had been handed on.

This was made even more apparent when, the following year, I was invited by both the Royal Shakespeare Company and Laurence Olivier's recently formed National Theatre Company to join their ranks. One was immediately faced with the dilemma that continually confronts all actors: choice. What to do next? Where to go? To accept or to refuse? "If to do were as easy as to know what were good to do, chapels had been churches, and poor men's cottages princes' palaces." In the theater, unlike most professions, there is no set pattern of progress from apprentice spark to executive luminary. All one had to rely on were fine-tuned instincts: the "divinity that shapes our ends, / Rough-hew them how we will." I was offered small speaking roles by the R.S.C, but something prompted me to accept Olivier's offer to join him at the National, walking on in a production of *Much Ado* to be directed by Zeffirelli.

We were based at the Old Vic theatre, that august cultural temple that had born witness to so much Shakespeare worship and where myself and Adrian had been such avid acolytes. Its new high priest, Olivier, set a noble example with his dedication to the work both on stage and in rehearsal. As well as being an exemplar of physical fitness, he stressed the importance of ancillary class work on voice and movement. I learned to breathe from the diaphragm and to give the iambic pentameter a long line, and generally filled in those gaps occasioned by lack of formal drama schooling.

The old yet again entwined with the new as the Bard was rediscovered and re-assessed, and never more so than in Zeffirelli's "Sicilian" version of *Much Ado.* Now graduated magna cum laude from O.U.D.S. neophyte to leading lady, Maggie Smith gave a star-dancing turn as Beatrice. Unrecognizable in thick, black wig and Mafioso mustache, I was also Second Watchman as well as Gentleman, contributing gleefully to the potpourri of Mediterranean accents, and even snatches of opera, that replaced the usual rustic English stage vowels emanating from that bucolic thespian locale, "Mummersetshire."

It was a measure of Shakespeare's genius and generosity that he survived such unusual treatment. Nay, he thrived, for it even served to enhance the exuberant Italian qualities inherent in the play. "Sigh no more, ladies" was transformed into a tonsil-teasing Neapolitan love song while such awkward moments as Beatrice's "Kill Claudio" were now rationalized. Long upsetting Anglo-Saxon sensibilities, in this hot-blooded setting as exotic as Claudio's "rotten orange" imagery, it became a natural vendetta.

It was at this time that Olivier was embellishing his reputation with a negroid Othello that fulfilled his avowed intention of providing a showcase of acting for acting's sake. His voice plummeted an octave and his signature makeup and swaying gait was of a startling authenticity. (Maggie Smith, also his acclaimed Desdemona, and yet still the recipient of his criticism for her singular, unorthodox vowel sounds, once peeked round his dressing room door while he was still smothered in Moorish makeup and enunciated perfectly, "How now brown cow!")

There was another famously revealing occasion when his performance was so extraordinary that not only the audience, but the cast, were aware of the magic being wrought on stage. Both applauded him at the final curtain. Olivier's reaction, however, was to storm off to his dressing room and, on being reassured that he had surpassed himself that night, to bewail the fact that he knew he had done so, but he didn't know *how* he had done so, so how could he be sure that he could do so again? It came as a humbling revelation to realize that the learning process was an ongoing one and, however experienced, one never quite knew the answer.

Shakespeare, however, seemed to have the uncanny ability of tapping into a stream of universal knowledge. "The longer you live, the more you experience, the more you find Shakespeare has *been there before*," Adrian wrote in confirmation. "I mean, you undergo an emotion, a thought occurs to you, you think this is silly, it's only me that imagines such things—and a few days later you find it in Shakespeare. I'm constantly finding that life imitates Shakespeare."

Certainly my own life reflected this. All too recently an amorous undergraduate, I was invited by Zeffirelli to the real Italy to play Lucentio, the young student and lover, in his screen version of *The Taming of the Shrew*. Filming in Rome, my wide-eyed excitement totally unfeigned, I rode into a re-creation of medieval Padua and into the unknown new realm of cinema, leaving behind the familiar purlieus of the theater—"As he that leaves / A shallow plash, to plunge him in the deep / And with satiety seeks to quench his thirst."

# "HIS WHOLE FUNCTION SUITING WITH FORMS TO HIS CONCEIT"

Although film acting required a shift of technique—something that I will attempt to address in the Afterword—the search for plausible characterization was the same. As with rehearsal of a stage play, you had to plan out the role beforehand, while still allowing for a certain flexibility that would permit interaction with fellow performers and the physical demands of the setting, not to mention those of the director. This was especially crucial as scenes were rarely filmed sequentially, calling for imaginative leaps and specific commitments.

Fortunately, playing Lucentio was relatively straightforward, the only sticky part being the daily gluing on of an elegant beard to set off the curled locks and renaissance finery. There was little of the kind of subtext so beloved of Stanislavski, where a character who says, "I can't find my galoshes," really means, "I hate my life in provincial Russia."

"People don't lie in Shakespeare," Adrian suggested. If someone says he 'met a fool in the forest,' he probably did; and Iago, Richard III and Prince Hal all tell the audience they're going to be deceitful first."

One looked for this internal truthfulness of character—most often revealed in soliloquies and asides—that identified the soul rather than the outward personality. This was the "secret life" that the great Harley Granville Barker had emphasized in his writings about Shakespeare.

"A key phrase, I think," Adrian noted. "W.S. showing us indeed the secret lives of Hamlet, Richard II, Lear, Macbeth—the things they whispered to their pillows were different from their public images. Hamlet seems to me a *different person* when he is 'alone': feelings boil up inside him when he's in company, and boil over when he's solitary."

"I have unclasp'd to thee the book even of my secret soul,'

says Orsino to Viola, and often a play itself would seem to contain the same hidden agenda—a secret other drama embedded in it. "Find that and you've found the key," Adrian confirmed. "For example, *Henry IV,* as everyone knows, has a morality play inside it—Hal, torn between vice and virtue (Falstaff and Father)."

Later, in 1980, Adrian would add: "Shakespeare, for the English is one thing: for Continentals, who not only don't get the jeweled language, but get him in modern words (and completely and immediately comprehensible), he comes across as something else. What if his stuff was written last week? I see Tom Stoppard's preparing a lecture on theater as text opposed to theater as event—a valid distinction, which often gets forgotten."

"You get additional barriers when foreigners play Shakespeare. They are more respectful than we are, because less familiar. They find it hardest to rise to the great moments—a whole life summed up in the way an actress says 'I am dying, Egypt, dying,' or an actor, 'She should have died hereafter.' We think quite often that many British actors are crummy: but one misses their fantasy and panache."

Working on Shakespeare in these fresh and unfettered circumstances seemed to liberate Adrian's imagination: "Came up with the idea that the Chorus in *Henry V* is a great role, and W.S. should have thought of him sooner. So why shouldn't he appear in *Richard II* and *Henry IV* also? Frequently there were roles in these plays whose function is purely descriptive—look at Vernon in *Richard II.* He's only there to describe poetically the young Hal 'Plum'd like estridges'; look at Burgundy in *Henry V,* his description of France in disarray. Let him be present and play small practical parts—the gardener in *Richard II* who's written for a good verse speaker; immediately the four plays have a unity, and the 'unworthy scaffold' idea prevents the director from Beerbohm Tree spectacularity."

In a production of *Romeo and Juliet* Adrian even transformed my old nemesis, the Old Apothecary, into a much more significant figure by making him the Chorus, "a sort of fate/death figure who appears among the crowd sometimes when something's looming. R & J both have so many presentiments of their own deaths, dreams of destiny still hanging in the stars."

But Adrian would also occasionally confess: "I often feel I have an albatross about my neck when it comes to Shakespeare—the weight of too much Bradley, Granville Barker, Dover Wilson, Quiller-Couch; too many Old Vic and Shakespeare Memorial Theatre Productions seen at a formative age; too much Gielgud and Olivier stamped on my retina.…

"There's a young Flemish director (Ivo Van Hove), who does things with Wm. Sh. that make my blood tingle, though he doesn't *know* as much about W.S. as I do, so expressly I try to do W.S. as often as I can to try and break free from my over-literary approach."

And yet, teaching at drama school all those "hungry little nestlings, beaks open for any tidbits I've picked up on my flights," Adrian could acknowledge the benefits of this literary training: "We're doing Shakespeare at the moment. What an advantage one has being English! I mean, being cognizant of all the groundwork that's been done by Poel and Granville Barker (not to mention Wilson Knight and Quiller-Couch). I realize that foreign directors tackle Shakespeare without knowing anything of these gentlemen. Maybe they've read Jan Kott—which for me is like trying to learn the piano without a teacher."


## "AND ONE MAN IN HIS TIME PLAYS MANY PARTS"

As I think this book will demonstrate, Adrian is a born teacher, and all his accumulated wealth of academic wisdom, allied to his international experience of practical stagecraft, has produced remarkable results.

In the mid 1970s Adrian described a *Merry Wives* he was directing in Brussels: "Not everyone's favorite play—'No-one,' as Dr. Johnson said, 'ever wished it longer'—but a clever scenario for character actors with funny faces, in which Belgium is rich—all descendants from Breughel's models; and innumerable scenes of people gulling each other, à la Ben Jonson, which are always fun to play.

"In England, one's heart sinks at the first mention of buck-baskets, but here they hardly know the play, and I hope they'll react to it in a more primitive way. Directing and playing Shakespeare in England is rather like an exercise in athletics: how will they get over the hurdles? Here they experience it more freshly."

This reminded me of a story about the actor Esmé Percy who, set to play Hamlet, searched everywhere for someone who had never ever seen the drama to direct him in it. *Hamlet,* however familiar, was undeniable and well-nigh irresistible. As P. G. Wodehouse noted ruefully in 1905: "It's *Hamlet* here and *Hamlet* there and *Hamlet* on next week, / An actor not in *Hamlet* is regarded as a freak."

It was the major test of a young actor's skills. Inevitably, one's perception of Hamlet himself, was filtered through many subconscious layers of previous performances. There was, of course, Olivier's film version, where his silver blonde hair shone as if spotlit amidst the black-and-white imagery. More recently, Richard Burton's rehearsal-clad Broadway turn left hosts of fans "blasted with ecstasy," while David Warner's shuffling, hirsute, muffler-wrapped 1960s Hamlet had seemed to embody the very spirit of rebellious youth that was then challenging old values—even bringing down governments.

My readiness was all, and, finally, in the early 1970s, it did come—an opportunity to play this extraordinary role in a repertory theater production in England. I had just returned from America, where the Vietnam war and the Watergate scandal had polarized and demoralized the nation. A parallel climate of "something rotten in the state" was quite palpable and overwhelming. Nixon's fall had emphasized the fact that Shakespearean tragedy was not so much about what happened to a man, but what happened in a man once the process of self-destruction had been initiated.

Our rehearsals were as abbreviated as the word *rep* itself, approximating to the short time in which the plays were originally rehearsed in Elizabethan times. It soon became apparent that the soliloquies worked best when spoken, as in their author's day, directly to the audience, taking everyone into one's confidence and unburdening the soul. The energy of the line was further galvanized when it was realized that the beginning of a sentence was usually of less import than its conclusion. This also helped to prevent the verse from tailing off into inaudibility and obscurity. We did experiment, though, with Hamlet addressing his "To be, or not to be" speech to his fellow student, Horatio, as if it were an exercise in academic logic, reflecting the Elizabethan enthusiasm for rhetoric and Shakespeare's abiding passion for antithesis. However, a sense of parallels and contrasts suffused the entire work and hardly required such passionless, donnish elaboration.

"Shakespeare really discovered Jekyll and Hyde," Adrian commented. "All those great roles encompass opposite poles of human behavior. Hamlet's half man of action, half thinker with 'puzzled will,' paralyzed by indecision. Macbeth—poet and slaughterer. Othello, peace-loving soldier and beastly murderer. Iago, clubbable fellow *and* serpent. That's what make them so bloody difficult to play!"

Much later, in the midst of writing this book, Adrian refined this insight further: "Those who claim that W.S. must have studied law, worked for a lawyer's firm, etc. have got a point. He has a lawyer's mind, able to separate 'this' from 'that.' The kernel of most speeches is a clash of opposites... 'So shows a snowy dove trooping with crows.' And this *duality* runs right through his plays (night/day, girl/boy, king/Falstaff, age/youth, Othello/Iago). It splits a line of verse just as it splits the theme of a play. He couldn't think of black, without at the same time thinking of white. So, trying to write something about him is like digging up Troy—you always find another Troy underneath."

Another essential feature of Shakespeare's creative process was that, just as he eschewed absolutes, so he never entirely "owned" the character by circumscribing it into an inflexible type. Rather, he encouraged the actor to share in the shaping of the role. That is why a Shakespearean character is never predictable, but as varied as the human personality itself.

There were also the physical demands of these roles to be reckoned with, especially in repertory with its minimum rehearsal and maximum performance schedule. As someone once remarked: "Playing Shakespeare is so tiring. You never get to sit down unless you're a king." Hamlet demanded especial stamina and mental activity with so much unpacking of the heart with words, and a duel of "best violence" to round it all off. The matinees for schoolchildren were an especial pleasure. Even when one's speeches were chorused by the rapt assembly, it was not unduly disturbing, for I recognized that I was playing to my former self, the schoolboy for whom these glorious words opened up a treasure-house of inexhaustible pleasures.

## "WITH A HEY, AND HO, AND A HEY NONINO"

My own perspective on Shakespeare was further enhanced by my good fortune in being involved in filming more of his plays. Just as it had seemed natural to be playing the young student, Lucentio, so soon after leaving Oxford, so it also seemed wonderfully appropriate to find myself wooing my future wife, Pat, on the seductively romantic location of Zeffirelli's next bonding with the Bard, *Romeo and Juliet*—moreover playing the suitably hotheaded and lusty Tybalt. (Pat had been asked to work on the film, too, as a photographer, thereby vindicating its author's pithy observation that "the ancient saying is no heresy, hanging and wiving goes by destiny.")

"O spirit of love, how quick and fresh are thou!" Orsino had enthused, and it was intoxicating to revel in a parallel world where my own real passions were mirrored by those played out daily on the film set. It was not difficult to imagine that Shakespeare was writing from experience, so acute were his amorous insights. Indeed, the recent popular, enjoyable, and successful film, *Shakespeare In Love* has presented a further parallel by showing the Bard himself as Romeo's alter ego.

"Lovers and madmen have such seething brains, / Such shaping fantasies, that apprehend / More than cool reason ever comprehends." Describing a production of *As You Like It,* Adrian confirmed this: "All the commentators go on about 'pastoral comedies' and 'sermons in stones,' when what counts is Rosalind telling Orlando that women are not goddesses, they have feet of clay. The other theme is love is madness… People in love do lunatic things. All the rest is secondary. I saw a silly production recently—evening dress, white bowler hats, and white sheets—but when Rosalind said she was "fathoms deep in love" you felt moved and "O go away silly director!"

## "WHY, THEN THE WORLD'S MINE OYSTER"

Not long after playing Hamlet, I put on "a truant disposition" and lived and travelled out of England. My expatriate move was matched by Adrian's: but whereas he remained in Europe, I struck out for a brave new world. There, among the natives of America, I encountered a curious and irrational lack of confidence where performing Shakespeare was concerned. There was much muttering about motivation—normally less emphasized by their more pragmatic, transatlantic colleagues of the speak-up-and-

...oid-falling-over-the-furniture school. James Fenimore Cooper had once declared that Shakespeare was "The great author of America," a sentiment shared by another theater lover, Abraham Lincoln, who went so far as to state: "It matters not to me whether Shakespeare be well or ill acted; with him the thought suffices." Now, however, the received wisdom had degenerated into a vague assumption that the Bard only sounded correct when voiced by a Briton, and in elocutionary tones.

As much as I shamefully, yet gratefully, acquiesced in this unwarranted perception, I was also at pains to point out that the Elizabethan accent of Shakespeare's day had been imported into America where it had taken root and flourished relatively intact. British English, on the other hand, had suffered a significant sound change, along with a certain thespian gentrification. A more "authentic" Shakespeare performance could probably now be heard on the other side of the "still-vexed Bermoothes" where, I was delighted to find, the Elizabethan word *sides* for scripts was still current.

Moreover, I added, American actors had enjoyed considerable success playing Shakespeare in Britain. Dustin Hoffman was a recent notable Shylock, but as long ago as the 1850s the Cushman sisters had made a sensation in *Romeo and Juliet.* I am the proud owner of a Staffordshire china portrait figure—the only example known to have survived—of Charlotte Cushman as Romeo that commemorates this triumph. I also have one of William Charles Macready as Macbeth—a reminder that, on the contrary, English actors were not always as well received by their American cousins.

"I went on; they would not let me speak," Macready noted in his diary in 1849 about a notorious New York performance of that unlucky play that provoked a riot, resulting in several deaths. "Someone flung a rotten egg close to me. I smiled in contempt, persisting in my endeavor to be heard. At last there was nothing for it: the play proceeded in dumb show. Copper cents were thrown, some struck me, four or five eggs, a great many apples, nearly—if not quite—a peck of potatoes, lemons, pieces of wood, a bottle of asafoetida (a vilely pungent gum), which splashed my own dress, smelling of course most horribly." Ambition in the theater, it seemed, should indeed be made of sterner stuff.

Fundamentally, it must be accepted that, just as audiences are unpredictable, so is Shakespeare. He is what he is: There is no "correct" version. (The best *Tempest* I have ever seen happens to be a "foreign" one by Giorgio Strehler performed in Italian in Paris.) His plots touch universal nerves and so have been co-opted successfully into other media, notably ballet and opera as well as film. Verdi gave Falstaff a melodic dimension and Wagner was drawn to the moral conundrum of *Measure for Measure* for his "*Das Liebesverbot.*" Shakespeare's imagination is too strong and illimitable to be neatly nationalized or tidily hidebound. It remains a huge, whirling, ever-expanding dramatic vortex, exploding and re-ordering Polonius' rigid categorization of "historical-pastoral, tragical historical, pastoral-comical."

We live in an age of statistical normalizing. So, is there a certain international, timeless standard by which a performance can be measured, one that survives in the collective consciousness, transcending the vagaries of language and of fashion in acting and theater design?

"I certainly don't try to define what acting is," Adrian commented. "It's like a color—you recognize it when you see it. Stanislavski, bless him, tried to pin it down—but he, in his time, was putting bridles on Russian ham actors: but his system's no good when there's no bloody horse. And you can't apply him to Shakespeare—because Shakespeare is concerned with the *in*consistencies of people's behavior, the *ill*ogicalities, the *in*explicables.

"'Through-lines' and 'super-objectives' dissolve into thin air halfway through the role. Why? Because Shakespeare's secret agent is at work—time. Time is fiddling with the controls all the time.

Hamlet's bloody, bold and resolute when he sees the Norwegian army, but not when he sees the King praying. Cleopatra beats up the slave who tells her Antony's married—and a few *lines* later, she's all sugar and spice to him because she wants to know the color of Octavia's hair.

"Stanislavski—Freud's contemporary—urges us to find out how people 'tick'; 300 years before, Shakespeare was telling us that they don't 'tick,' not in the predictable way a clock ticks anyway. Forgive me for going on in this windy way—struggling with Shakespeare daily tends to blow the mind!"

## "FEEDING OF THE DAINTIES THAT ARE BRED IN A BOOK"

A few years ago Adrian and I started to discuss the idea of coalescing our continuing correspondence into a collaboration on a book about acting. The international faxes flew and, after mulling several ideas, we narrowed our choice down to compiling a *vademecum,* or companionable guide both for the general reader, but especially for the Shakespearean actor: much ado's and don'ts, as it were. Performing in most plays was technically straightforward, but scaling Shakespearean peaks required well-tested methods and the correct equipment. Also perhaps a map for, as Adrian affirmed, "A book on how to *act* W.S. is basically a book on how to *decode* W.S. I keep getting all kinds of new theories. We have so little evidence about Shakespeare. Do you think he *deliberately* burned all letters, bills, rough sketches, etc. to preserve his anonymity? (or did they go up when the Globe blazed?)"

With regard to this anonymity, one of the few Shakespearean issues that will not be pursued in these pages is the long-disputed question of the authorship of the plays and poems. Was "Shakespeare" a name or a pseudonym? Who was the mortal behind the immortal words? We can hear him but we cannot identify him.

Like other actors—Leslie Howard, Orson Welles, Charlie Chaplin—I have an instinctive feeling that there is something that does not quite add up. The glorious renaissance mind revealed by the plays does not square with the crabbed, litigious personality of the Stratford claimant with his trivial, almost anonymous, legacy of a few scrawled signatures, a second-best bed and not one single book. Whereas Edward de Vere, the 17th Earl of Oxford appears an ideal candidate.

This Hamlet alter ego was a precocious scholar trained in all the princely arts, a great European traveller and, significantly, a published poet as well as patron of an acting troupe. Passionate about the theater, but constrained by his high birth to "put an antic disposition on," his true identity is both concealed and subtly revealed within the "Shakespeare" plays. As Joseph Sobran has urged, once one accepts this most Shakespearean device of disguise, "The candid reader will find a thousand pieces falling into place and the towering plays and poems will sound more resonantly than ever before." Certainly the Sonnets take on a whole new startling relevance and urgency. Meanwhile, until the "smoking Canon," as it were, of indisputable truth is found, Adrian and I have agreed to disagree and, for the purposes of this book, I have acquiesced in the accepted Stratfordian biography, or rather, mythology.

"Re. Oxford," Adrian argued "the more I read W.S., the more convinced I am that it was written by an actor—you feel it even in the shape of the speeches. Far more actable than Marlowe or Jonson. Perhaps in 400 years' time they'll 'discover' that Tom Stoppard was written by A.J. Ayer and S.J. Perelman!"

Much of our discussion centered around the staging of Shakespeare and the fresh insights that had been brought to bear on this by the recent discoveries of the sixteenth century foundations of London's Rose and Fortune theaters. With so little documentary evidence to hand, recreating the Elizabethan theater and its methods relied a great deal on inspired guesswork. "I found this theory in a book (*Shakespeare In His Age* by F.E. Halliday, very respectable prof. who wrote *The Cultural History of England*, which you gave me once in 1966, by the way)," Adrian noted, "The 'pit' area, where everyone says the 'groundlings' stood, pushing right up to the stage, was in fact used as an *acting area*. So 'Enter X Above' didn't necessarily mean X entered on the balcony, but 'above' the lower acting area.

"But where were the groundlings? (Did they *really* stand for three hours, shoulder to shoulder, fidgeting and moving and spreading colds and flu? Hadn't the Burbages more consideration for their public than that?—or were they fewer, leaning perhaps on the lower galleries (standing room only)? And the dandies we all hear about, who 'sat on the stage' and showed off? If they had seats around the *pit*, they wouldn't be in the sightlines: whereas on *stage* they would."

All these considerations are being put to the practical test now that Sam Wanamaker's extraordinary efforts—in the teeth of bureaucratic indifference and local philistinism—to rebuild a replica of the Globe Theatre, as close as possible to its original site on the south bank of the Thames, have been realized. I was privileged to join the ranks of those enlisted worldwide to try to help Sam achieve his impossible dream and to now enjoy the fruits of his heroic vision and indefatigable labors. Once more a London institution and an audience magnet, the open-air playhouse is providing invaluable information about Elizabethan stagecraft.

Framed anew within the sacred geometry of the space, the actor has returned to the center of his cosmos. It has become startlingly apparent that his forebears must have possessed remarkable qualities, including an ability to speak with precision and projection, "trippingly on the tongue" and yet with the newfangled realism that Hamlet also requested. They constituted overwhelmingly a *cry* of Players—not a murmur. Shakespeare was well aware of the problem of commanding attention and knew how easily it could be lost:

"As in a theatre, the eyes of men, / After a well grac'd actor leaves the stage, / Are idly bent on him that enters next, / Thinking his prattle to be tedious."

Three thousand day-lit spectators sitting in the round, some answering back, others buying and eating food, had to be compelled to attention by sheer acting skill and charisma. Shakespeare created the firmament in which a star actor could shine.

The new Globe has swiftly proven that it is no mere thatch-and-wattle Tudor theme park but once more a vital part of England's cultural life. The true nature of the author of the plays of William Shakespeare may remain open to debate, but his playhouse is an indisputable reality and, once more, a success.

"I'm trying to write about WS's theater at the moment," reported a fax last year from Amsterdam, "despite all the volumes that have been written about it, though a lot by university people who don't know much about sightlines!

"About that Chorus (which I saw you do once on T.V.!), the 'Muse of Fire.' The explanation (so-called) of the Elizabethan theater. What! After writing *H. VI: 1, 2, 3; Love's L.L.; R & J; M.N.Dream; Merchant of Venice; K. John; Rich II,* and *Henry IV: 1, 2*—he feels in 1599 a need to explain to Joe Public that he's supposed to use his imaginary forces?! and see imaginary horses?! *Why so late?*

"And all this groveling! 'Gentles all… (we) flat unraised spirits… so great an object, this war-like Harry…port of Mars…' He wasn't half so smarmy about the other kings! What's going on?

"A lot of Elizabethan Political Correctness, if you ask me. Everyone's wild about Harry, and thinking, "I hope Will's not going to do a Lytton Strachey on *him*, as he did with the Richards and the Henrys.

"But you won't catch Will giving an opinion. 'I'm just showing what happened.' 'Demand me nothing, what you know you know,' as Iago put it. Of course this is roughly put—but I cannot find any other reason for this 'credo' so late, except to deflect the patriots who thought 'Agincourt' is above criticism."

"How much there is to say (how much has already been said); and how to keep it in order, and how to avoid waffle…"

I was delighted that, in the midst of all these cerebrations, Adrian had not forworn his propensity for collecting the Bard's more bizarre interpretations. "The only WS play I've seen recently," he reported last year, "was a renowned Italian production in the Holland Festival, of *Giulio Cesare*. Brutus and Cassius were played by two extremely anorexic girls, like stick insects, and Marc A was (deliberately) a man with throat cancer. He had no voice, only a hole in his throat, and croaked his slow way through the long oration. The setting seemed to be a burned-out cinema, gray twisted carbonized chairs. Director's view-point: why are plays always done with *beautiful* people? What about the others?…Don't think I'll mention it in The Book!"

Among the material that *did* appear to merit mention was, yet again, the significance of dreams that suffuse Shakespeare to the degree that sometimes "drama" seems synonymous with "dreamer." " 'Dreams' is a good pointer," Adrian noted, "not because we are such stuff etc., but because you cannot understand him if you do not dream. I mean, the method actor says, 'How can I play Macbeth since I've never killed a king?' No—who has?— you have to dream it! You meet your dead father's doppelgänger— your wife, who died years before… You dream, like Clarence, your own death… How to bring over this incoherence to audiences, who demand coherence? To actors who don't ask enough questions ('Just play what's there') and to actors who ask too many ('How can I forgive Capulet in two lines when I've hated him for twenty years?'). In short, how to find the law of the Shakespearean universe? In other words—how to get on his wavelength?

"Anyway, writing about Acting is always a dodgy thing. You cannot write a how-to book: there isn't any how-to—except how to read what's there. How to see first what WS was up to before we start displaying our own egos. At the same time, unless we bring our own experience and imagination to bear on it, it remains just words, words, words… The craft of acting is full of paradoxes!"

And so, it seemed, was the craft of writing: With Shakespeare, there was never enough time and one was never "finished." Even though one tried to avoid the prolixity of Don Armado who "draweth out the thread of his verbosity finer than the staple of his argument," both Adrian and I became preoccupied with professional matters and missed one publishing deadline after another. "Fair flowers that are not gathered in their prime / Rot and consume themselves in little time," the subject of our book gently chided us, dismissing our stalled efforts with such pertinent observations as "striving to better, oft we mar what's well."

"If I'm horribly slow," Adrian responded, "it's because I have to prevent myself from going off at a tangent all the time. WS is so indivisible—when you talk about the words, you talk about the character, and the theater, and the verse—it's all one. You can talk about 'the world of Turgenev' or of Dickens or Joyce—but not about 'the world of W.S.'—it's like the universe, nothing seems outside it. And it's probably expanding…"

In the chapters that follow, I think that Adrian has provided a telling, intelligent response to his own interrogations and questioning. The modesty of "our bending author" and his confessions of inadequacy are typical, and positively Chaucerian in their scope and unjustifiability: "I get blocked by thinking of all the people who know so much more about it than I: so I have to think of all those who know less! As someone said of Canon Chasuble (in *The Importance of Being Earnest*), 'He has never written a single book, so you can imagine how much he knows.' "

I am certain that the rest of this book, earnest in places, important, I hope at all times, so full of wise saws and modern instances, will give you as much pleasure and as many keen fresh insights as it has me. It has been written with both passion and integrity.

To borrow Othello's phrase with regard to Adrian, "I know thou'rt full of love and honesty, and weigh'st thy words before thou giv'st them breath."

I am delighted that, Boswell-like, I have had the good fortune to be both "a snapper-up of unconsidered trifles" as far as Adrian's letters are concerned and also the successful petitioner for all the weightier words that follow. I now pass them on for your deliberation and, hopefully, your delectation.

Introduction

# "NOT OF AN AGE,
# BUT FOR ALL TIME"

We should try to see Shakespeare plain. In the (nearly) four hundred years since his death, so much has been written commenting on his writings and conjecturing about his life that he risks being buried under a mountain of books. He is dissected by scholars, he is misquoted by politicians, and he is idolized by art-fanciers. He has become a monument, and the characteristic of monuments is that they glorify the dead and obstruct the traffic.

At first sight he looks forbiddingly grand. In his own time he was already classed with Ovid, Plautus, and Seneca. For many he was simply "sweet Mr Shakespeare." For Ben Jonson he was "the wonder of our stage." Only one dissenting voice is heard, that of an embittered rival playwright, Robert Greene: "…an upstart Crow, beautified with our feathers…in his own conceit the onely Shake-scene in a countrey." Greene was piqued that a mere actor should presume to write plays—and succeed.

Later generations have dubbed him "the Immortal Bard," "Sweet Swan of Avon," "the Master," "myriad-minded Shakespeare."

Coming to praise, they have buried him. To turn a writer into an idol is to make him seem remote and unattainable. Better acquaintance will show how close to us he is—like one of those Elizabethan portraits by Nicholas Hilliard, where between the ringlets and the ruff a face looks out that you might have seen yesterday in the street.

The face we need to see plain is that of Shakespeare the playwright, the man himself remains a mystery. The attested facts of his life would hardly fill a page. We know from church registers the date of his christening—26 April 1564—but not his date of birth; and we know the day he died—23 April 1616, (this has led many to suppose that he died on his birthday). Further, church registers record the births, deaths, and marriages of his children, and the deaths of his parents, and legal documents reveal that he had problems with the tax inspector, that he bought some property, and that he chased down debtors. Only six copies of his signature are known to have survived.

He left behind only his professional writing in its published form. No letters, no shopping lists, not even a note to his landlady about feeding the cat, have ever come to light. Historians still hope that a cache of letters, or rough drafts of plays, or manuscripts of lost plays, will be found in some country house library, but this is dreaming of the pot of gold. No word has been recorded of anything he actually *said.* "We have the man Shakespeare with us" wrote the Countess of Pembroke, casually, in one of the few Elizabethan letters that refer to him, and one could only wish that she had been more of a gossip.

Now "the man Shakespeare" has disappeared, and probably had a hand in his own disappearance. We know no more about him than he wished us to know. It would not be surprising if he himself destroyed all his private papers. On his tomb in Holy Trinity Church, Stratford, runs the inscription:

GOOD FREND FOR IESUS SAKE FORBEARE,
TO DIGG THE DVST ENCLOASED HEARE:
BLESTE BE YE MAN Y SPARES THES STONES
AND CVRST BE HE YT MOVES MY BONES.[1]

Some think this is the last thing he ever wrote; others say that this doggerel is not worthy of the hand that wrote the Sonnets—but Shakespeare was such a chameleon writer, that it's possible he did write it. If so (and it cannot have taken him long) he is not, one fancies, addressing himself to body snatchers. Rather it is a message to future biographers not to go muckraking (or dust-digging) into his private affairs. Knowing mankind's curiosity for gossip, he may have feared that public interest in his personal life would overshadow its interest in his literary achievement. The man Shakespeare is dust and bones, and future generations should concern themselves only with Shakespeare the writer. He knew his worth and predicted that his works would last:

Nor marble, nor the gilded monuments
Of princes, shall outlive this powerful rhyme...
                                              (Sonnet 55)

So long as men can breathe, and eyes can see,
So long lives this,[2] and this gives life to thee.
                                              (Sonnet 18)

And, as we shall see later, while writing for the theater of his time, he consciously wrote also for actors and audiences yet unborn.

---

[1] GOOD FRIEND FOR JESUS SAKE FORBEARE
TO DIG THE DUST ENCLOSED HERE:
BLESSED BE THE MAN WHO SPARES THESE STONES
AND CURSED BE HE THAT MOVES MY BONES.

[2] Meaning, this poem.

Yet during his lifetime only seventeen of his plays were published, most of them in garbled versions. The plays belonged to the company, who kept the original manuscripts under lock and key. After all, for a theater a good play is a capital asset. Even the actors were provided only with their own speeches and cues. (These scripts were not in book form but copied out on rolls—from which we get the word *role*.) Unscrupulous booksellers, anxious to profit from a play's success in the theater, would use any means to get hold of a play and rush it into print. Stenographers would be sent into the theater to take down the play in a primitive form of shorthand. Dishonest actors would sell their "rolls" and what they remembered of the rest of the play to printers. There were no laws of copyright, and the idea was not to honor the author but to make a quick buck.

Sometimes the company itself would arrange to have the play printed, either to counteract these pirated editions, or because they had finished with the play. By publishing they were tacitly allowing other companies to perform it. Even these were badly edited, with cast lists and stage directions missing, and verse being set up as prose and vice versa. It was not until seven years after Shakespeare's death that all the plays were printed in an authenticated "omnibus" version, known as the Folio. Indeed, we would probably never have heard of Shakespeare at all, were it not for the labor of love of its editors, two actors of his company called John Heminges and Henry Condell. After that, Shakespeare's original manuscripts vanished for ever.

Playwriting took up only so much of his time. He was, in fact, a complete man of the theater—even his rival Robert Greene sneered at him as a "Johannes Factotum," a Jack-of-all-trades. As a "shareholder" in his company, the Lord Chamberlain's Men, he would have been involved with the day-to-day running of the theater, dealing with actors, musicians, carpenters, tailors, joiners, weavers, and bellows-menders; probably organizing rehearsals for other people's plays, and keeping an eye on the accounts and watching the box-office returns. Plays were quickly played out, and he would have had constantly to find new dramatic material that would provide good parts for his actors, and that the public would willingly pay to see. He faced the same problems as any theatrical manager today.

He was also an important actor; not the leading actor, that role was reserved for Richard Burbage, but when the names of the Lord Chamberlain's Men are listed, his name appears among the "principall Actors." He knew at first hand the difficulties of learning lines, of speaking clearly, and of commanding an audience's attention; of timing laughs so as to set the house upon a roar, and of creating those electric moments when three thousand people are holding their breath as one.

This talent for holding an audience rapt suffuses his plays. Even today actors are in no doubt that his plays were written by an actor. And as house-dramatist he could provide his company with exactly the kind of plays that he, as manager, was looking for.

His theater, the Globe, was the most successful in Elizabethan London—and there were seventeen others. When James I came to the throne, after the death of Queen Elizabeth, he gave the company royal status: The Lord Chamberlain's Men were promoted to be the King's Men. When Shakespeare retired to Stratford-upon-Avon, he had earned enough money to buy the second biggest house in the town.

The Globe—and this is often forgotten—was a commercial theater: It had to pay for itself. The Lord Chamberlain's patronage was simply a form of protection, for actors and entertainers were classed as vagrants ("rogues and vagabonds") unless they were listed as "servants" of some great nobleman.

Theatrical managers know that their task is twofold. Firstly you have to announce something that will bring the public into the theater; and secondly, once they're inside, you have to give them their money's worth. You have to keep their interest alive for some two or three hours, and at the Globe this was no easy task since half the audience was standing. Shakespeare, supreme showman as he was, was as expert at the first task as at the second.

He picked up the wavelength of his audience's curiosity. He knew that many people go to the play for the same reason they line up outside Madame Tussaud's Waxworks—to see historical or legendary figures close up, and to visit the Chamber of Horrors. He knew their taste for pageantry. When the playbills went up announcing plays about English kings, the public would count on battle scenes, coronations, royal processions, and funerals. Besides, they were eager to know about the men who had made England what it was, and how their forefathers lived. The Wars of the Roses were no more distant to them than the American Civil War is to us, and Richard III had been dead for only a hundred years.

Latin was a kind of second language. It was taught in the grammar schools and used at court when foreign diplomats were received. New translations of Latin writers were appearing, whetting the audience's appetite for knowing more about Julius Caesar, Marc Antony, and Cleopatra.

Foreign travel was becoming a craze—men would "sell their lands to see other men's." A typical figure in London society was the traveller who returned from Europe with exaggerated stories of how the grass was greener across the water, especially in Italy. So the playwright gave his romantic comedies a whiff of exoticism by setting them in Venice, Verona, Padua, Messina, or half-invented countries like Illyria and Bohemia. His Athens, with its English woodlands, and his spooky city of Ephesus, have no more connection with the real places than does Brecht's use of Chicago as the setting for *Arturo Ui*. Distance lent enchantment. Citing these romantic-sounding places gave him leave to lift his stories to the world of fable—"Once upon a time…" begins every fairy tale.

Even in his more ambitious works he would carry his audience back to worlds elsewhere—Troy, Ancient Rome, medieval Scotland, Denmark—or to the England of his ancestors. By so doing, he offered his public a way of being taken "out of them-selves," and he gave himself a freedom to comment about con-temporary England, where freedom of speech was severely curtailed.

The public that jostled for places at the Globe Theatre was the same public who, the day before had been to watch the bear-baiting in the Paris Garden—it was just down the road. Out-wardly the Bear Pit and the Globe so resembled each other that in some old prints of London the names are reversed. The sportive spectacle offered there was that of a bear tied to a stake being set on by hungry mastiff dogs: The dogs, fangs bared, fly at his throat; the bear fights back with claws and teeth, which were often filed down to prevent him biting too deeply. Nevertheless, some of the dogs are torn to pieces, and others get their heads bitten off like rotten apples. Shakespeare makes reference to this when Macbeth is cornered by his enemies:

> They have tied me to a stake; I cannot fly
> But bear-like I must fight the course.

It is unlikely that Shakespeare himself appreciated this cruel spectacle. On the contrary, his plays frequently show an un-Elizabethan sympathy for cornered animals (and men), the hunted deer, the trapped bird, the tyrant overwhelmed by his enemies. But his public liked to see blood spilt.

Once they were inside the theater, he offered them blood galore—murders, assassinations, suicides, duels, scenes of torture, and fights to the death in battles.

And for those with a taste for the supernatural he produced ghosts, fairies, hobgoblins, witches, sorcerers, aerial spirits, and visions. The leading character of his next-to-last play was a magi-cian with powers over the four elements.

It might seem invidious to emphasize Shakespeare's talents as a showman. Many nontheatrical people take a blinkered view of this side of him—some even look upon it as an aberration. But we cannot see Shakespeare plain if we ignore it. He was not writing for a select coterie, an in-crowd, he was writing for the theater of his time, that was how he earned his living, and the playgoers of his time demanded sensational effects.

He was not, however, the kind of commercial manager, who says cynically, "Give the public what it wants." His attitude was that of the enlightened manager who prefers to say, "Give the public what it doesn't (yet) know it wants." The greatness of Shakespeare comes to the fore when we see what use he made of all these special effects. He didn't invent them—they were part of the dramatist's tool kit.

If the public wanted a ghost (or an assassination, or a battle), they should have it. But what interested the playwright was not the thing itself, but the effect it has on the people who experience it.

Dead King Hamlet's appearance to his son sets in motion the series of actions, and lack of action, that makes *Hamlet* the most famous play in the world. It is irrelevant to ask whether Shakespeare himself "believed in" ghosts: For the purpose of the play, he creates a group of people who do.

Macbeth murders a virtuous and innocent old King. The murder itself is not the point—indeed, it is committed offstage. The play concerns us with the heart searching that leads up to the deed, and its awful consequences: It's the first step on a slippery slope that leads to mass murder, war, a broken conscience, and, for the regicide himself who is a Christian—eternal damnation.

*Henry V* centers round the Battle of Agincourt. Curiously enough, there are no stage directions in the play concerning the battle itself. The drama lies in the preparations for war, and those dreadful last minutes before dawn before the fighting breaks out; and in the aftermath where England and France join hands over fields drenched in the blood of soldiers who died for their countries.

The promise of tumult and bloodshed lured men into the theater. What the author gave them, once they were inside, were portraits of the men who caused the battle, as well as those who suffered from it.

For every two spectators who came to the Globe, fresh from the bear-baiting spectacles, avid to see fights and murders and ghosts, there was always one who was carrying in his pocket the essays of Bacon and Montaigne, and who, like them, was preoccupied with the vital question, "What is Man? What governs him, between the time he makes his entrance to the cradle, and his exit to the grave? What, as we say nowadays, makes him tick?"

This was Shakespeare in his time—a figurehead of the theater in one of the theater's golden ages. That age came to an end twenty five years after his death when all London theaters were shut down for a period of eighteen years by the Puritans. The Globe Theatre became a cowshed. For many people the date of this, 1642, is the most significant date in the history of English drama.

A whole generation went by when there was no call for actors or playwrights. Those actors who had worked with Shakespeare died off, and they had no reason to pass on their skills or their knowledge to their children.

When the theaters reopened at the Restoration of the Monarchy, nobody knew any more how the plays had been staged or acted—or wanted to know. A kind of unofficial censorship was imposed on the culture of the time that led up to the Civil War. A new leaf was turned. Theater had to be reinvented, and theater men turned to Paris for their inspiration. Yet still the ember of Shakespeare kept glowing in the ashes. In the 1660s we find the Vicar of Stratford (his home town) noting quaintly in his diary:

> Remember to peruse Shakespeares plays and bee vers'd in them that I bee not ignorant in that matter.

No doubt his curiosity was aroused by the tombstone.

The idea has not died out that Shakespeare was merely an Elizabethan playwright, working in a primitive playhouse with only clumsy technical resources, writing comedies about Elizabethan life, or historical dramas about the Middle Ages or the Ancient World—all peopled with colorful characters speaking old-fashioned English. Many people have his Complete Works on the shelves (books do furnish a room), think of him as a classic—cultural and educational—and even visit his plays from time to time, to see how people lived in the past. Even a hundred years ago Bernard Shaw was surprised at "the consequent submission of the British public to be mercilessly bored by each of his plays once in their lives for the sake of being able to say they had actually seen it."

Treating Shakespeare as a cultural icon only diminishes his stature. Elizabethan playwright he certainly was, although he spent the last ten years of his writing life under the reign of King James, which makes him also a Jacobean. But when his friend Ben Jonson said that "he was not of an age, but for all time," he was implying that Shakespeare had access to some underground stream of knowledge about humanity that flowed from ancient times and would go on flowing into the unforeseeable future.

In the domain of science, certain discoveries—like that of the wheel, the Law of Gravity, the phenomenon of electricity, or DNA structure—were not doomed to be superceded and discarded—like the flat earth theory. They have proved to be *laws of physics*, showing us the mechanisms of nature and how nature works. The date of their discovery has no bearing on their truthfulness. Apples were falling to the ground long before Newton formulated the law of gravity, the DNA molecule existed before it was discovered.

Shakespeare's field of interest was human nature, and human nature also has its laws and patterns and syndromes. These are hard to formulate scientifically (although psychologists are still trying), but they can be illustrated. Man can be shown in action, the workings of his mind made audible. Shakespeare knew more about mankind than Mankind has yet learned. We do not yet speak of a Hamlet Complex, or an Iago Syndrome, in the same way as we use the phrase Oedipus Complex, but those who know the plays well will recognize time and again, among their fellow men, the same symptoms—Hamlet's fatal leaning toward procrastination (being unready to answer life's challenges when they appear), and Iago's urge to destroy something (or someone) that is beyond his comprehension.

To understand Shakespeare today we have to realize that he is not merely an Elizabethan writer who is attractive, and worth staging, for historical reasons. More, we should look on his Elizabethan-ness as an accident of history rather than as something essential. His comedies are not meant to be realistic pictures of Elizabethan life. His historical plays would not get high marks for historical accuracy. He has tradesmen with Anglo-Saxon names rehearsing a play in a wood near Athens; he plumps Falstaff and his Elizabethan cronies at the Boar's Head Tavern into a drama about Henry IV, who died 180 years before (which is like setting the Marx Brothers loose in a film about George Washington).

If we look in the plays for what we expect to get from historical novels, they can seem clumsy and ill-informed. It helps to regard them as myths, legends, fairy tales, allegories, and parables—those tales that, free from time and place, tell us immutable truths about ourselves.

Few stones remain of Elizabethan London, the English language has changed, and the theater Shakespeare wrote for is long since demolished. These facts make him seem distant to us.

But the bonds that link human beings—lovers and friends, husbands and wives, fathers and children, the powerful and the powerless—these, with all the stresses and tensions that attend on such relationships, have not changed. Neither have the dreams and nightmares that haunt our imagination. The desire for perfect love, the anxiety about being betrayed, the fear of death (a loved one's as much as one's own) still keep people awake at night. These are the stuff of Shakespeare's plays.

Treat them as chronicles of everyday life, accurate transcriptions of reality, and they may be found wanting. But treat them as dramatized dreams, where hidden hopes and fears take on the appearance of reality, and the demands for literal, workaday truth melt away.

It is the property of dreams to demand interpretation but in the end to defy explanation. Even Freud was often baffled by his patients' dreams. With time the explanations are forgotten, but the dream remains—the dream outlives its explanation.

In the same way, over four hundred years, Shakespeare's plays have been rewritten, reinterpreted, reexamined, but still they stand upright, demanding to be rediscovered, "It shall be called Bottom's dream" says Bottom the weaver after a night of love with the Fairy Queen, "because it hath no bottom." Shakespeare's dramatized dreams also seem, like the sea, bottomless and inexhaustible.

Peter Brook put it clearly:

> I saw the other day an interview on French television with Orson Welles, when he started by saying something like "We all betray Shakespeare." The history of the plays shows them constantly being re-interpreted and re-interpreted, and yet remaining untouched and intact. Therefore they are always more than the last interpretation trying to say the last word on something on which the last word cannot be said.[3]

However, interpretation is not our immediate business. Interpretation can be taken to mean what the actor brings to the written material, while we are concerned with what the written material brings to the actor.

Frequently an actor is given a role in a film or a television play to which the author's contribution is quite sketchy. Dialogue

---

[3] Peter Brook, *The Shifting Point*, 1988.

is minimal, characterization almost nonexistent, and the player has to put his talent and imagination to work to make the part come alive at all. The written material lies inert like an empty glove, and the actor becomes the hand that animates it.

With Shakespeare, the situation is reversed. It is the actor who is the glove, and Shakespeare the hand that gives him body and strength and movement. So complete a playwright is he that, if listened to, he will do three-quarters of the actor's work for him. Of course, this demands a greater dose of humility than some actors are capable of producing, but paradoxically, *the more the actor relies on Shakespeare the better he acts.*

A familiar sight is the actor who reads the play a couple of times, has a number of bright ideas about his part, and sets off developing his own ideas at all costs. After a while, he's taken a wrong turn and cannot find the way back. Another actor, *before even thinking about interpretation*, begins by asking himself what the words are actually saying, why they are in that particular order, why certain metaphors or images are used (and are they merely decorative?), and what directions to actors lie embedded in them; in short—what is Shakespeare actually doing?

This is as necessary as the runway to the airplane, which needs it to gather speed before taking off. This runway groundwork is the subject of the present book.

We propose to proceed from the inside outwards, from the detail to the whole. Just as a scientist studying the composition of a river will take a glass of the water and examine the forms of life swimming about inside it, for that sample is a microcosm of the river, so we shall find that if we start by looking at a few simple speeches, and their dynamics, we shall find them typical of Shakespeare's mindset, and this will lead us on to more complex questions about characterization and about Shakespeare's theater.

# I

# WHAT IS THE
# LANGUAGE DOING?

~

"I could play this scene all right," said the drama student rehearsing Othello, "only the words keep getting in the way." The tutor was taken aback by this claim, and looked around for an apt reply.

He remembered reading that certain high schools, while purporting to teach English Literature, think that it taxes the young too much to ask them to study the written word, and prefer a more active approach. Studying *Romeo and Juliet,* for example, they improvise the street fights between the Capulets and Montagues, or the scene where Romeo infiltrates the Capulets' ball (imagining this takes place in a disco), and then go on to examine *West Side Story.* They, too, do not let Shakespeare's words get in the way.

"The words," he told the Othello-pupil, "are not just any old words; *Othello* is not a B-film, for which a dialogue writer has been hired to provide the actors with a few lines to keep them occupied while they act out the situation. On the contrary, the words are the scene and the scene is the words, and you can no more separate them than you can separate the ingredients of a mayonnaise."

No doubt, went on the tutor, the student could work himself up into a state of excitement where he could show *someone* (himself probably) in the throes of an emotion that *could resemble* jealousy (such as he would feel it)—but the result would be woolly and generalized, whereas Shakespeare is as specific and precise as music.

Suddenly he realized that the student was in fact saying something quite preposterous: "*I* could play the scene all right, only *Shakespeare* keeps getting in the way."

The student was putting his own feelings up front, and using the text as a mere reinforcement—whereas it should have been the other way round! Shakespeare is a master at creating strong dramatic situations—and his plays contain ample material for improvization classes—but the essence of his plays, and the level where the drama is being fought out—is the language.

In any play it is essential to ask oneself, "What are the characters doing to each other?" In a Shakespeare play you also have to ask, "What is the language doing?"

Yet for many people Shakespeare's language appears to be a barrier. It is helpful to think of it as an old walled city—it can look forbidding from the outside, but once the explorer has passed within the gates and walked about a bit, and familiarized himself with the layout of the streets and the lack of modern traffic, he finds it very like the world outside.

The reader must get used to certain usages that have changed, such as the second person singular form ("thou art"), although this is still perfectly normal English in many parts of Yorkshire. He must expect a conversation to open with "How now?" rather than "How are you?" and to close with "Go to" rather than "Off you go." ("Go to" is not a broken-off expletive!) He will find that certain words have changed their meaning. "What is the matter?"

now means "What is all the fuss about?" but previously it meant "What is the subject (of a book or a quarrel)?"

> POLONIUS: ...What do you read, my lord?
> HAMLET: Words, words, words.
> POLONIUS: What is the matter, my lord?
> HAMLET: Between who?
> POLONIUS: I mean the matter that you read, my lord.
>
> (II.2)

And we will often stumble over a word that has dropped out of use, or an expression we can make no sense of. Hamlet asks "Who would fardels bear...?" and we don't know what a *fardel* is (though the context makes it clear). We cannot immediately identify Hyperion, say, or "Niobe all tears." We shall not understand Othello's intention when he says:

> If I do prove her haggard,
> Though that her jesses were my dear heartstrings,
> I'd whistle her off and let her down the wind
> To prey at fortune...
>
> (III.3)

unless we know something about falconry. And as for the archaic sexual innuendoes and doubles entendres, the smuttiest-minded schoolboy could not spot how many of these are deliberately embedded (as one might say) in the text.

The reader needs a guidebook. No actor or director should be without a good annotated edition. The modern Arden Shakespeare (edited by T.J.B. Spencer) is highly to be recommended— although it is too heavy to rehearse with: It should be kept on a table in the rehearsal room. The New Penguin series has the advantage of being much lighter and less academic. The introductions are illuminating, and the footnotes are collected at the end of the book, which leaves the pages of text uncluttered.

The editors not only explain difficult words, but shed light into dark corners that the reader might otherwise pass by without noticing. The actor's imagination will not be stifled by consulting these studies. On the contrary. As T.S. Eliot put it, "When a poet is as great a poet as Shakespeare was, we cannot judge of his greatness unaided."

Since these glossaries are indispensable, the question has more than once arisen, shouldn't his plays be "translated into modern English"? It is difficult to know what kind of English the questioner has in mind. An awful warning of what might happen was provided, jestingly, by the eminent Cambridge professor, Sir Arthur Quiller-Couch, when he imagined a soliloquy of Hamlet as it might be expressed today by, say, the leader writer of an upmarket newspaper:

> To be, or the contrary? Whether the former or the latter be preferable would seem to admit of some difference of opinion; the answer in the present case being of an affirmative or of a negative character according as to whether one elects on the one hand to mentally suffer the disfavour of fortune, albeit in an extreme degree, or on the other to boldly envisage adverse conditions in the prospect of eventually bringing them to a conclusion.[1]

"Fog," Quiller-Couch calls this kind of writing. Compare it with the clarity of Shakespeare's words:

> To be, or not to be, that is the question:
> Whether 'tis nobler in the mind to suffer
> The slings and arrows of outrageous fortune,
> Or to take arms against a sea of troubles
> And by opposing—end them.
>
> (III.1)

---

[1] *On the Art of Writing*, 1912. Chapter on "Jargon."

The main problem of understanding Shakespeare is not one of archaic words and references to legendary persons, it is that his language is compact, multilayered, and unexpected. Besides, it was not meant in the first place to be read, but to be spoken and heard.

The great King James Version of the Bible, which was being prepared during the second half of Shakespeare's life, bears on the title page the subscript "Appointed to be read in churches." The secret of its great rhythms and harmonious language is that it was designed to be read aloud. A phrase like "Consider the lilies, how they grow" rings round the church in a way that "Consider how the lilies grow" does not. Just so, Shakespeare's plays could be marked, "Appointed to be spoken in theaters."

Shakespeare perfected a style of writing that was not literary, but oral. A simple example will be enough to show how this Oral Style works. Let us look at the opening lines of *Richard III*.

Now is the winter of our discontent
Made glorious summer by this sun of York,
And all the clouds that lour'd upon our house
In the deep bosom of the ocean buried.

If we change the order of two words only, the sense will not be altered:

The winter of our discontent is now
Made glorious summer by this sun of York,
And all the clouds that lour'd upon our house
Buried in the deep bosom of the ocean.

but all the life has gone out of it—it's like a flat tire. It has become a mere announcement, a piece of information. It starts before we are ready to listen, and it trails off at the end. The first and last words make a mighty difference.

The first word—

Now…

is not only the opening word of the speech, and the scene, but of the whole play. To see how this works in performance, we have to imagine a theater, with the audience abuzz with apprehension about the play they are going to see. A man steps on to the stage. Is there opening music? Perhaps, we don't know. Silence falls— or the man silences the audience. He looks pleased about something—what? He starts to speak.

Now…

There's urgency in the word. He's not talking about yesterday, or last week, or even next week, it's Now. A short sharp word that bites. The "ou" sound will come back a few lines later in "clouds… lour'd…our house."

Now… (now what?)

and our curiosity is fed, spoonful by spoonful. A different layout will illustrate how.

Now
is the winter of our discontent
Made glorious summer by this sun of York,

Sun, or son? The listener hears both.[2] With the summer comes the *sun*. The emblem that the House of York bore on their shields was that of a blazing *sun*. But the new king is also a *son* of the House of York. One word is thus doing the work of three.

---

[2] Or Hamlet's "O, that this too, too solid flesh would melt…" Some editors claim Shakespeare wrote "sullied flesh." But since *solid* and *sullied* had, in his day, the same sound, it doesn't matter. The listener hears both.

And all the clouds that lour'd upon our house

(the House of York)

in the deep bosom of the ocean…

We expect the next word to be "melted" or "drowned" or "swallowed up" or "sunken"—but Shakespeare surprises us:

buried.

We notice the word all the more because we had to wait for it. The sentence was not complete without it. "Buried" suggests dead and gone for ever, and the finality of burial is reinforced by making it the final word of the sentence. And what a gift for an actor, that plosive *b* of buried! ("Melted," "sunken," or "drowned" would not give a like effect.) After the lines, the audience is left with an image of an ocean with a clear horizon under a cloudless summer sky.

The first word of the sentence ("Now…") grabs us by the lapels and makes us listen. The sentence itself keeps us alert, in suspense, and the last word carries the most weight of all, dropping like a guillotine. The actor—if he felt so inclined, could leave a little pause after "Now…" and another before "…buried," and still hold our attention.

Oral Style means shaping the sentence so that the actor can make the maximum effect.

Words—as anyone knows who has tried to make a speech in public—perform differently when spoken. The reader's eye can pick and choose, pause, puzzle, skim, and even daydream. But the listener gets carried along by the flow of what he hears; sound and rhythm add to his understanding.

Faced with a phrase like:

If it were done when 'tis done then 'twere well
It were done quickly,

the reader might pause to look at the syntax. But, in the theater,
even a half-attentive listener will hear a man, on the point of committing a murder, saying

If...*done*...*done*...well...*done* quickly...

the repeated "done" sounding like an ominous knocking at a
door...

He may not know what "fardels" are, but hearing

Who would fardels bear
To grunt and sweat under a weary life

the words "grunt," "sweat," and "weary" conjure up the image of
a beast of burden. Shakespeare's repetitions— ("the very torrent,
tempest, and...whirlwind of passion," "the origin and com-
mencement of his grief") are all part of this Oral Style. If a cough
in the audience should blot out a word or two, the sense still
comes across.

What appears difficult on the page often becomes clear when
aptly spoken. The rhythm of a sentence expresses the sense as well
as the words. Punctuation is all-important, as John Gielgud confirms:

It seemed to me that if you were not quite sure of a difficult
speech in Shakespeare, and you studied the punctuation and
got it right, the sense would in some way emerge. Much later,
in both *A Winter's Tale* and *Measure for Measure* I was alarmed
to find that so much of the verse was very obscure but I tried

to trust to the sweep of every speech, and to mark the commas and full stops and semi-colons, and if I observed these correctly, as a bad swimmer begins to trust the water, the text seemed to hold me up.[3]

There are two different ways of looking at a Shakespeare speech. One is to look for the sense of it and the emotion—and you will find these confirmed by the rhythm and the sounds. Alternatively, look at the rhythm and the sounds—and these will lead you to the sense and the emotion. It's been compared to a hill with a tunnel running from west to east. The man who goes in by the western entrance will eventually find himself at the eastern exit, and vice versa.

A speech from *Othello* will help to illustrate this.

Othello is in a mood to avenge himself on his wife for her supposed unfaithfulness. His cry of "Arise, black vengeance" is countered by Iago's "Patience, I say; your mind, perhaps, may change." Perhaps Othello answers:

Never, Iago. Like to the Pontick sea,
Whose icy current and compulsive course
Ne'er feels retiring ebb, but keeps due on
To the Propontic and the Hellespont,
Even so my bloody thoughts, with violent pace
Shall ne'er look back, ne'er ebb to humble love,
Till that a capable and wide revenge
Swallow them up.

(III.3)

At first, this might look like a purple passage, a poetic jewel stuck in the scene to make it glitter. Let us take both "entrances to the tunnel." First, the sense. Othello's "bloody thoughts" will go on relentlessly until they express themselves in revenge. They

[3] John Gielgud, *Shakespeare—Hit or Miss?*, 1991.

are as unstoppable as the current of the Pontick or Black Sea, as it sweeps down the Bosporus,[4] through the Sea of Marmara, as far as the Dardanelles, (the "Hellespont") where it loses itself in the Aegean. The mood is one of grim, bloodthirsty determination. The intention: to convince Iago that his mind will not change.

Now let us look at it technically—for the rhythm and the sounds.

The speech goes on for seven lines before it reaches a full stop. The speech gathers strength, keeps due on, neither ebbing nor looking back, until it reaches the climax:

revenge

Swallow them up.

Its relentlessness is underlined by the repetitions. The opening "Never" recurs three times: "ne'er feels retiring ebb...ne'er look back, ne'er ebb to humble love." The dark *o* of Pontick is hammered on in Propontic and Hellespont. If he had chosen to say Black Sea or Dardanelles (as those who wish to "translate" him would probably do), he would not achieve the same sinister effect. For when the current dissolves itself into the open sea, the vowels, too, open into *a*'s and *i*'s and *e*'s: "capable (in the sense of "capacious") and wide revenge." The speech has its own "compulsive course."

So in its length and its relentlessness the speech is *imitating* both the currents from the Pontick sea and the onward-going movements of his bloody thoughts. It does not merely *describe* Othello's determination, it *embodies* it.

The one period suggests that the sentence is written to be uttered without drawing breath, the actor building all the time— the commas are mere aids to comprehension. The actor who

---

[4] He could not have known that while the current of the Bosporus flows in one direction (from the Black Sea to the Dardanelles) the *under*current, denser and more saline, flows in the opposite direction. See Neil Ascherson, *Black Sea,* 1995.

"chops it up" will find he is *explaining* the emotion; the actor who can do it in one, will be *expressing* the emotion. Besides, the speech is typical of Othello's character—he sticks to one idea and is not easily deflected. How better can he prove to Iago that his mind will not change?

And so we see that sense, sound, rhythm, and even dramatic intention, are all fused together.

The words can no more be said to "get in the actor's way" than a railway track can be said to get in the way of a train.

Othello was a soldier who had travelled. Indeed, he won Desdemona's heart with his stories of adventures in distant lands. When he cites the Pontick sea, we can assume that this is not merely an example plucked out of the air, but a memory of something he saw one day, standing on a hill in Asia Minor, watching its inexorable current. An actor playing Othello would recognize this as a glimpse of Othello's past.

This one sentence, then, is doing a lot of work. It is refuting Iago's surmise; it is illustrating Othello's steadfastness of purpose; it is advancing the plot—for henceforth, there will be no turning back; and it is also offering us a sliver of autobiography. Far from using many words to make one simple point, as may at first appear, it is using relatively few words to make a good many points.

# II
# MOVING PICTURES

Shakespeare used words like no one else. When his language looks unfamiliar, many people assume that he was writing sixteenth-century English and that that idiom has passed away. If this were so, his contemporaries would have written like him. But look at Jonson, Marlowe, Webster, Ford. None of them possessed his audacity with words and images. Shakespeare's language was his own invention.

His skill with words gets taken for granted, but in fact it is the nucleus of his talent. He had a mind like a thesaurus. It is difficult to imagine him searching for a word—they presented themselves to him in batches, and he only had to pick the one he wanted. Ben Jonson says that "he never blotted (crossed out) a line," and when the mood was on him, he evidently wrote swiftly and frenziedly, breaking rules, inventing, improvising, experimenting, playing a kind of verbal jazz.

He yoked together words that sounded similar:

*swill'd* with the *wild* and wasteful ocean

With many ho*liday* and *lady* terms he question'd me

and paired off words that had not been introduced:

Disdain and scorn *ride sparkling* in her eyes

He juxtaposed rolling Latin words with short flat Saxon ones:

*holla* your name to the *reverberate* hills

No, this my hand will rather
The *multitudinous* seas *incarnadine*
Making the *green one red.*

He made adjectives do the work of nouns, and both of them
behave like verbs:

in the dead *vast* and middle of the night

There are a sort of men whose visages
Do *cream* and *mantle* like a standing pond

Look, love, what *envious* streaks
Do *lace* the *sev'ring* clouds in yonder east…

He capers nimbly in a lady's chamber
To the *lascivious pleasing* of a lute

Simple words, but they stop us in our tracks because we have not
seen them used that way before.

He could take such liberties with language because in his time
the rules of English were not yet hard and fast. Grammarians were
only just beginning to put it in order. English was not the universal language it is today—only the English spoke it.

Grammar schools, such as the one Shakespeare attended,
existed to teach Latin grammar, not English, for a man was not
considered to be educated unless he could write and read Latin
fluently. (Shakespeare, according to Ben Jonson—himself a classicist—
had "small Latin and less Greek.") Foreign diplomats visiting

London would not even bother to learn English, they would converse in Latin, because it was lucid and unambiguous, offering fewer chances of misunderstandings. Besides, Latin had a literature that served as a model for good style and correct usage, while English literature had yet to be created. English was simply the language of "the people."

But under the hard piecrust of Latin, the fruit of the pie, native English, was boiling and bubbling. The language was expanding as never before. People were coming to London from the provinces with their local dialects. (Sir Walter Raleigh always spoke with a strong Devonshire accent.) Travellers were arriving from abroad, speaking French and Italian and Dutch, and bringing foreign books. Words from their tongues were rapidly adopted and anglicized. New words were appearing every day.

The Elizabethans relished a felicitous word or a well-turned phrase. Like language students today, men would carry notebooks, or "tablets," in which to note down new words or expressions that caught their fancy. Such men were often in evidence in the playhouses. "Where are my tablets? Meet it is I set it down," cries Hamlet, in front of an audience many of whom are at that very moment noting down his own newly minted phrases.

Bernard Shaw, in an amusing playlet *The Dark Lady of the Sonnets,* shows Shakespeare, in conversation with a Beefeater and with Queen Elizabeth, doing it himself, noting down felicitous phrases for later use in his plays. This is not unlikely. Word collecting was a fashion, and Shakespeare one of the most zealous of collectors.

Scholars make much of the enormity of his vocabulary. It has been calculated that he possessed some 25,000 to 30,000 words. This is twice as many as his nearest rival, John Milton, and over ten times as many as Racine used—or chose to use. Many of these words came from reading, although there is no evidence that he possessed a large library, and no books are mentioned in his will.

And Dr. A.L. Rowse has pointed out[1] that the notable influences of the Bible and of Ovid in his works come only from the first books of the Old and New Testaments and from the first books of *Metamorphoses,* which suggests that he could not read for long before he felt the itch to write.

The majority of words he must have learned from talking, and above all listening, to people from all walks of life and from all parts of England. (The Elizabethans, like the Irish, were ebullient talkers.)

He knew the terminologies of medicine, sports, music, and cooking. He used so accurately the professional jargon of soldiers and sailors and lawyers, that later commentators have conjectured that he himself must have once served on land or sea, or worked in a lawyer's office. Politicians, too, have argued that he could not have written as he did unless he himself had been in the corridors of power; just as we—theater people—are certain that he was an actor.

Many find it impossible to imagine that a "poor player," with a mere grammar school education, should possess such a wealth of words. Indeed, the extraordinary idea has been put forward by some envious academics that no one man could master such a phenomenal vocabulary, and that "William Shakespeare" was a pen-name shared by a number of different writers—that Shakespeare was a committee!

What matters, of course, is not how many words a writer knows, but what he does with them—the patterns he creates, the combinations he achieves. Many linguists of genius are execrable stylists, and few professors of literature have shown that they can write one line of poetry.

> You taught me language; and my profit on't
> Is I know how to curse…
>
> (I.2)

says Caliban.

---

[1] A.L. Rowse, *William Shakespeare A Biography.*

Computers can tell us how many times the word *bird* or *late* appear in the Collected Works, but a computer has no aesthetic sense and cannot measure why clusters of simple words can take the breath away with their beauty and harmony:

bare ruin'd choirs where late the sweet birds sang

daffodils
That come before the swallow dares and take
The winds of March with beauty...

With fairest flowers
While summer lasts, and I live here, Fidele,
I'll sweeten thy sad grave...

...the music crept by me on the waters...

What scourge for perjury can this dark monarchy
Afford poor Clarence?

(All those dark vowels! and one open *a* at the end!)

An immense vocabulary he may have had, but often it's the way he combines the plainest of words that moves us most.

Time and again one is struck by his ability to capture in words what would otherwise seem to elude description. G.K. Chesterton once said that anybody who could describe clearly how to tie a knot must be a master of English prose, but Shakespeare could sum up more complicated actions than that. No phenomenon of nature seemed to be beyond him. On a woman's increasing sexual attraction:

Other women cloy
The appetites they feed; but she makes hungry
Where most she satisfies...

on sorrow, how persistent it can be:

> Sorrow, like a heavy-hanging bell,
> Once set on ringing, with its own weight goes...

on the movement of a feather:

> Look, as I blow this feather from my face,
> And as the air blows it to me again,
> Obeying, with my wind when I do blow,
> And yielding to another when it blows,
> Commanded always by the greater gust...

(this image to illustrate the fickleness of public opinion!)—or the sudden fall into disgrace of a politician who had occupied the highest post in the land:

> I have ventured
> Like little wanton boys that swim on bladders
> This many summers in a sea of glory;
> But far beyond my depth: my high-blown pride
> At length broke under me; and now has left me
> Weary and old with service, to the mercy
> Of a rude stream, that must for ever hide me...

We cannot help noticing how down-to-earth the comparisons are, how big subjects like sex, sorrow, or the ups and downs of politics, are likened to quite homely, familiar things—eating, a tolling bell, a feather, or boys swimming on inflated balloons. We have seen Othello's craving for revenge likened to the sea in flood, and God's mercy to "the gentle rain from heaven."

His contemporary playwrights, highly educated men like Marlowe and Ben Jonson, would often put in high-flown metaphors—mostly drawn from books—to give their speeches a bit of a poetic lift. But Shakespeare does the contrary—he brings us down to earth, his images are not there to embellish, or to display his learning, but to help the listener to understand, and—in his mind's eye, to see. He draws little word-pictures, based on every-day things.

They'll take suggestion as a cat laps milk...

This fellow picks up wit as pigeons peas...

...and is become to bellows and the fan
To cool a gypsy's lust.

—Take you me for a sponge, my lord?
—Ay, sir, that soaks up the king's
countenance, his rewards, his authorities...

Northumberland, thou ladder, wherewithal
The mounting Bolingbroke ascends my throne...

Now is this golden crown like a deep well
That owes* two buckets filling one another;            (*owns)
The emptier ever dancing in the air,
The other down, unseen, and full of water...

There is, of course, a very good reason for all this. Shakespeare is relating directly to his audience. He is constantly making complicated matters accessible by likening them to objects that the listeners see and touch and use. Describing the relationship between two crafty usurpers to the throne by calling one the other's "ladder" makes the situation clear to every member of the audience. It is more than a word-picture, it is a little story—for everyone knows what a temporary utensil a ladder is, and how usually it gets kicked away after use (which is exactly what Bolingbroke does to Northumberland).

Shakespeare referred not only to the accessories of daily life that were familiar to his public, but to their most important preoccupations. They lived closer to nature than we do, and had less protection from it. Their lives were regulated by winter and summer, night and day, storms and sunshine. Their day started before dawn broke, sunrise was an important event shared by all— so that when a king is said to appear like the sun,[2] everybody had a picture in his mind of that moment; just as when Cleopatra at Antony's death says she feels as if the sun has burned itself to a cinder and left the world like a star in darkness,

> O sun!
> Burn the great sphere thou mov'st in; ...darkling stand
> The varying star of the world...

the whole audience could imagine how great her grief was. To an audience that had crops to tend, fruit trees to cultivate, and sheep to care for, the opening words of *Richard III,* the passage from winter to summer, were not mere figurative speaking, but the most direct way possible of conveying an atmosphere of well-being, and peace after war.

Shakespeare is not flowery, puffed up, vague, but hard, earthy, and specific. Here is the learned Ben Jonson celebrating a lady's charms:

> She is Venus when she smiles;
> But she's Juno when she walks
> And Minerva when she talks.

and here is Shakespeare:

> I grant I never saw a goddess go:
> My mistress, when she walks, treads on the ground.

---

[2] See, see, King Richard doth himself appear
As doth the blushing, discontented sun
From out the fiery portal of the east
When he perceives the envious clouds are bent
To dim his glory and to stain the track
Of his bright passage to the occident.

Or take the word *lamp*. When Marlowe talks of lamps, it is simply a pretty way of not using the word *stars:*

> the ceaseless lamps
> That gently look'd upon this loathsome earth...

But for Shakespeare—and for most members of his audience—a lamp is an imperfect household object, with a wick that gets used and oil that runs out (how many times, writing late at night, Shakespeare must have met this problem!). And when he gives an old man on the point of death these words to say:

> My oil-dried lamp and time-bewasted light
> Shall be extinct with age and endless night.
> My inch of taper will be burnt and done...

he is not being romantic about death, but realistic, using a daily domestic occurrence to bring home to his audience the fragility and brevity of human life; and, moreover, drawing a little picture in words that they all will recognize.

Reading, we cannot "see" Marlowe's ceaseless lamps, but we can see Shakespeare's oil-lamp, as it fizzles out. And if the actor, speaking the lines, can see it in his mind's eye, the audience too will see it in theirs.

The most extraordinary feature of the images he uses, the word-pictures that he draws, is the movement they contain. The word-pictures are moving pictures, the images show us not still lifes, but happenings. Movement is one of the hardest things to put into words (which made it for Chesterton so difficult to describe the tying of a knot), but movement never ceases to fascinate Shakespeare. Like a sculptor who delights in using immobile stone and bronze to capture a horse prancing or a dancer in movement, so Shakespeare uses language to show a world in motion. Watch his verbs.

Rough winds *shake* the buds of May, Mercy *droppeth* as the rain, sorrow's bell *goes on ringing*, a feather *yields* to the wind, small swimming boys *fall* into the stream, winter *turns* to summer, oil lamps *dry up* and their tapers *burn out*—and this is merely to quote the examples we have seen already. There is always something going on, ~~there is always a verb injecting life into the image.~~ The sun rises and kills the envious moon, winds blow and crack their cheeks, the lightning "doth cease to be / Ere one can say 'it lightens,'" the sea chafes and rages and takes up the shore, its currents turn awry or keep due on. Even stone has its life: Rocks impregnable get decayed by Time, and waterdrops wear out the stones of Troy.

Nature is never still. He must have noticed this from his earliest childhood, in watery Warwickshire, where he went "unwillingly to school" no doubt, preferring to watch what was going on in the kitchen, where the chickens trotted in and out while his mother was feeding his baby brother:

> Lo, as a careful housewife runs to catch
> One of her feather'd creatures broke away,
> Sets down her babe, and makes all quick despatch
> In pursuit of the thing she would have stay

or had problems with an ill-ventilated oven:

> Sorrow concealed, like an oven stopped,
> Doth burn the heart to cinders where it is

(No other dramatist of his time ever made any reference to something so domestic as a stopped oven.)[3] Or he went out to play in the surrounding fields and woods, and watched birds and little animals, always in motion. It takes a country boy to observe such details as this:

---

[3] Dr. Caroline Spurgeon has made an invaluable study of how Shakespeare unconsciously reveals himself through the images he uses: *Shakespeare's Imagery and What it Tells Us*, 1935.

...a dive-dapper, peering through a wave
Who, being look'd on, ducks as quickly in.

or:

The bird that hath been limed* in a bush     (*ensnared by glue on twig)
With trembling wings misdoubteth every bush

(We can see the bird, hovering above the branch, undecided whether to land or not.)

The pictures are already little stories, and he empathizes with the bird's emotions. A dramatist is being born. He even notices a crisis in the life of no lesser creature than a:

...snail, whose tender horns being hit,
Shrinks backward in his shelly cave with pain,
And there, all smother'd up, in shade doth sit,
Long after fearing to creep forth again.
                              (*Venus and Adonis*, 1033–36)

He is not looking at the snail from the outside—the words "shelly cave" and "in shade" suggest that, in his imagination, he is there inside, with the creature. He is, as it were, *identifying* himself with the snail. The writer who, later, would identify himself with King Lear and Cleopatra and Hamlet was also capable of perceiving the world from the point of view of a tiny gastropod!

If he were to turn his attention away from the snail, and lie on his back to gaze at the clouds, he would have seen them, too, changing shape:

Sometime we see a cloud that's dragonish,
A vapour sometime like a bear or lion,
A tower'd citadel, a pendant rock,
A forked mountain, or blue promontory
With trees upon't, that nod unto the world

And mock our eyes with air…
That which is now a horse, even with a thought
The rack dislimns, and makes it indistinct
As water is in water.

(*Antony and Cleopatra:* IV.14)

Seeing shapes in clouds is a thing children do. Discovering the world around them, they show a freshness of imagination denied to most adults. Yet when he wrote this, Shakespeare was in his forties, and the words are given to an even older character—the Emperor Antony, who just before his death feels that he is going to pieces and cannot any more find his identity:

…here I am Antony;
Yet cannot hold this visible shape…

and compares himself to clouds dissolving and melting into thin air.

It is remarkable that a writer in the prime of life should have such an insight into what it feels like, with death waiting in the wings, to lose one's grip on oneself and on the world; and to translate this feeling into an image that every child has seen.

As with Othello's advancing Pontick sea, so with Antony's melting clouds, a movement in the world of nature helps us to understand a character's state of mind.

Shakespeare's skill at capturing in words the restlessness of nature is not an end in itself, but a means to an end to revealing man's inner world, the world of his emotions. And just as a character in a drama is usually pulled this way and that by conflicting impulses (to take this action or that action? to commit a murder, or not? to go on living, or to die? to do one's duty, or to follow one's emotions?) his mind in a constant state of change, so nature in movement reflects this mental commotion. After all (Shakespeare might argue), Man himself is always slowly changing, growing up or growing old:

> And so, from hour to hour we ripe and ripe
> And then from hour to hour we rot and rot.

and his emotions are as changeable as English weather. Only a pompous old politician like Julius Caesar can claim "But I am constant as the northern star"; Shakespeare's most unforgettable characters are not constant at all; Hamlet, Cleopatra, and Richard II change tack from one moment to the next. They fascinate us just because they are so hard to pin down. (A butterfly that has been "pinned down" is a dead butterfly.)

There flourished in his day an avid curiosity about the nature of Man. What was he made of, this creature half way between an angel and an animal? His mind was like an undiscover'd country. And just as explorers like Sir Walter Raleigh were sailing abroad to examine that stretch of land called America, so philosophers and poets like Bacon and Montaigne and Shakespeare were charting that land that was Man's inner consciousness, his mind and heart, his secret life.

Society had allotted to each his role: One was a king, another a beggar; one was a judge who dealt out punishment, another was a whore who, if she was unlucky, suffered it. But being and seeming were two distinct things, a person could often be the opposite of what he or she seemed. A man admired for his honesty and integrity might be a calculating intriguer, a woman accounted a she-devil might be a woman full of love. What was the human being really like, under "the furred gown or tattered robes"?

However, Shakespeare could not write a play about Man, only about men, and women. Just as Kingsley Amis, when asked for an article on The English Mind, replied "Whose English mind?" so Shakespeare probably, if someone suggested he wrote about Man, would have retorted, "Which man?" Paradoxically, in rewriting an old play about Hamlet he put so much humanity into the role that through the ages men and women have identified themselves with the hero, and the play has become a sort of modern *Everyman*. But no doubt he set out simply to write a play about Hamlet.

His writing, and what we know of his life, show that he had a very practical mind. His characters are pulled hither and thither by forces like Love, Ambition, Jealousy, and Guilt. They feel Pity and Sorrow. Some seek Honor, others are prone to Melancholy. Many of them fear Death. A great number of his plays deal with Kingship, and Power, with War and Peace. But he was a visual writer—he needed to write about things he, and his audience— could see. A ladder, a bucket, an oil-lamp, a river in flood, a flash of lightning—these are visible things.

But Ambition? Guilt? Sorrow? Kingship?

Abstract words.

Invisible things needed to be made visible. He could not let an abstract word slip from his pen without straightaway linking it with a concrete image. "The poet" as Theseus says:

> gives to airy nothings
> A local habitation and a name.

Any page of his plays will offer dozens of examples.

We have seen Sorrow like "a heavy-hanging bell" and Sorrow concealed like a "stopped oven." We also find Sorrow conscripted:

> When sorrows come, they come not single spies
> But in battalions.

Ambition is embodied in a clumsy rider who misses his mount:

> Vaulting ambition, which o'erleaps itself
> And falls on the other.

But when ambition diminishes, it becomes a badly made coat:

Ill-weav'd ambition, how much art thou shrunk…

Beware of Jealousy,

> It is the green-eyed monster that doth mock
> The meat it feeds on.
> (Like a fly spreading germs on food)

Kingship can be protecting—and constricting:

> O majesty!
> When thou dost pinch thy bearer, thou dost sit
> Like a rich armour worn in heat of day
> That scalds with safety.

War is seen as hunting hounds:

> Cry "Havoc!" and let slip the dogs of war.
> Now for the bare-pick'd bone of majesty
> Doth dogged war bristle his angry crest
> And snarleth in the gentle eyes of peace.

A warrior king, Henry V, is pictured with three dogs of war, each with an abstract name.

> Then should the war-like Harry, like himself
> Assume the port* of Mars; and at his heels,          (*posture)
> Leash'd in like hounds, should famine, sword, and fire,
> Crouch for employment.

Hunting was a popular sport. For most Elizabethans the hunted animal was no more than meat. Shakespeare was the only poet to show feeling for the terrified deer, hare, or bird.

Death, in the popular imagination, was a ghoulish skeletal figure with a scythe, the Grim Reaper. Shakespeare invented other ways of looking at him.

...this fell sergeant, death,
Is strict in his arrest.

Reason thus with life:
Merely, thou art death's fool;
For him thou labour'st by thy flight to shun
And yet runst toward him still.

Juliet's father, finding her apparently lifeless, cries:

Death is my son-in-law, death is my heir,
My daughter he hath wedded.

Those who quote with amazement the extent of Shakespeare's vocabulary are perhaps on the wrong track. What deserves admiration is the number of *images* he had at his disposal.

The above selection has been made at random, simply to illustrate how abstract words are continually paired off with concrete word pictures. No apology need be made for putting his phrases, out of context, under the microscope, for his metaphors too often get taken for granted.

He did not, however, use them at random. Scrutinizing them, one finds a certain pattern appearing, which is of immense help to an actor.

The word *image* is, evidently, connected to "imagination." Shakespeare, creating a character, was less concerned with what that character looked like or how he walked, than with how he saw the world and how he expressed his feelings—in short, with how his imagination worked, and with the images that furnished it.

To return to Othello's "Pontick sea" speech, it is typical of him that he uses this example. Othello's language is full of references to such prodigies of nature—"antres (caverns) vast and deserts idle," "hills, whose heads touch heaven," "hills of seas," and eclipses of the sun and moon; he swears an oath "by this marble heaven." His sword is from Spain, and his handkerchief from

Egypt; in his last speech he talks of Arabian trees and of Aleppo. This is not only the landscape of his memories, it is the landscape of his mind.

Compare this with the language of Iago, full of lust and lechery. He harps on copulating animals—goats and monkeys and wolves. His philosophy is "Put money in thy purse," his oath, "Divinity of hell!"

The drama between the two men plays itself out even on the level of language. As Iago's poisonous ideas begin to work on Othello, Othello's language begins to change. He, too, starts to talk of toads and crocodiles, goats and monkeys, and refers to Desdemona as a "lewd minx."

One of the vital keys to understanding a Shakespearean character is a study of the images that character uses.

Many actors favor a quasi-psychological approach, asking themselves, "Has Othello known women before?" or "Did Iago have an unhappy childhood?" These are questions on which we can only speculate; there is no evidence one way or another. And in what way is the character's past relevant, while there, in black and white, are the images that make up the character's *present* mental world?

The language of Romeo and Juliet is often too flowery to be quite credible for a pair of adolescents. But Shakespeare was then quite young and was feeling his way as a writer. However, the young lovers constantly see each other as images of light in a dark setting.

O she doth teach the torches to burn bright!

Take him, and cut him out in little stars,
And he shall make the face of heaven so fine
That all the world shall be in love with night

For the actor, this gives emotions that might otherwise be blurred and sentimental a sharpness and a focus. "Act as if you're in love with Juliet" is a less helpful indication than "React to Juliet as if you're in a dark place, and she's a bright light." The focus of their love is that they *dazzle* each other.

Antony, who speaks continually of islands, continents, oceans, and empires, can be said to have a vast and global imagination. He'd throw away a third of the world to make love to Cleopatra:

> Let Rome in Tiber melt, and the wide arch
> Of the rang'd empire fall!...
> the nobleness of life
> Is to do thus; *(embracing)*

It is no accident that, dying, he looks at the sky and compares himself to a cloud-bank.

What a contrast with ancient Justice Shallow, (IV.2) a man of no imagination, only memories of long-dead friends, who with one foot in the grave himself can only bleat out platitudes about death:

> Death, as the psalmist said, is certain;
> all shall die...

and go on to ask about the current price of cattle.

Hamlet makes so many half-hidden references to fevers, ulcers, sores, and even sees his own tendency to think too much in terms of illness:

> And thus the native hue of resolution
> Is sicklied o'er with the pale cast of thought

that many biographers have concluded that Shakespeare himself was ill when he wrote it. If he was, it's none of our business. Hamlet is speaking, not Shakespeare.

Falstaff frequently quotes the Bible and the Prayer Book, and this is often used to prove that Shakespeare knew the Bible well.

Yes, certainly he did. "It has been estimated," says A.L. Rowse,[4] "that his Biblical range is five times that of Peele or Marlowe, and far greater than that of any contemporary dramatist." This is certainly interesting; but more to the point, is that Falstaff, materialist and earthy old glutton that he was, knew the Bible well. It suggests a whole chapter of his past life that he never refers to.

In fact we do Shakespeare a service if we assume that each character is alone responsible for his own words—to imagine that each had, as it were, written his own part; and to reduce the playwright's role to that of a kind of editor-in-chief. This means not blaming the author if a role appears underwritten or inconsistent.

Richard II, for instance, has a role coruscating with ideas and poetic fancies, while Bolingbroke the usurper speaks a much duller language, and is often given to bouts of silence. Many critics conclude that Shakespeare was more "inspired" when writing Richard's part, and nodded off when it came to writing lines for Bolingbroke. But let us assume that this is because "Bolingbroke" himself could not do any better. His lack of poetry is his own, not Shakespeare's. And if he is frequently speechless (Richard even calls him "silent king"), there is a good reason for it. He cannot follow Richard's verbal arabesques. He is simply a duller man. If he had talked in the same poetic vein as Richard, the play would mean something quite different—it would no longer be a play about a visionary king being deposed by a man with the mind of a crooked business man.

In the long run it would be more appropriate to talk of Shakespeare's languages in the plural, for each character has his own language, with its own rhythms, verse forms, and above all its own set of images. Like a character actor of genius, the author only appears in a series of virtually impenetrable disguises. In his work, as in his life, he has done a superb vanishing act.

---

[4] A.L. Rowse, *William Shakespeare: A Biography.*

Probably he thought himself (Will-the-man as opposed to Shakespeare-the-writer) as of no significance or interest to anyone outside his immediate circle, and his own life—or death as nothing exceptional. In his characters' mouths he put some of the most eloquent utterances about death in the English language, but when it came to his own demise, he had no literary pretentions. He did not take himself that seriously. So it seems more than likely that he, almighty poet that he was, did indeed write the flat, unpoetic doggerel that is inscribed on his tombstone.

A prime example of Shakespeare's "moving pictures" is this speech from *Henry V*, where Chorus, the play's presenter, urges the audience to imagine the last tense hours before the battle of Agincourt.

Note how cinematic the writing is—it reads almost like a shooting script, and in every "shot" there's movement. Watch the verbs—there are some forty of them—besides action words like *creeping,* and *poring.* And notice also the "sound track"—the whispers, the hammering the cock crows; not forgetting the "lighting," from the camp fires and the moon:

Now entertain conjecture of a time
When creeping murmur and the poring dark
Fills the wide vessel of the universe.
From camp to camp, through the foul womb of night,
The hum of either army stilly sounds,
That the fixed sentinels almost receive
The secret whispers of each other's watch.
Fire answers fire, and through their paly flames
Each battle sees the other's umbered face.
Steed threatens steed, in high and boastful neighs,
Piercing the night's dull ear; and from the tents
The armourers, accomplishing the knights,
With busy hammers closing rivets up,
Give dreadful note of preparation.
The country cocks do crow, the clocks do toll,

And the third hour of drowsy morning name.
Proud of their numbers, and secure in soul,
The confident and over-lusty French
Do the low-rated English play at dice,
And chide the cripple tardy-gaited night
Who like a foul and ugly witch doth limp
So tediously away. The poor condemnèd English
Like sacrifices, by their watchful fires
Sit patiently, and inly ruminate
The morning's danger; and their gesture sad,
investing lank-lean cheeks and war torn coats,
Presenteth them unto the gazing moon
So many horrid ghosts. O now, who will behold
The royal Captain of this ruined band
Walking from watch to watch, from tent to tent,
Let him cry, "Praise and glory on his head!"
For forth he goes and visits all his host,
Bids them good morrow with a modest smile,
And calls them brothers, friends and countrymen.
Upon his royal face there is no note
How dread an army hath enrounded him,
Nor doth he dedicate one jot of color
unto the weary and all-watchèd night,
But freshly looks, and overbears attaint
With cheerful semblance and sweet majesty;
That every wretch, pining and pale before,
Beholding him, plucks comfort from his looks.
A largess universal, like the sun,
His liberal eye doth give to every one,
Thawing cold fear, that mean and gentle all
Behold, as may unworthiness define,
A little touch of Harry in the night.
And so our scene must to the battle fly;
Where—O for pity!—we shall much disgrace,
With four or five most vile and ragged foils,

Right ill-disposed in brawl ridiculous,
The name of Agincourt. Yet sit and see,
Minding true things by what their mockeries be.
                              (*Henry V:* IV.Prologue)

# III

# FINDING THE FORM

⁓

The British are reputed to have a tradition of playing Shakespeare. Certainly they are used to him. Few British stage actors can have got through their careers without, at one time or another, playing something of his. If we were to take a map of England and stick a pin on every town or village where Shakespeare is being played tonight, the map would look like a hedgehog. A popular play like *Twelfth Night*, it has been estimated, gets up to 150 different productions a year.

A cursory glance at the list of the major English actors over the last four hundred years reminds us that their names are *all* associated with Shakespeare. Burbage, Betterton, Kean, Garrick, Mrs. Siddons, Macready, Irving, Ellen Terry, Beerbohm Tree, Forbes Robertson; and in the twentieth century, Gielgud, Olivier, Redgrave, Sybil Thorndike, Peggy Ashcroft, Edith Evans, Paul Scofield; and lately, Vanessa Redgrave, Derek Jacobi, Ian McKellen, Kenneth Branagh, Anthony Sher, Judi Dench, and Maggie Smith—all are remembered for, and some owe their reputations to, their excellence in one or more Shakespearean roles. Evidently he gave them wings. Conversely, many an excellent player has died and fallen into oblivion, whose name was not connected with Shakespeare.

But if we were able, by some kind of time machine, to "see" Garrick's Hamlet or Irving's Lear today, we would probably find that they had very little in common with Scofield or McKellen, apart from speaking the same words. And often, not even that. We would be astounded by the disparity in acting styles, and often equally astounded by the different versions used.

There does exist an early silent film of the Hamlet of the nineteenth-century actor, Sir Johnston Forbes Robertson. When he made it, he was over sixty—he didn't start playing the part until he was middle-aged, but in those days that was no drawback. We see a gaunt weather-beaten figure with flowing hair and what John Gielgud has called "large Gothik gestures." Even without the voice, his magnetism comes through. But today no audiences would accept this as Hamlet, since he was at an age when many actors would find themselves too old to play Lear. But it is not absurd. In its day it was a pinnacle of the actor's art. "See all that; and you have seen a true classical Hamlet," wrote Bernard Shaw. "It will bear seeing again and again."

If there is a tradition of playing Shakespeare in England, it lies in the freedom and diversity, and often the irreverence and impertinence with which his plays are handled. But there's one common denominator among all the actors listed in the twentieth century, and that is their belief in, and respect for, Shakespeare's text. This is no pedantic notion suggesting that his works were sacred, and that no word may be altered or cut, but a conviction that he was a supreme craftsman of the theater, and a truthful portraitist of human beings.

This was not always the general view. For some two hundred and fifty years he had been looked upon as a quarry from which lines and scenes could be hewn to suit theater managers' needs.

When the London theaters reopened in 1660, after the Restoration of the monarchy, actors must have forgotten how to play him. Samuel Pepys noted in his diary (and he was a keen theatergoer) that *A Midsummer Night's Dream* was "the most insipid ridiculous play that ever I saw in my life," and that *Twelfth Night* was "but a silly play, and not related at all to the name or day."

The eighteenth century thought Shakespeare a sort of wild man of the woods—crude, vulgar, tasteless, and his plays as gems of poetry imprisoned in a load of dross. Voltaire called him "a barbarian of genius." Play-doctors and actor managers set about improving and rewriting the plays. Colley Cibber and Nahum Tate set out to ensure, like Hollywood producers, that his plays had positive, upbeat endings. Romeo and Juliet were reunited at the end, and given an extra love scene to boot. King Lear and Cordelia, and even poor old Gloucester, were kept alive at the end—and Cordelia married Edgar. Vulgar characters like Lear's Fool were given the sack, and the Drunken Porter in Macbeth was replaced by a respectable serving man, as Decency demanded. Even old Antigonus in *A Winter's Tale,* whom Shakespeare killed off in Act II, devoured by a bear, reappeared at the end of Act V (sixteen years later) with the unlikely story that he had killed the bear, preserved it in ice, and had been living on its meat ever since. And Shakespeare's language was laundered. Macbeth's crude cry:

> The devil damn thee black, thou cream-fac'd loon,
> Where got'st thou that goose look?

became, "Now, friend, what means thy change of countenance?"

The nineteenth century saw the rise of the scene painter and the inventor of stage machinery. It seemed that nothing could not be imitated—snowstorms, train crashes, even horse races. Shakespeare, with his battle scenes and pageantry, his Roman forums, his Sphinx, his coronations series and his enchanted forests, provided them with many an excuse for spectacle. Besides, the nineteenth century loved nothing more than a hero it could admire, a Great Man standing head and shoulders above his fellows, and here the great actor-managers saw their opportunity to excel. The plays were cut and reshaped to make garments for Henry Irving and Beerbohm Tree. The leading actors and the scenic artists did the work; secondary roles were hacked about or chopped out to give more elbow room for the star, and the public was often kept waiting for quarters of an hour at a time staring at a red curtain, while elaborate scene changes went on behind it. Traditionally *Hamlet* ended when the prince said "The rest is silence" and expired; and Henry Irving brought the curtain down on *The Merchant of Venice* after Shylock (played by himself) had made his final exit—thus excising the whole fifth act.

In 1888, however, an important discovery was made. A German critic discovered in the University Library of Utrecht a drawing made in 1596 of the interior of the Swan Theatre in London. This was the first view anyone had ever had of the interior of an Elizabethan playhouse, with its thrust stage and galleries. Copied from a drawing by a Dutch priest, Johannes de Witt, who had been a tourist in London, it is puzzling and probably inaccurate, but it proved to be the thin end of the wedge as far as opulent Victorian Shakespeare staging was concerned. It stimulated speculation about how Shakespeare was originally performed. It led to his being reassessed and treated with more respect. Shakespeare started to become himself again. In England three remarkable men contributed to his restoration.

One of them was William Poel, a scholarly strolling player with the zeal of a missionary and the obstinacy of a fanatic. He was convinced that the picture-frame stage with its curtain and its decorative scenery was the opposite to what Shakespeare required: He wanted to reconstitute Elizabethan staging. Many thought him a crank, but Poel was overmastered by his vision, He dropped out of the commercial theater, and with a small band of adherents set up productions on stages denuded of scenery that imitated the Elizabethan playhouse.

He studied the original editions of the plays, and became convinced that the eccentric punctuation, the ubiquitous commas and the illogical brackets, were not printers' errors but score marking for actors, indicating pace, rhythm, and breathing. He discovered that the Elizabethan actors had a very quick and musical delivery, quite the opposite of the sonorous and overstressed declamation to be heard at the Lyceum and Her Majesty's, the theaters of Irving and Tree, and that the quicker Shakespeare was played, the more easy it was to understand. Above all, he made discoveries about verse speaking that still hold good today.

Producing *Richard II* in 1899, Poel engaged a handsome, Italianate young actor of twenty-two for the leading part, a man then unknown and fairly inexperienced, but destined to become the most influential director of the twentieth century—Harley Granville Barker. Barker later recounted how Poel had locked the whole cast of the play in the rehearsal room, refusing to release them until they had mastered his special ways of verse speaking—and that they were not freed until the early hours of the morning.

Barker said that Poel taught him more about the staging of Shakespeare "and the spirit of playing in it" than anyone else in Europe. Barker's own productions of *Twelfth Night* and *A Winter's Tale* at the Savoy Theatre just before the First World War became legendary. He did not follow Poel's extremist belief in bare stages and madrigals, what he called his "Elizabethan Methodism," but created something "essentially Elizabethan and dynamically modern," according to the actor-historian Robert Speaight, who went on to say "Barker's productions at the Savoy from 1912 to 1914 looked ahead in a pretty straight line to Peter Brook's *A Midsummer Night's Dream* at Stratford more than fifty years later."[1]

At the end of the First War, Barker suddenly withdrew from the theater. He married an American heiress, Helen Huntington, ten years his senior—according to Shaw she cut him off from the theater—and retired to live in France, returning to England only to supervise productions of his own plays (he was a notable and serious playwright), and finally in 1940 he came back to codirect

---

[1] Robert Speaight, *Shakespeare on the Stage,* 1973.

John Gielgud in *King Lear* at the Old Vic. "He had only ten days to work with us on King Lear, but they were the fullest in experience that I have ever had in all my years upon the stage," Gielgud wrote later, "Of his supremacy as a director no one who had the good fortune to attend those rehearsals can have any possible doubt."[2]

Barker's withdrawal from the practical theater scene was a great loss, but what the theater lost on the swings it gained on the merry-go-rounds. He spent his exile in France writing. His chief activity was a series of *Prefaces to Shakespeare*. He took ten plays for analysis, suggesting modestly that they were "some research into Shakespeare's stagecraft," while they are in fact the most thorough and imaginative studies of the plays, written from the point of view of a fellow dramatist, with an unearthly insight into how Shakespeare functioned. Many modern directors swear that they will always carry Granville Barker in their pocket when directing Shakespeare. As one critic wrote on their appearance, "After Mr. Granville Barker there will never again be the same excuse for misinterpretation."

In his youth, as an actor, Barker was a disciple of Bernard Shaw. Barker played the leads in Shaw's early plays (which Shaw himself directed). Shaw treated him as a surrogate son, and there were even rumours that he was his natural son.[3] Shaw is the third man partly responsible for the reappraisal of Shakespeare.

His attitude toward him was ambivalent. Shaw was contemptuous of what he thought of as Shakespeare's lack of political ideas, and of serving up platitudes expressed in fine words so that they sounded like profound truths:

> With the single exception of Homer, there is no eminent writer, not even Sir Walter Scott, whom I can despise so entirely as I despise Shakespeare when I measure my mind against his.

---

[2] John Gielgud, *Stage Directions*, 1963.

[3] Eric Salmon, *Granville Barker, A Secret Life*, 1983.

is one of Shaw's more cheeky sayings. He wrote this at a time when he was preparing to become a dramatist himself, and he was probably simply angry at Shakespeare for not being Bernard Shaw, and for not wanting to change the world.

Shaw, however, knew Shakespeare inside and out, and was full of admiration for him as a wordsmith, and a technically expert playwright. He professed to admire what he called with astonishing foresight his "twentieth century plays" like *Troilus and Cressida* and *All's Well that Ends Well* more than the acknowledged masterpieces.

He had been a music critic, and was himself an accomplished musician. Claiming that he composed his own plays like operas, he admired a similar musical quality in Shakespeare's. He praised Granville Barker as "a producer who has an ear for music"; and Barker himself referred to Shakespeare's plays as "a score awaiting performance."

As a drama critic, between 1895–98 on the *Saturday Review,* Shaw used his column to attack, wittily and virulently, the actor-managers who traduced Shakespeare's purposes, and used him "as a cuckoo uses a sparrow's nest" and "breaking (the plays) up and trying to jerry-build modern plays with them, as the Romans broke up the Coliseum to build hovels." Irving especially came under his lash:

> His Hamlet was not Shakespear's Hamlet, nor his Lear Shakespear's Lear…an impertinent intrusion of a quite silly conceit of his own into a great play…[4]

Shaw's views on Shakespeare, however irritating sometimes, are still enlightening today. This is partly because he does not consider him an impeccable playwright (but neither did Barker) and

---

[4] Bernard Shaw, *Our Theatres in the Nineties,*1895–98. Reassembled as Shaw's *Dramatic Criticism,* ed. John F. Matthews, and *Shaw on Shakespeare,* ed. Edwin Wilson.

because he knew how Shakespeare should be played and spoken. Nobody has expressed it better than he. If there is a key to speaking Shakespeare, he has found it.

In a letter to Ellen Terry, when she was playing at Irving's Lyceum, he wrote:

> In playing Shakespear, play *to* the lines, *through* the lines, *on* the lines, but never between the lines. There simply isn't time. You would not stick a five-bar rest into a Beethoven symphony to pick up your drumsticks and similarly you must not stop the Shakespear orchestra for business. Nothing short of a procession or a fight should make anything so extraordinary as a silence during a Shakespear performance.

Barker was to write a similar advice to John Gielgud in 1937:

> Everything the actor does must be done w*ithin the frame of the verse...* [5]

Shaw expanded his remarks in a favorable review he gave Johnston Forbes Robertson's *Hamlet* in 1897, that same Forbes Robertson whose silent film was mentioned previously. He professed himself astonished that the actor had kept so close to the text: the production was "really not at all unlike Shakespear's play of the same name." Analyzing the actor's performance, he writes:

> He does not utter half a line; then stop to act; then go on with another half line; and then stop to act again, with the clock running away with Shakespear's chances all the time. He plays as Shakespear should be played, on the line and to the line, with the utterance and acting simultaneous, inseparable, and in fact identical.

---

[5] Quoted in Robert Speaight, *William Poel and the Elizabethan Revival*, 1954.

# TRIPPINGLY ON THE TONGUE

A warning should be given to actors who, often unconsciously, insert little bridge words (like "oh," "yes, but…" and "well," or hesitations, to make dialogue sound more "natural." To hear someone say:

> To be, or er, well, yeah, *not* to be, that's the, er, that's the question. I mean, whether 'tis nobler in the um mind to, er, to *suffer* the…the slings and *arrows* of, of, of outrageous fortune, or to, to take arms *against* a, well, *sea* of troubles…

is more like listening to a piano tuner than to a pianist.

The actor's first aim is clarity. He must make us listen to him, and to carry us along with him.

But Shakespeare needs no "poetry voice." He was not writing high-flown literature, like Alfred Lord Tennyson or Dylan Thomas. His raw material was human speech, and what he produced was speeches to be spoken by human beings, and the actor's task is to find the human speech within the writing.

Here is a speech that has found its way into innumerable anthologies, and has been quoted in countless elocution recitals, so that many people think it's a poem, and forget that it's part of a play.

> The quality of mercy is not strain'd,
> It droppeth as the gentle rain from heaven
> Upon the place beneath: it is twice bless'd;
> It blesseth him that gives and him that takes:
> 'Tis mightiest in the mightiest; it becomes
> The throned monarch better than his crown;
> His sceptre shows the force of temporal power,
> The attribute to awe and majesty,
> Wherein doth sit the dread and fear of kings;

But mercy is above this sceptred sway,
It is enthroned in the heart of kings,
It is an attribute to God himself,
And earthly power doth then show likest God's
When mercy tempers justice.

*(Merchant of Venice:* IV.1)

To ask what this speech is "about" is to ask the wrong question—it gets a stillborn answer, "It's about mercy." Which is like Woody Allen who read *War and Peace,* and when he asked himself what it was all about, came to the conclusion, "It's about Russia."

It is more helpful to ask ourselves again, "What's the speech doing?" for then we will discover that it is not a poem, but an *argument;* that there's movement in it.

We must first try to get the meaning clear—for how can an actor expect to be understood if he does not himself understand?

This means grouping the thoughts. The meaning becomes much clearer if we ignore (for the moment) the verse form, and give it a different shape on the page.

The quality of mercy is not strain'd: it droppeth as the gentle rain from heaven upon the place beneath.

It is twice bless'd: it blesseth him that gives and him that takes.

It is mightiest in the mightiest: it becomes the throned monarch better than his crown.

His *sceptre* shows the force of temporal power— (it is) the attribute of awe and majesty, wherein doth sit the dread and fear of kings: but *mercy* is above this sceptred sway.

It is enthroned in the heart of kings.

It is an attribute of God himself.

And earthly power doth then show likest God's, when mercy seasons justice.

Each paragraph is a *new thought*, and since we can see that the speech has a buildup, each idea leads us like steps on a staircase, upwards, towards the point of the argument.

Mercy is like the rain, and (up a step) it is found to be a double blessing. (Another step.) It suits a king better than his crown or sceptre. Why? (Up again.) Because these things symbolize fear and dread, but mercy is above that. (Up.) It sits in the king's *heart*. (Further up.) Mercy belongs to God. (Top of the staircase.) Those who exercise earthly power show a Godlike power when, dispensing justice, they show mercy. This is what the speaker is leading up to say.

This is ongoing writing—each thought adds something to the one before. It never stays still. It goes on building to the point of the argument, taking us along with it. It is like the tide coming in, wave following upon wave, as the sea encroaches on the land—which is an image that Shakespeare himself uses about death:

> Like as the waves make towards the pebbled shore
> So do our minutes hasten to their end;
> Each changing place with that which goes before.

This is a typical feature of any Shakespearean speech—it builds up; it might change direction, but it is never static and never goes backwards.

Now, if we go back to the original verse form in which it is printed, we find that the second half of the line is always more important than the first half:

> it becomes
> The throned monarch *better than his crown;*
> His sceptre shows the force of *temporal power,*
> The attribute to *awe and majesty*
> Wherein doth sit the *dread and fear of kings*
> But mercy is *above* this sceptered sway....

To advance the argument, the speaker is juggling with two ideas, playing off one against the other. On the one hand, (in the first four lines)—mercy; on the other hand, (in the next five lines)—earthly power. The two ideas fuse at the end—when earthly power, exercising mercy, can resemble God's power.

All the words have their part to play—there is not one word too many—but some words are more important than others, as we have seen. The "poetic voice" would tend to give each word equal value, and even to put the sound above the sense—to go for what is called "the music of the verse." But if we agree that, dramatically speaking, the *speech is an argument,* and that the speaker is out to prove something, to convince his or her listeners of a certain point of view, then the "musical" approach must take second place to clarity.

This is where William Poel's innovatory discoveries about verse speaking come in.

Recalling that Elizabethan actors spoke "trippingly on the tongue"—which Irving and Tree patently did not, (old recordings of their performances confirm this)—Poel set up to imagine what Elizabethan stage speech was like, and drew some marvellous conclusions. More important directors than he would later adopt and practice his ideas.

Textbooks tell us that most of Shakespeare's verse is written in lines of ten (sometimes eleven) syllables, each line having five "feet," and that most of these feet are made up of a short syllable followed by a long one (tee-túm), as in the words *esteem, defeat, disdain;* such feet are called iambs. The iambic pentameter goes: tee-túm tee-túm tee-túm tee-túm tee-túm. Speaking everyday English we often drop into the iambic pentameter without realizing it: "I think I'll go and fix myself a drink" is one, as is Eliza Doolittle's "I washed my face and hands afore I come."

In Portia's speech we have seen:

The át/tribúte/ to áwe/ and máj/esty´
Wherein/ doth sít/ the dréad/ and féar/ of kíngs
(tee-túm tee-túm tee-túm tee-túm tee-túm)

In Shakespeare's earlier plays, this rhythm predominates. As he matured, he started to smash these rhythms up, and make something less smooth, more jagged, in tune with the characters' mental states.

Actors used to believe that since there were supposed to be five stresses in a line, then, effectively, five words in the line should be, in speaking, stressed.

Yet it's obvious that a phrase like "I'll go now" alters its meaning, depending on whether the speaker says "*I'll* go now," "I'll *go* now" or "I'll go *now*," and which stress is the right one depends on the circumstances.

William Poel advanced the revolutionary theory that, in speaking Shakespeare there are not five stresses to a line, but usually only *two* (sometimes one or three); and where these fall depends on the meaning. So before Poel's time, an actor would probably have said:

> The *quality* of *mercy* is not *strain'd,*
> It *drop*peth as the *gentle rain* from *heaven*
> Upon the *place beneath:* it is *twice bless'd.*
> It *bles*seth *him* that *gives* and *him* that *takes.*

and so on. But this stressing every second word is as monotonous as a sewing machine, and throws meaning out of the window. Squeezing the last drop of significance from every line (perhaps because of the idea that Shakespeare was a Great Poet) only causes the audience to lose the thread: The sentences are often too long, and sometimes too convoluted for us to hear, at first go, all the nuances.

Poel explained himself:

If elocution is to imitate nature, a dozen or more words must be sacrificed so that one word may predominate and thus give the keynote to the whole sentence. In this way only can the sound be made to echo the sense. [6]

This means, of course, that the actor has to make a choice of what the keynotes are. Applying Poel's theory to Portia's speech, we should probably come up with something like this:

The quality of *mercy* is not *strained,*
It droppeth as the gentle *rain* from *heaven*
Upon the place *beneath:* it is *twice bless'd;*
It blesseth him that gives *and* him that takes
'Tis mightiest in the *mightiest;* it becomes
The throned monarch *better* than his crown;
His *sceptre* shows the force of *temporal* power
The attribute to *awe* and *majesty,*
Wherein doth sit the dread and *fear* of kings.
But *mercy* is *above* this sceptred sway,
It is enthroned in the *heart* of kings,
It is an attribute to *God* him*self,*
And *earthly power* doth then show *likest God's*
When *mercy seasons justice.*

Poel points out that if the keywords

are rapped out and heard distinctly, the listener knows what the rest of the sentence means, and *the whole can be said very quickly.* [7]

The speed was the secret. The Prologue to *Romeo and Juliet* famously mentions "the two hours' traffick of our stage." Allowing

---

[6] Letter to *The Saturday Review,* 31 July 1909, quoted in Robert Speaight, *William Poel and the Elizabethan Revival.*

[7] Ibid.

for the fact that the poet was deliberately underestimating the time span—for he was unlikely to begin a play by telling the audience they were in for a long performance—it is not conceivable that performances at the Globe went on for twice that length. Yet even on radio today, with no time spent on changing scenery, or entering and exiting, and no actors' pauses, *Hamlet* unabridged cannot be got through in less than three and a half hours; and a recent German production on the stage took up to six hours.

This suggests, not only that Elizabethan actors had excellent diction, and a rapid way of speaking that was clear and flexible enough to be understood by more than 3,000 people (the capacity of the Globe Theatre), but also that the text was written—not to be declaimed, but to be spoken swiftly and lightly. Shakespeare's rhythms probably had more in common with Rossini than with Beethoven.

William Poel, in opposing a too emphatic style of delivery, and insisting on the importance of key words that, like pylons, held up the sense of the lines, had Shakespeare's own authority for it. Hamlet, giving notes to the travelling actors who arrive at Elsinore, tells them:

> Speak the speech, I pray you, as I pronounced it to you,
> trippingly on the tongue; but if you mouth it, as many of your
> players do, I had as lief the town-crier spoke my lines.
>
> (III.2)

Readers might like to try for themselves to discover the key words in the following passage and to mark them. There are five "beats" to a line, but when we go for the sense, seldom more than two stresses.

The speech is again from *Henry V*—it illustrates what Chorus called "a little touch of Harry in the night." The King overhears one of the English officers expressing his dismay that the French

army outnumbers the English by five to one—and gives him and
his fellows a pep talk:

WESTMORELAND:
O that we now had here
But one ten thousand of those men in England
That do no work today.
KING HENRY:
What's he that wishes so?
My cousin Westmoreland? No, my fair cousin.
If we are marked to die, we are enow
To do our country loss: and if to live,
The fewer men, the greater share of honor.
God's will! I pray thee wish not one man more.
By Jove, I am not covetous for gold,
Nor care I who doth feed upon my cost;
It yearns me not if men my garments wear;
Such outward things dwell not in my desires.
But if it be a sin to covet honor,
I am the most offending soul alive.
No, faith, my coz, wish not a man from England:
God's peace! I would not lose so great an honor
As one man more methinks would share from me
For the best hope I have. O, do not wish one more!
Rather proclaim it Westmoreland, through my host,
That he which hath no stomach to this fight,
Let him depart: his passport shall be made,
And crowns for convoy put into his purse.
We would not die in that man's company
That fears his fellowship to die with us.
This day is called the Feast of Crispian:
He that outlives this day, and comes safe home,
Will stand a-tiptoe when this day is named,
And rouse him at the name of Crispian.
He that shall see this day, and live old age,

Will yearly on the vigil feast his neighbors,
And say, "Tomorrow is Saint Crispian."
Then will he strip his sleeve, and show his scars,
And say, "These wounds I had on Crispin's day."
Old men forget; yet all shall be forgot,
But he'll remember, with advantages,
What feats he did that day. Then shall our names,
Familiar in his mouth as household words,
Harry the King, Bedford and Exeter,
Warwick and Talbot, Salisbury and Gloucester,
Be in their flowing cups freshly remembered.
This story shall the good man teach his son;
And Crispin Crispian shall ne'er go by,
From this day to the ending of the world,
But we in it shall be remembered—
We few, we happy few, we band of brothers:
For he today that sheds his blood with me
Shall be my brother; be he ne'er so vile,
This day shall gentle his condition;
And gentlemen in England now abed
Shall think themselves accursed they were not here,
And hold their manhoods cheap, whiles any speaks
That fought with us upon Saint Crispin's day.

# IV

# A SHAKESPEAREAN SHAPE

On the page they look daunting, those solid blocks of Shakespearean verse and prose—so unlike the to-and-fro dialogue of modern plays. The actor may be pardoned if he wonders how he will keep our interest.

Certain actors refer to particularly long speeches as "tunnels." ("Hold on, lads,"—I remember a Henry V saying at rehearsal—"I've got another tunnel coming up!") It's a misnomer, for the only thing you can do about a tunnel is to get to the other end as quickly as possible.

The actor's primary task is to make the audience listen to him. Evidently it's not enough to say the words "because they're there."

It's no solution, either, to invent all kinds of unexpected movements and gestures (to give the audience something to watch) nor to indulge in ingenious stage "business" to keep them amused—the word says it, "busy-ness." I once saw an Iago who carried a tame rat on his shoulder, to which he addressed all his soliloquies, and, yes, the audience was fascinated—by the rat.

Nor is it enough to enchant the audience with "the music of the verse" as our predecessors did in the nineteenth century.

The listeners should be asking themselves, "What will he say next?" This is not difficult when the speaker is telling a story, and quite a number of Shakespeare's long speeches are stories.[1]

The whole world loves a story: In Sir Philip Sidney's much-quoted phrase, it "holdeth children from play, and old men from the chimney corner," it unites the village gossip with the professor of history, the reader of airport thrillers with the reader of Tolstoy. I have frequently noticed in plays that when a character starts telling a story, the audience's attention quickens. A young girl of ten, whom I know, once told an experienced theater director that she knew Richard III"s first speech by heart, but she didn't know how to do it—and his reply was, "Tell it like a story."

A story contains movement and conflict. Most of Shakespeare's other speeches, those that are not stories, also contain movement and conflict, and it is the actor's job to find these out. They are not like lakes of still-standing water, but more like mountain streams or swiftly coursing rivers. The actor does not need laboriously to row, but to find the current and let it carry him along.

Even in speeches that do not narrate a story, Shakespeare uses storytelling devices to give the speech life. The most remarkable of these is the way he makes a speech into a little battlefield where opposing forces fight it out. There are conflicts of words, of ideas, and—most interestingly, of intentions: The character is debating within himself which of two actions to take.

For simplicity's sake we might call this device, "Black vs. White." A speech can often be boiled down to the formula, "Black exists; but White also exists." In a speech they can be said to be in conflict. Here are a few examples, culled at random. Notice how the little hinge-word *but* indicates the switch from one to the other.

---

[1] Think of *Othello's* address to the Senate (I.3); Clarence's dream (*Richard III:* I.4); the Ghost's account of his own death (*Hamlet* I.5); Hotspur's denial of rebellion (*Henry IV, Part 1:* I.3); Jacques' "A fool! A fool! I met a fool in the forest!" (*As You Like It:* II.2)

I thank you: I am not of many words *but*
I thank you.

(*Much Ado About Nothing:* I.2)

When sorrows come, they come not single spies
*But* in battalions.

(*Hamlet:* IV.5)

Now, fair Hyppolita, our nuptial hour
Draws on apace: four happy days bring in
Another moon;
 *but* O! methinks how slow
This old moon wanes; she lingers my desires
Like to a step-dame or a dowager
Long withering out a young man's revenue.

(*A Midsummer Night's Dream:* I.1)

Good name in man and woman, dear my lord,
Is the immediate jewel of their souls:
Who steals my purse, steals trash; 'tis something, nothing,
'T was mine, 'tis his, and has been slave to thousands;
*But* he that filches from me my good name
Robs me of that which not enriches him
And makes me poor indeed.

(*Othello:* III.3)

In peace there's nothing so becomes a man
As modest stillness and humility;
*But* when the blast of war blows in our ears
Then imitate the action of the tiger...

(*Henry V:* III.1)

My liege, I did deny no prisoners:
*But* I remember, when the fight was done,
When I was dry with rage and éxtreme toil,
Breathless and faint, leaning upon my sword,
Came there a certain lord, neat, and trimly dress'd,...

(*Henry IV:* I.3)

In many a long speech, the speaker goes on about "Black" at some length before opposing it with "White"; the word *but,* which changes the subject, and often the tone of the sp⁄ch, is always waiting round the corner to ambush us. The first Chorus of *Henry V* elaborates about the advantages of a Muse of Fire that would bring the warlike King before us looking as mighty as Mars, the God of War, before interrupting himself:

> *But* pardon! gentles all,
> The flat unraised spirits that hath dar'd
> On this unworthy scaffold to bring forth
> So great an object…

Marc Antony, speaking at Caesar's funeral, ("I come to bury Caesar, not to praise him") says nothing that would irritate Caesar's assassins, for several minutes, before letting a note of caustic irony creep in:

> He was my friend, faithful and just to me:
> *But* Brutus says he was ambitious,
> And Brutus is an honorable man…
> (Julius Caesar:III.2)

And from that moment the tide has turned.

And again, Richard of Gloucester, in his opening speech, seems for all the world to be welcoming peace and the end of hostilities, until he grabs us by the throat with that terrible,

> *But I,* that am not shap'd for sportive tricks…
> (Richard III: I.1)

In short, *but* must be the most *dramatic* word in the language. *But* indicates that all is not harmonious; *but* signals where the shoe pinches. Lyric poetry and short stories can be written without excessive use of the word *but,* they can flow from beginning to end without bumping over obstacles. But drama cannot do without it.

You cannot even summarize the plot of a play without using it—it can be a key word for a director when he examines a play's shape.

Oedipus sets out to find the cause of the plague that besets Thebes—but he himself is its origin.

Two tramps cannot leave their field because they are waiting for a Mr. Godot—but he never arrives.

Like the germ that turns milk into yogurt, the "but" element turns a mere situation into a dramatic one.

"But" can give the actor an invaluable handle when he tries to form an idea of a role, for it notes the inconsistency that gives the character its humanity. ("He was powerful—but insecure."— "She was loving, but ambitious."—"He was brave, but hesitant.") When people say that a character is a play or a film script is one-dimensional, or a cardboard figure, it is usually because this "but" element, the contradictory factor, is missing.

Shakespeare's whole way of thinking is permeated by the notion of "but." He is always conscious that there are two sides to every question, that nothing exists without its opposite.

It is as if he couldn't think of "night," without the idea of "day" occurring to him, at the same moment.

—O! now, be gone; more *light and light* it grows.
—More light and light; more *dark and dark* our woes
(*Romeo and Juliet:* III.5)

—If after every *tempest* come such *calms,*
May the winds blow till they have waken'd death.
(*Othello:* III.1)

…With one *auspicious* and one *dropping* eye
With *mirth in funeral* and with *dirge in marriage*
In equal scale weighing *delight* and *dole*…
(*Hamlet:* I.2)

Time and again the opposites come, yoked in pairs: light/darkness; man/beast; life/death; saint/devil; foul/fair; youth/old age; war/peace; summer/winter. Creating Othello, he simultaneously imagines an Iago. Inventing two brothers, he makes one good, the other bad (*Hamlet, King Lear, Much Ado About Nothing*). When tiny, pert Hermia appears (*A Midsummer Night's Dream*). along comes tall complaining Helena. The fruits of Shakespeare's imagination were, indeed, "like to a double cherry."

And so down to single speeches, which become arenas where one word, or one idea, takes arms against another. Grammarians call this antithesis. Richard II talks of "setting the word against the word." Once the actor is aware of this device, he should look out for its use. By this means he can bring out the conflict in the speech, and keep the audience interested as they watch the battle.

His first task, faced with a long speech, is to break it down to its component parts, and note where one thought becomes another, or contradicts another.

The blank verse typography (where every line is roughly equal) or the blocks of prose paragraphs, can often be a visual hindrance. The verse form leads some actors into thinking that there should be a break at the end of every line. In reality, the breaks come at the end of every *thought*. It is refreshing to rewrite a difficult speech in free verse (the sort Walt Whitman used) thus regrouping the thoughts.

If we try this with an important speech of Richard II's, we shall see how the thought becomes clearer. Richard appears on the walls of Flint Castle: Below him are the rebels, out to dethrone him. They send forward a messenger, the Earl of Northumberland, but before he can utter his message, Richard takes exception to the fact that Northumberland has not knelt down before him, a sign of disrespect—verging on sacrilege toward a king who sees himself as God's representative on earth.

We are amazed; and thus long have we stood
To watch the fearful bending of thy knee,
Because we thought ourself thy lawful king.
And if we be, how dare thy joints forget
To pay their awful duty to our presence?
If we be not, show us the hand of God
That hath dismissed us from our stewardship;
For well we know no hand of blood and bone
Can gripe the sacred handle of our scepter
Unless he do profane, steal or usurp.
And though you think that all, as you have done,
Have torn their souls by turning them from us,
And we are barren and bereft of friends,
Yet know my master, God Omnipotent,
Is mustering in His clouds on our behalf
Armies of pestilence; and they shall strike
Your children yet unborn and unbegot,
That lift your vassal hands against my head
And threat the glory of my precious crown.
                                        (*Richard II:* III.3)

Regrouping the thoughts in free verse might look like this:

We are amazed;

and thus long have we stood to watch the fearful
bending of thy knee
because we thought ourself thy lawful king.

And if we be,
how dare thy joints forget to pay their awful
duty to our presence?

If we be not,
show us the hand of God
that hath dismissed us from our stewardship.

For well we know
no hand of flesh and bone
can gripe the sacred handle of our scepter
unless he do profane, steal, or usurp.

And though you think
that all (as you have done) have torn their
souls by turning from us,
and we are barren and bereft of friends;

yet know—
my master, God omnipotent,
is mustering in his clouds armies of pestilence;
and they shall strike your children
(yet unborn and unbegot)
that lift your vassal hands against my head,
and threat the glory of my precious crown.

(*Richard II:* III. 3)

This regrouping shows how Black v. White is at play again: "You think… (you can defy me)" versus "I know… (God will defend me)."

And the "but" element appears—and Richard's tone changes—at "Yet know…" (*Yet* is a synonym for *but*.) Finally, Richard affirms himself. At "Yet know…" he pulls out the stops and delivers his terrible threat against the descendants yet unborn of those vassals who have dared to usurp his sacred kingship.

This layout shows, when we are regrouping the thoughts in a speech, and watching to see how one conflicts with another, how important are all those little words which a learned grammarian has called "the traffic signs of language:" *and, if, yet, but, so, thus, for, since, although, whether, or…* They indicate that a speech, far from being a "tunnel" (long and straight), is full of left turns and right turns and reversals, and requires constant changes of gear.

Moreover they indicate, by their very frequency, that the speech is not a mere expression of emotion, but a closely reasoned argument.

Many actors have a tendency to think themselves into the emotional state of the character, work themselves up—and *then* add the lines. (This is why some aver that "the lines get in the way.") With Shakespeare a different approach is required.

The actor needs first to make sense of the speech, understand the argument, and then defend it. The emotion comes later. The emotions come *through* the words, not before them. The actor has no need to invent a "subtext" or try to make the words mean anything else than what they say: He needs to "play the lines." Peremptory commands like "how dare," "show us" and "yet know" indicate the tone of the speech. How will Richard pronounce words like *king, duty, God, sacred, glory, crown?* And how words like *joints, profane, steal, usurp, vassal, threat?*

Rhythms, too, give us an inescapable key to the emotions. Set out like this, the speech draws attention to the way the king hammers his dissatisfaction home with repeated double and triple stresses:

| We are amazed…      | (— — v —) |
| …thus long…         | (— —)     |
| And if we be,…      | (v — — —) |
| If we be not…       | (— — — —) |
| For well we know…   | (v — — —) |
| And though you think… | (v — — —) |
| Yet know…           | (— —)     |

If you read the speech aloud, paying attention to the suggested breaks, and to the key words (the words that are important to Richard), and to the heavy stresses, you will probably find a patrician fury welling up inside you—almost of its own accord.

This is an example of a dictum that has been remarked upon by many Shakespeare interpreters:

If you play the sense, you get the rhythm.
If you play the rhythm, you get the sense.
If you play the sense, you get the emotion.
If you play the rhythm, you get the emotion.

It is an unique feature of Shakespeare's best writing that rhythm, sense, and emotion are all one.

In other words, if you just go for the emotion, and neglect the rhythm and the sense, you cannot play the emotion.

☾ ☾ ☾

The supreme example of the Black vs. White syndrome is Hamlet's over-famous soliloquy. "To be, or not to be"—the opening words indicate that there will be a clash of opposites, that Hamlet's mind is the arena where conflicting ideas are to fight it out.

So much has been written about this speech, that the attempt might appear superfluous. However, we shall avoid going into such questions as who Hamlet is (is he a portrait of the author? or is he based on, say, the Earl of Essex?), whether he suffers from manic depression or melancholy or madness, what prompts him at this point of the play to utter this question, or what philosophers have influenced him in his thoughts, or even what does he "mean." In other words, we shall eschew all "interpretation," that is, someone else's views on the speech and stick purely to *what is said:* what words are used, and in what order, and whether the thought groups are short or long.

Even to ask the question, "What is the speech about?" is to get a leaden answer ("It's about Life and Death") because the question is wrongly formulated. A speech is an action. We need to ask, *Where is Hamlet going in the speech?* A speech is movement. At the end of it, the speaker thinks differently from the way he thought at the beginning. His mind-set has—even if slightly—changed: And the play has taken a few steps forward.

So it is essential to say that the speech is not a meditation. Hamlet hasn't come on to give us a lecture called "My Thoughts on Life and Death." He is not telling us about conclusions he arrived at last week. On the contrary—and the hesitant opening proves this—he is thinking in front of us. He has not been down this path before. When he starts out he has no idea where he will end up. We, the spectators, are in the privileged position of being able to watch his mind at work.

And the lengths of the sentences show that sometimes it works in fits and starts, and sometimes when he has made a discovery—it works at full speed, the thoughts tumbling over one another to find expression. He discovers things he'd forgotten he knew. An actor may find helpful the phrase: "I don't know what I think till I hear what I say."

To jog the memory, let us set out the speech as it is usually presented in editions of the play.

> *Enter* Hamlet.
> HAMLET: To be, or not to be: that is the question:
> Whether 'tis nobler in the mind to suffer
> The slings and arrows of outrageous fortune,
> Or to take arms against a sea of troubles
> And by opposing end them? To die: to sleep;
> No more; and, by a sleep to say we end
> The heart-ache and the thousand natural shocks
> That flesh is heir to, 'tis a consummation
> Devoutly to be wish'd. To die, to sleep;
> To sleep: perchance to dream: ay, there's the rub;
> For in that sleep of death what dreams may come
> When we have shuffled off this mortal coil,
> Must give us pause. There's the respect
> That makes calamity of so long life;
> For who would bear the whips and scorns of time,

The oppressor's wrong, the proud man's contumely,
The pangs of dispriz'd love, the law's delay,
The insolence of office, and the spurns
That patient merit of the unworthy takes,
When he himself might his quietus make
With a bare bodkin? who would fardels bear,
To grunt and sweat under a weary life,
But that the dread of something after death,
The undiscover'd country from whose bourn
No traveller returns, puzzles the will,
And makes us rather bear those ills we have
Than fly to others that we know not of?
Thus conscience does make cowards of us all;
And thus the native hue of resolution
Is sicklied o'er with the pale cast of thought,
And enterprises of great pith and moment
With this regard their currents turn awry,
And lose the name of action.

Hamlet is weighing up the "question" of being and not being.
If the speech is a battlefield of ideas, then Life and Death are the
names of the opposing armies. Most people infer that he is con-
templating suicide; this is nowhere stated, though the phrases
about ending a sea of troubles, making one's quietus (an old word
for settling one's accounts) with a bare bodkin, and flying to other
ills "that we know not of" might suggest it.

In the conflict between White and Black, let us suppose that
White stands for living, or staying alive, and that Black suggests
Death, or dying (or committing suicide.)

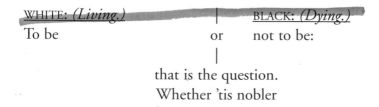

WHITE: *(Living.)*                              BLACK: *(Dying.)*
To be                       or        not to be:

                    that is the question.
                    Whether 'tis nobler

in the mind to suffer the slings
and arrows of outrageous fortune,

|

or

|

|           to take arms against a sea of
|           troubles and by opposing—
|           end them—
|           To die,

|

to sleep;
no more;

|

|           and by a sleep to say we end
|           the heartache and the thou-
|           sand natural shocks that
|           flesh is heir to,
|           'tis a consummation
|           devoutly to be wished.
|           To die,

|

to sleep; to sleep:

|

perchance to dream!     |

|

Ay, there's the rub;

|

for in that sleep of death what
dreams may come when we have
shuffled off this mortal coil   |
must gives us pause.        |

|

There's the respect

|

that makes calamity of so long
life; for who would bear the
whips and scorns of time, the
oppressor's wrong, the proud
man's contumely, the pangs of
dispriz'd love, the law's delay,
the insolence of office

when he himself might his
quietus make
with a bare bodkin?

Who would fardels bear, to
grunt and sweat under a
weary life, but that the dread
of something after death

(the undiscover'd country
from whose bourn no
traveller returns)

puzzles the will,
and makes us rather
bear those ills we have

than fly to others that
we know not of?
Thus
conscience doth make cowards of us all,
And thus the native hue of resolution
Is sicklied o'er with the pale cast of thought,
and enterprises of great pith and moment.
With this regard their currents turn awry,
And lose the name of action.

The layout shows that at the beginning Black seems to be winning. Hamlet is inclined toward Death. Death and Sleep are like identical twins: If Death is "no more" than Sleep, it is "devoutly to be wish'd."

Suddenly there's a turning point, when he discovers an essential flaw in the argument: What if Death, too, has its dreams?— a gruesome perspective for Hamlet who—he has told us—is already prone to nightmares:

> I could he bounded in a nutshell, and count myself a king of infinite space, but that I have bad dreams.

"Ay, there's the rub" he cries, as one might say "That's the catch!" and for the actor, it marks a change of gear. His thoughts are coming more quickly now: We can see this by the length of the sentences that follow. He even repeats it: "There's the respect"— and the world's ills come pouring out, one scarcely uttered before another takes its place.

In this second movement, White is starting to win—Life is proving preferable to Death. But only just! What does Life mean to Hamlet? We have only to look at the synonyms he uses to see:

> heartache…thousand natural shocks…this mortal coil… calamity… weary life…the ills we bear…

It's little wonder that nineteenth-century actors spoke of him as "the gloomy Dane."

There is a third movement to come. If the speech is a battle, it ends with a peace treaty. At "Thus…" he draws a conclusion,

> …conscience doth make cowards of us all

(which reminds one of what Oscar Wilde said: "Conscience and cowardice are really the same things. Conscience is the name of the firm."). We can understand Hamlet's conclusion better if we draw on two things we have learned about Shakespeare's writing technique.

One is that he thought in pairs of opposites. And if we look for the opposite of "cowardice," we find it back at the beginning of the speech: the idea of "nobility." Hamlet is not asking whether it is preferable, or easier, or more comfortable, "to suffer the slings and arrows of outrageous fortune," but "Whether 'tis *nobler...*"

The other is to remember that the essential part of a line of verse lies in the second half; the lines "build." So what Hamlet has discovered is that "conscience doth make cowards *of us all.*" In this matter, all humanity is alike.

These points clarify the A to Z of the speech. Looking for a "noble" solution for himself, he finds only cowardice in all Mankind—a universal fear of undertaking any "enterprises of great pith and moment."

We have tried to put into focus what Hamlet says, without any interpolations, simply by looking at the words, and by re-aligning the speech. We could, however, be accused of changing the sense by altering the punctuation.

In any case, the "accepted" punctuation of Shakespeare's plays, as found in most editions, is not Shakespeare's own. Later scholars have inserted commas and colons and semicolons, like schoolmasters correcting an essay, to make it clear for us, and to conform to the rules of punctuation. (No doubt there are purists who would like to restore the capital letters to e.e. cummings.) Since we do not know for certain how Shakespeare punctuated the speech, since the manuscript is lost, nothing prevents us from putting forward our own suggestions. The First Folio—the first collected edition of the plays, printed seven years after his death—gives a totally different punctuation, which is worth looking at.

This may be the work of a careless printer. If it is, however, a reproduction of the author's manuscript, then it suggests that either he was writing too quickly to bother about the stops ("We'll sort that out in rehearsal"); *or* he was using an alternative form of punctuation whose purpose was not to make the sense clear, but to signal to the actor the phrasing, the breathing stops or beats, and the tempo.

*Enter Hamlet,*
POL.: I heare him comming, with-draw my Lord.
HAM.: To be, or not to be, that is the question,
Whether tis nobler in the minde to suffer
The slings and arrowes of outragious fortune,
Or to take Armes against a sea of troubles,
And by opposing, end them, to die to sleepe
No more, and by a sleepe, to say we end
The hart-ake, and the thousand naturall shocks
That flesh is heire to; tis a consumation
Devoutly to be wisht to die to sleepe,
To sleepe, perchance to dreame, I there's the rub,
For in that sleepe of death what dreames may come
When we have shuffled off this mortall coyle
Must give us pause, there's the respect
That makes calamitie of so long life:
For who would beare the whips and scornes of time,
Th'oppressors wrong, the proude mans contumely,
The pangs of despiz'd love, the lawes delay,
The insolence of office, and the spurnes
That patient merrit of th'unworthy takes,
When he himselfe might his quietas make
With a bare bodkin; who would fardels beare,
To grunt and sweat under a wearie life,
But that the dread of something after death,
The undiscover'd country, from whose borne...

If this is, indeed, the way Shakespeare wrote it, the commas—and lack of them—being his scoremarks, his way of "directing" the actor's timing, gives us one essential indication: that Hamlet's mind is racing. The ideas are coming thick and fast.

He doesn't press down on a word and listen to its echo before passing on to the next. He doesn't, as many of your players do, say:

> To die… (*thinks*) to sleep… (*thinks) no more!… (thinks)* and
> by a sleep, to say we end the heartache…

All this comes out in a rush. There's an urgency about his reasoning, as if he's thinking "I have to hammer this out *now.*" The fact that the first semicolon appears only in the eighth line (after "flesh is heir to") suggests that the wheels of his mind are already whirring fast when he comes on—as though we catch him in the middle of a thought process; perhaps (but this is conjecture) arriving on stage at the moment he manages to formulate his problem—("Got it! To be, or not to be, *that* is the question!") and going on from there in a state of wild excitement.

Nobody expects an actor nowadays to adhere to this Folio punctuation. If it is authentic, it was scored for a particular actor, centuries ago, to deliver to audiences with perceptions very different from our own. Life was less noisy in those days, so their sense of hearing was probably more acute; and Elizabethan actors spoke rapidly. If it isn't exactly Shakespeare's scoring, it is nevertheless the one proposed in the great commemorative edition edited by two members of his company, both of whom are said to have played in the first production, one as Horatio, the other as Polonius.

We have quoted it to show how the literary scholars, who long after the author's death tidied up his punctuation, and whose emendations have become accepted, did, in fact, indicate a much slower rhythm for the speech, and inadvertently led to many actors treating the speech like a portentous sermon that holds up the play, rather than as a battle of ideas that advances it. At this battle even Hamlet is partially a spectator, for the ideas *occur to him* as he speaks (the "whips and scorns of time" passage is bitterly autobiographical); and the outcome of the battle is certainly unknown to him when at the start he sets "to be" in conflict with "not to be."

All plays show characters in conflict with each other. Shakespeare specializes in showing characters in conflict with themselves. Single speeches are the arenas where these conflicts are fought out. For an actor, this conflict-within-a-speech is a gift. What is more challenging than to portray somebody at odds with himself?

Sometimes it seems as if one part of a character rises up and struggles with another part:

> My *stronger guilt* defeats my *strong intent*
> And, like a man to double business bound,
> I stand in pause where I shall first begin
> And both neglect.

This is from *Hamlet;* but it is not Hamlet who is speaking, though the sentiments might be his, for he frequently stood in pause where he should first begin. The words are the King's, when he is trying to pray. (III. 3)

And here is Prospero:

> Though with their high wrongs I am struck to the quick,
> Yet with my *noble reason* 'gainst my *fury*
> Do I take part:
>
> > (*The Tempest:* V.1)

Shakespeare himself was familiar with these internal struggles, as we can see in the Sonnets:

> Mine *eye* and *heart* are at a mortal war...     (46)

> Thine *eyes* I love, and they as pitying me
> Knowing thy *heart* torment me with disdain...     (132)

> In faith, I do not love thee with *mine eyes,*
> For they in thee a thousand errors note;

But 'tis my *heart* that loves what they despise,
Who, in despite of *view,* is pleas'd to dote.     (14)

Nowadays we talk about somebody's "identity." In Elizabethan times this was not current. It was the contradictions in a person's character that made them much more interesting. And Shakespeare, concrete-minded as he was, personified these contradictions. Your Eye can love someone, while your Heart resists. Or, Your Heart can urge you to love someone, while your Mind, or Judgment, can push you in the opposite direction.

The Mind and the Heart can sometimes be identified as the forces opposing each other on the battleground that is a speech.

A typical victim of this struggle is the shepherdess, Phebe, in *As You Like It.* Phebe is in a dilemma. She is wooed by a kind peasant boy, Sylvius, whom she—little minx that she is—treats like a dog. She has just met (and been affronted by) a handsome young aristocrat called "Ganymede"—and this is love at first sight. On the one hand, her Mind (her Judgment) tells her it would be unwise to cut off relations with Sylvius; on the other, her Heart is beating wildly for "Ganymede." (Poor girl, she hasn't realized that this Ganymede "gentleman" is a lady in disguise.)

When she tries to tell Sylvius of her feelings (and to sort them out for herself too) her Heart and Mind appear to be having an argument. She sounds like two people talking:

Think not I love him, though I ask for him.
'Tis but a peevish boy, yet he talks well.
But what care I for words? Yet words do well
When he that speaks them pleases those that hear.
It is a pretty youth—not very pretty—
But, sure, he's proud, and yet his pride becomes him.
He'll make a proper man. The best thing in him
Is his complexion, and faster than his tongue
Did make offense his eye did heal it up.
He is not very tall, yet for his years he's tall.

His leg is but so-so, and yet 'tis well.
There was a pretty redness in his lip,
A little riper and more lusty red
Than that mixed in his cheek, 'twas just the difference
Betwixt the constant red and mingled damask.
There be some women, Sylvius, had they marked him
In parcels as I did, would have gone near
To fall in love with him. But for my part,
I love him not nor hate him not, and yet
I have more cause to hate him than to love him.
For what had he to do to chide at me?
He said mine eyes were black and my hair black,
And, now I am remembered, scorned at me.
I marvel why I answered not again.
But that's all one, omittance is no quittance.

(III.5)

Again, by playing about with the layout, and dramatizing Phebe's speech as a *duo*logue between her Heart and her Mind, we can understand more clearly Phebe's dilemma. Her Heart is talking to itself; her Mind wants to be overheard by Sylvius.

MIND: Think not I love him, though I ask for him.
'Tis but a peevish boy;
HEART: yet he talks well;
MIND: But what care I for words?
HEART: yet words do well
When he that speaks them pleases those that hear.
'Tis a pretty youth:
MIND: not very pretty:
But sure he's proud;
HEART: and yet his pride becomes him:
He'll make a proper man: the best thing in him
Is his complexion, and faster than his tongue
Did give offence his eye did heal it up.
MIND: He's not very tall;

HEART: yet for his years he's tall:
MIND: His leg is but so-so;
HEART: and yet 'tis well:
There was a pretty ripeness in his lip,
A little riper and more rusty red
Than that mix'd in his cheek: 'twas just the difference
Between the constant red and mingled damask.
MIND: There be some women, Sylvius, had they mark'd him
In parcels as I did, would have gone near
To fall in love with him; but for my part
I love him not
HEART: nor hate him not;
MIND: and yet
Have more cause to hate him than to love him:
for what had he to do to chide at me?
He said my eyes were black and my hair black,
And now I am remember'd, scorn'd at me.
I marvel why I answer'd not again.
HEART: But that's all one, omittance is no quittance.

Finally Phebe's Heart and Mind reach a truce. She resolves the
problem in a way that keeps Ganymede warm and Sylvius occupied:

I'll write to him a very taunting letter,
And thou shalt bear it, wilt thou, Sylvius?

Phebe is divided between Ganymede and Sylvius just as
Hamlet's mind was split between two questions: Is it nobler to
suffer? or is it nobler to die by one's own hand?
Both these speeches show a character in a dilemma. Hamlet
and Phebe are like travellers who have followed a certain path and
find that the road ahead forks. We hear them debating with themselves which way to follow. They both have to make a choice: and
the choice they make both moves the play forward, and tells us
something about their character.

Hamlet *could have* argued that it was nobler to make his quietus with a bare bodkin than bear the calamity of life, and in consequence he might have killed himself: *but* he chose not to—"the dread of something after death" was too strong.

Phebe *could have* decided that "Ganymede" was so rude to her that she never wanted to set eyes upon "him" again; *but* she chose to find Ganymede's scolding more stimulating than Sylvius' billing and cooing.

Shakespeare constantly puts his characters in suchlike dilemmas, revealing their character by the choice they make. This is part of his humanism. They are not predestined by fate of the Gods or by anything outside themselves. They are not programmed like robots, or beasts. A lion that spots an antelope has no choice but to hunt it down and kill it—it's in his nature. But Macbeth can choose whether or not to kill his king, and Othello can choose whether or not to give ear to Iago's insinuations, and Henry V can choose whether or not to declare war on France, and Hamlet can choose whether not to heed Horatio's warnings about the danger of following the Ghost's beckoning.

So many a Shakespeare speech is a kind of minidrama in itself, showing a character at war with himself as he fights his way out of a dilemma. And as the great voice teacher Cicely Berry[2] wrote (using another word for "dilemma"): "We should always be concerned with the predicament, and not the feeling, that will take care of itself."

((    ((    ((

Here is Macbeth in a predicament. He is set upon killing the King of Scotland, Duncan, in order to gain his place. He has given a banquet in the king's honor—where, no doubt, he sat next to his victim. In the middle of the banquet he leaves the table and goes to another room because the idea of "the deed" is beginning to

---

[2] See *Voice and the Actor*, p. 285.

horrify him. His Conscience is fighting his Ambition. (This time we will leave the layout as it is.)

*For* Killing Duncan:

MACBETH:
If it were done when 'tis done, then 'twere well
It were done quickly. If the assassination
Could trammel up the consequence, and catch
With his surcease success—that but this blow
Might be the be-all and the end-all!—here,
But here, upon this bank and shoal of time,
We'd jump the life to come.

*Against* Killing Duncan:

But in these cases
We still have judgement here—that we but teach
Bloody instructions, which, being taught, return
To plague the inventor. This even-handed justice
Commends the ingredience of our poisoned chalice
To our own lips. He's here in double trust:
First, as I am his kinsman and his subject,
Strong both against the deed; then, as his host,
Who should against his murderer shut the door,
Not bear the knife myself. Besides, this Duncan
Hath borne his faculties so meek, hath been
So clear in his great office, that his virtues
Will plead like angels, trumpet-tongued against
The deep damnation of his taking-off;
And Pity, like a naked new-born babe
Striding the blast, or heaven's cherubin, horsed
Upon the sightless curriers of the air,
Shall blow the horrid deed in every eye,
That tears shall drown the wind.

*Conclusion:*

I have no spur
To prick the sides of my intent but only
Vaulting ambition which o'erleaps itself
And falls on the other.

It has become clear that these three speeches (Hamlet's, Phebe's and Macbeth's) all have the same three-part shape:

Black vs. White ⇒ Outcome

The outcome is not simply the football score after the match, but a new element. It can be a discovery made ("Conscience doth make cowards of us all"), a new idea ("I'll write to him a very taunting letter") or a decision made (Macbeth's "I have no spur..."—triple-stressed again!—shows that he has decided against killing the king. Two lines later he will say to his wife, "We will proceed no further in this business.").

This pattern can be found through and through the plays.

Sometimes the outcome is arrived at quickly: Iago juggles with his hatred of the Moor and his despisal of Cassio to form a new plan that will destroy them both: "I have 't, 'tis engendered..."

Sometimes the outcome is postponed over a whole scene: Marc Antony, in his funeral oration, tells the people of Rome how Caesar loved them. He sets this off against an apparent defense of Caesar's assassins ("Brutus is an honorable man"), only at a late moment producing Caesar's will—a surprise—because he holds the outcome in his own hands: "mutiny."

Sometimes the outcome is left open: Othello, bending over the sleeping Desdemona, is torn between his love for her, (Heart) and his conviction that she should be killed (Mind). The outcome is the murder itself.

The formula, Black vs. White ⇒ Outcome, is basically as simple as: Prosecution vs. Defense ⇒ Judgment.

If we turn to Shakespeare's nondramatic writings for a moment, we find the same pattern recurring in many of the Sonnets—those brief poems he wrote when he was not acting or writing for the theater; and when the theater was closed because of the plague.

Here is the most familiar one, number 18. The poet is gently making fun of the kind of love poetry in which the loved one is compared to anything beautiful in nature—"your eyes are like the stars," "My love is like a red red rose."

We might imagine that someone has commissioned him to write a verse comparing the beloved to "a summer's day." On the one hand he shows the drawbacks of such a day; on the other hand, he promises that the beloved will live longer, defying even Death; and in the outcome he explains why: "This" in the last line means "this poem," which he predicts—and correctly!—will become immortal.

## XVIII

Shall I compare thee to a summer's day?
Thou art more lovely and more temperate:
Rough winds do shake the darling buds of May,
And summer's lease hath all too short a date:
Sometime too hot the eye of heaven shines,
And often is his gold complexion dimm'd;
And every fair from fair sometime declines,
By chance, or nature's changing course untrimm'd;

But thy eternal summer shall not fade,
Nor lose possession of that fair thou ow'st,
Nor shall death brag thou wander'st in his shade,
When in eternal lines to time thou grow'st;
So long as men can breathe, or eyes can see,
So long lives this, and this gives life to thee.

Writing sonnets was a form of game, with its own special rules. The sonnet has fourteen lines, and the "point" lies in the last couplet—which rhymes. The other twelve deal with some kind of paradox, or absurdity, or inconsistency; and they can be divided up into either two groups (eight lines and six lines) or four groups (four and four and four and two). "Summer's day" obviously belongs to the first group:

This is true... (1–8)
But the opposite is also true... } (9–14)
Because...

The 4-4-4-2 group is more repetitious. Its formula is often:

This is so... (1–4)
This is so... (5–8)
This is so... (9–12)
But... (13–14)

We can see this at work in Sonnet 30:

XXX

When to the sessions of sweet silent thought
I summon up remembrance of things past,
I sigh the lack of many a thing I sought,
And with old woes new wail my dear time's waste:

Then can I drown an eye, unus'd to flow
For precious friends hid in death's dateless night,
And weep afresh love's long since cancell'd woe,
And moan the expense of many a vanish'd sight:

Then can I grieve at grievances foregone,
And heavily from woe to woe tell o'er
The sad account of fore-bemoaned moan,
Which I new pay as if not paid before.

But if the while I think on thee, dear friend,
All losses are restor'd and sorrows end.

Shakespeare wrote some 154 sonnets—that is to say, 154 of his sonnets have been discovered. Since he was adept at thinking in this form, it is not surprising to find the thought pattern recurring in his plays. Perhaps the Sonnet is the father of all those speeches that are shaped Black v. White ⇒ Outcome.

We are not digressing in mentioning the Sonnets in a chapter on Shakespearean speech. Although they were not written to be performed, and their verbal texture is often much denser than material he wrote for the stage, they are invaluable as a first step to understanding how to play Shakespeare.

Drama teachers would be well advised to start work on Shakespeare by exercises on the Sonnets. Students can be encouraged to recite a sonnet before the class, and the listeners (who have their books shut) are then asked, "Did you understand it?"

The Sonnets contain many of the same features as the dramatic writing—oppositions, images, arguments. As in a play, the lines "build." Simon Callow, in *Being an Actor,* tells of the lessons he had in sonnet speaking from Sir Peter Hall:

> Finally he told me something surprising but immediately effective: the meaning of the line very often resides in the second half, so go towards that, which has the additional advantage of sustaining the forward movement of the verse. I tried it out on:
>
> *Like as the waves make towards the pebbled shore*
> *So do our minutes hasten to their end.*
>
> I had been sweeping into the line: "Like as the WAVES maketowardsthepebbledshore / So do our MINUTES hastentowardstheirend"—a false apposition and an energy rundown. The moment one says: "Like as the waves make TOWARDS THE PEBBLED SHORE, So do our minutes HASTEN

TO THEIR END," the meaning becomes clear and the poem starts to move. Giving the metaphor its life is the secret of the whole undertaking. A poem should be like a piece of wood that the microscope reveals to be, not a solid mass, but a kingdom seething with life, swarming multitudes of molecules. "I think you may have a tendency to fall in love with the wrong word," Peter gently said.

Reciting a sonnet, the actor is clear or he is nothing. He cannot hide behind interesting gestures or stage business; he cannot pretend to be someone else, or wallow in "feelings" instead of making the lines heard. The Sonnets are merciless.

The student might ask, "But who is speaking?"

— The person who wrote the poem. Pretend it's you. Speak as if the sentiments are your own.

"But who am I talking to?"

— That's up to you. Think of someone to whom you want to express these sentiments. "Cast" someone for the mental image of the person you're talking to. We don't know for certain who were the objects of these poems, but that doesn't rob them of their intensity.

"How much emotion do I put into it?"

— Don't worry about that at first. Speak the lines in such a way as to convince us you mean them, and the emotion will follow.

The Sonnets are wonderfully corrective for those students who like showing off—who want to rush into "feeling" things, or pretending to be someone they are not.

When Laurence Olivier was at the height of his fame, he was interviewed on TV and presented as "the greatest actor in the world." Came the inevitable silly question, "Would you perform something for us?" Sir Laurence chose, very simply, to recite Sonnet 18. "Shall I compare thee…?"

An actor who can speak a sonnet clearly before a group of people, so that they can understand it, and so that they believe him or her, is on the way to understanding how to speak Shakespeare's dramatic verse.

((    ((    ((

Playing Shakespeare is, of course, not simply an exercise in elocution. We have spent some time discussing the structure of speeches, and played down the role that emotion plays. This is a question of priorities. Just as an architect ensures that the walls of a house be solid before the doors and windows and curtains are put in, so we believe (to paraphrase Cicely Berry) that the "predicament" must be understood before the emotions are let loose.

It's the shape of the speech that indicates the rise and fall of the emotional temperature. We have seen how Shakespeare gives us "traffic signs" to indicate changes of thought and mood. These are also indications to the driver—the actor driving the speech along—that he must change gear.

How these gear changes operate, and how they are indicated in the text, can be seen if we finally look in full at a speech we have often quoted: the opening speech of *Richard III* when the hunchback Richard of Gloucester (he is not yet king) addresses the public.

We shall find the same tripartite shape (Black vs. White ⇒ Outcome). We shall find moreover that the speech is almost composed of three sonnets.

Each block is made up of fourteen lines—except the first, which has thirteen. Now the public of Shakespeare's time knew the sonnet form and recognized it, just as today people are familiar with the limerick—or, when hearing music in 3/4 time, recognize a waltz. So watch how Shakespeare, after the thirteenth line, when the listeners are expecting the "point," deliberately changes the subject, changes the tone, and disorientates them, with what we have called the "But" element.

GLO.: Now is the winter of our discontent
Made glorious summer by this sun of York;
And all the clouds that lour'd upon our house
In the deep bosom of the ocean buried.       4
Now are our brows bound with victorious wreaths;
Our bruised arms hung up for monuments;
Our stern alarums changed to merry meetings;
Our dreadful marches to delightful measures. 8
Grim-visag'd war hath smooth'd his wrinkled front;
And now,—instead of mounting barbed steeds,
To fright the souls of fearful adversaries,—
He capers nimbly in a lady's chamber 12
To the lascivious pleasing of a lute.       13

But I, that am not shap'd for sportive tricks,
Nor made to court an amorous looking-glass;
I, that am rudely stamp'd, and want love's majesty       16
To strut before a wanton ambling nymph;
I, that am curtail'd of this fair proportion,
Cheated of feature by dissembling nature,
Deform'd, unfinish'd, sent before my time       20
Into this breathing world, scarce half made up,
And that so lamely and unfashionable
That dogs bark at me, as I halt by them;
Why, I, in this weak piping time of peace,       24
Have no delight to pass away the time,
Unless to see my shadow in the sun
And descant on mine own deformity:

And therefore, since I cannot prove a lover,       28
To entertain these fair well-spoken days,
I am determined to prove a villain,
And hate the idle pleasures of these days.
Plots have I laid, inductions dangerous,       32
By drunken prophecies, libels, and dreams,
To set my brother Clarence and the king
In deadly hate the one against the other:

And if King Edward be as true and just.       36
As I am subtle, false, and treacherous
This day should Clarence closely be mew'd up,
About a prophecy, which says, that G
Of Edward's heirs the murderer shall be.       40
Dive, thoughts, down to my soul: here Clarence comes.

Breaking the speech down into its component parts not only helps to make the sense clear, but shows how the emotions fluctuate. Many speeches (like this one) have a high emotional content, but if the actor peaks too early and tries to keep the emotion high, he will soon run out of energy. The traffic signs show how emotions can be released and sometimes held back.

Richard's speech has three major signs: "Now...," "But I...," "And therefore..."

For an actor the most interesting part is evidently the middle section, where indeed he "descants on his own deformity"—for fourteen lines! At first sight this passage might seem over-repetitive. The author, we might think, could have reduced it to:

But I, that am not shap'd for sportive tricks,
Nor made to court an amorous looking glass...
Why I, in this weak, piping time of Peace,
Have no delight to pass away the time
Unless to see my shadow in the sun
And descant on mine own deformity.

and we should have all the information we need. Indeed so—if information is our goal. But we should lose Richard's feelings. There's a very good reason why he goes on at such length about himself. His deformity is his preoccupation. It colors his every thought, it drags on his every movement, it stands in the way of his ambition. How can a crippled hunchback become king of England? He cannot let the subject drop—he is obsessed by it.

Even if he tries to be ironical about it at the start, ("not shap'd for sportive tricks" is an understatement), emotion takes him over. The repeated hammer blows of "I... I... I..." are like an angry child banging on a door that stays obstinately shut. The hated words pile up: "not shap'd," "rudely stamp'd," "curtail'd," "cheated," deform'd." "unfinish'd," "sent before my time," "half made up," "lamely and unfashionably"—the more he talks, the more his blood boils—until he reaches the three final words that sum up his frustration: "...mine own deformity." A director might say, "Give a little more gas with each example—and more—and more—until, when you reach "deformity" you cannot go any further. In this passage Richard builds up from first gear to fourth.

When he enters, Richard already seems in a state of high excitement. A Shakespearean speech, more often than not, begins in a high gear, and then throttles back. Somebody entering a room in an emotional state is evidently more theatrically interesting than somebody who wanders on calmly as if arriving early for a committee meeting; and an actor does well to ask himself, at the moment of making an entrance, just how high the pitch of his emotions is.

Richard's language shows us that he is very animated about this peace that has occurred. He is lavish with adjectives: *glorious* summer, *merry* meetings, *delightful* measures, *nimble* caperings, *lascivious* pleasing. He seems to be pleased as Punch. Everybody else is. (Henry Irving used to open the play with the joyous sound of victory bells.)

"But I,..." startles us, as if he has whipped off a mask.

He thrashes himself into a state of fury about being excluded from this peace—and especially about the soldiers from the wars returning who are making love in every lady's chamber.

In the third part, "And therefore..." marks another gear change. The language suddenly becomes practical. "Plots have I laid..." No images anymore, nothing resembling poetry. The rhythms become choppy and often monosyllabic.

He's in a hurry. At the end a note of urgency comes in:

*This day* should Clarence closely be mew'd up. Not "one day" or "next week" we notice—but "this day"—an echo of the snapping, urgent "Now…" that began the speech. (This is a favorite device of Shakespeare's: to compress time so that events follow closely upon each other.) And Richard has scarcely spoken when Clarence appears, arrested already ("guarded") on his way to the Tower; and, ready to dissemble, Richard changes gear again:

Dive, thoughts, down to my soul;…

And the play, proper begins.

If we were to make a graph of the rise and fall of feelings in this speech, it might look like this:

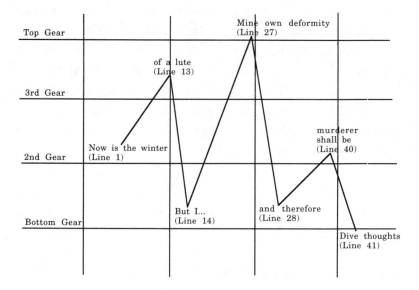

Although we have touched on only two or three well-known passages in this chapter, we have tried to show that a speech has a shape.

The Scottish playwright John McGrath once said that "a play doesn't have a message, it has a shape"—and a speech is often like a little playlet in itself. Even if it doesn't contain a story, it frequently tells a story.

The shape starts to become clear when we watch where a character changes his mind, or changes the subject. These changes indicate to the actor possible changes of tone, and mood. They tell him when he is speaking with the voice of Reason, and when Emotion overmasters him.

To ignore the shape is like swimming against the current. The actor who observes the shape finds Shakespeare's directing hand lifting him up and guiding him along with the stream.

V

# WORDS, WORDS, WORDS

I n chapter three we spoke disparagingly of "the poetry voice."
It is worth looking at this phenomenon, since it is also called
"the Shakespeare voice."

It occurs when an actor is overconscious of the sound of his
own voice. It occurs when he tries to "color" the words from the
outside. It occurs often when an actor loves Shakespeare not
wisely, but too well. (You hear it on old recordings of nineteenth
century actors.) It's as if the actor is saying, "Wonderful poet, this
Shakespeare! Listen to this—the play of vowel sounds, the
cadences, the rich language:

> This royal throne of kings, this scepter'd isle,
> This earth of majesty, this seat of Mars,
> This other eden, demi-paradise,
> This fortress built by nature for herself
> Against infection and the hand of war... (*Richard II:* II.1)

And so he goes on, rolling the words round his mouth like a wine-
taster, forgetting he's in a play; forgetting two signals that the
author is sending out:

a) if the language is heightened, it's a sign of some deeply felt emotion on the character's part;
b) if the text is repetitious, and the speaker goes on hammering the same nail for lines on end, then it's because he needs to: The subject is of capital importance to him.
c) repetitions are always building up to something.

Here, John of Gaunt is deeply upset about the decline of "this realm, this England," brought down low by the King, Richard II. He goes on about it because he cares. It's not the moment for the actor to invite Shakespeare on the stage to take a bow.

This looks like an overblown, patriotic speech, as though Shakespeare is playing Poet Laureate. But the twist is in the tail. At the end, Gaunt will lament that "this dear, dear land" is now, because of Richard's misrule, no more than a tenement or a farm, "leas'd out," and will use words like "shameful," "rotten," "scandal." Put back in its context, the speech is a cry of rage from a dying elder statesman. The tone throughout is anger. It is not Shakespeare speaking, it is Gaunt. The rich vowels and the cadences belong to him.

Shakespeare here is subsuming himself into Gaunt. The best compliment an actor can pay him is to do likewise—to imagine that John of Gaunt himself actually said these things, at that moment, and that Shakespeare simply wrote them down.

At this stage, the actor might feel bewildered. He knows that if you speak Shakespeare in an everyday way, like normal conversation, it doesn't work. The language is too dense, and the sentences too long.

On the other hand, if he plays "the music" of the verse, and tries to make it ring, he is accused of using "a Shakespeare voice." Where is the happy medium?

After all, words are Shakespeare's magic wand. Say, "Here comes the King," and for the audience, the next actor who enters is a King. Say, for example, "I am giddy: expectation whirls me round," and the audience knows your state of mind. With words, the scenery is changed, without the help of scene shifters and flymen pulling up heavy flats:

— How far is it my lord, to Berkeley now?
— Believe me, noble lord,
I am a stranger here to Gloucestershire:
These high wild hills and rough uneven ways...

And we have moved from London to Gloucestershire.

With words, Shakespeare makes us see things that are not there—like an enchanter who, by evoking the name of a spirit, conjures that spirit up.

How is the actor to do this?

This is an account of an exercise that deserves a place at the basis of all Shakespeare training. It helps the beginner in his first attempts at speaking Shakespeare, and it serves the seasoned performer in some of the trickier stretches of his role.


## FIRST EXERCISE

The class is divided into two groups, each member sits facing a partner. The instructor gives privately to each one a slip of paper on which an everyday word is written, such as:

house—dream—dog—holiday—toy—tree—mother

INSTRUCTOR: First I want you to use your memory. I want each person to think back and recall one specific example of the word you have, in its context. So if your word is *lamp,* you might remember a night-light burning at your bedside when you were ill, as a child; or it might be the great lamp the dentist switched on above you, when you were about to have a tooth out; or it might be a lamp you saw on a dark night, burning in a distant farmhouse window. Concentrate hard on your mental picture of this lamp.

When your turn comes, say to your partner the word *lamp* three times, and as you say it, picture your lamp and try to communicate your image. The partner will then say what image has come over. After that, the rest of the class can say what image—if any—they received.

This is not a guessing game, nor an exercise in telepathy or extrasensory perception.

What can happen is this.

Robert starts; his word is *house;* his partner, Amy, concentrates. "House...house...house..."

AMY: It's a small house, in the country...you're inside the house...it's warm, there are lots of lights on, small lights...lots of colored cushions...outside the window it's terribly cold, maybe snowing...you were very small...

OTHERS: Yes, I saw the window...he was scared of something outside...he was a kid...

INSTRUCTOR: Well, Robert, what were you remembering?

ROBERT: It was the house in the country we used to spend Christmas in, when I was a kid. We had a Christmas tree by the window, and, yes, there were coloured cushions on the window seat. I was about seven, I remember looking out of the window, and thinking how cosy it was indoors, and how grey and cold it was outside...

Robert was amazed that Amy "saw" the lights on the Christmas tree, and the cushions.

The instructor pointed out how notable it was that everybody agreed that he was inside the house, looking out; and that he was very small at the time.

Robert's memory was very clear-cut, like a photograph. He

was recalling one particular moment, from one particular viewpoint.

What can also happen is this.

It's Mary's turn to speak and John's to listen.

MARY: Holiday…holiday…holiday
JOHN: You were in…a hot country…by the seaside?…you were happy… *(He dries up.)* Well, Mary?
MARY: Last year we went to Mexico…we had a great time.
OTHERS: Go on…
MARY: Well, it was just a great holiday!
OTHERS: What moment were you remembering?
MARY: Lots of moments, really. It was great all the time.

Mary was remembering a *general feeling* of happiness (a feeling quite often associated with holidays) but no specific moment. So John couldn't "see" a clear image.

This exercise has been tried out over many years, in drama schools in different countries. It is striking how, time and again, when the speaker has a clear image to convey, the listener picks it up accurately, and with circumstantial details (e.g., the cushions, the fairy lights). Conversely, when the image is vague, the listener sees only fog.

Note that the instructor asked only for an "image." He didn't say, "What were your feelings toward that night-light, or dentist's lamp, or farmhouse light?" Mary was unsuccessful because she tried to communicate her *feelings* about the holiday, rather than something specific in the holiday that impressed her. Inevitably, since the students were delving back into their own memories, their feelings also came into play. But in second place, if the image is clear, the feelings will come.

Before going on to the second part of the exercise, somebody asked the instructor, "Why do we have to say the word three times?"

Because it needs a bit of practice to align your image of the thing with the word you speak. The first or second time, you might miss. It's like playing darts.


## SECOND EXERCISE

The first part was about memory, this part is about imagination. The setup is the same, only the words on the paper have changed. Many of the things listed will be outside the students' direct experience:

Crown—dagger—blood—dream—ghost—poison— sword—wound—monster—cloud—corpse

INSTRUCTOR: All these words are important in Shakespeare's plays—you'll probably recognize a lot of them. This time, however, it's not your own memory you're recalling, but someone else's. It doesn't matter whose. Invent an incident centering round your words, or if you like, borrow one from a Shakespeare play you know.

Your word might be *ghost*. You might imagine you're a general on the eve of a battle, that you are likely to lose, and you are visited by the ghost of someone you once murdered.

Who you are doesn't matter, it's the imaginary ghost that counts. You'll need to see how it's dressed, what it does, who it was when it lived, how far away it is, what it wants of you. But it's not your feelings that interest us in the first place: Try to help your partner to "see" the ghost.

You can get up and move about if you like, and use your bodies. Only if your word is a thing, don't mime it.

Again—say nothing but the word. And this, by the way, is not a vocal exercise. You're not asked consciously to inflect the word, or sing it, or emphasize it specially: simply to "see" the image, and let the word come out while doing so.

Once more, experience has proved that some players can convey a whole story in one word. In Switzerland, among a class whose knowledge of Shakespeare's plays was limited, one student made a class see a dagger, stuck upright in a table, and dripping with blood, although no murder had yet been committed; and another made us see the ghost of a Cardinal in red.

The more talented the speaker, the more clear the transmitted image tends to be. But the listeners need to be talented, too.

((       ((       ((

One object of the exercise is to help the actor to be specific, and not general; to be committed, and not neutral.

Many words in Shakespeare have acquired "poetic" associations—moon, stars, sun, flowers, dawn, ocean, spring—that is to say, they are thought to be the stuff of poetry (and sentimental love songs) and some actors think this is a sign to fall into a "poetic" way of speaking. Other actors, to counterbalance this, take on a neutral tone. Both ways avoid the issue.

If you take a word like *daybreak* and say it neutrally, you are only saying that the time is about five in the morning. If you say it "poetically," you will be communicating no more than the ideas that daybreak is (usually) something vaguely pleasant.

But in a play, the word means something very different when spoken by—

a) a man in a condemned cell on the morning of his execution,

b) a young bride on the morning of her wedding day, and

c) a soldier on a night out who has to be back in barracks at 6 A.M.

In each of these characters' mouths, the word acquires all kinds of echoes and reverberations, according to what each one is imagining.

The actor, then, faced with a speech to prepare, (after he has asked himself, What do these words mean?) does well to ask himself, What do these words mean *to me/my character?*

Another object of the exercise is to help the actor to use the words as a funnel, into which he pours the images and implications of the word, *at the moment of pronouncing it.*

As in music, it's the actual moment the notes are played that is important—it is then that the musical thought is conveyed. When G.B. Shaw said that Shakespeare must be played "on the line, and to the line, with the utterance and acting simultaneous," this is what he meant.

The actor who, at the moment he says the word "winter," conjures up a mental image of icy winds rushing through bare branches, can bring that image over to his listeners. If, straightway afterwards, he says "summer," and visualizes those same trees, drenched in sunlight and heavy with leaves, he provides the audience with a contrary image. If then he talks of "clouds," and projects a picture of dark, rolling thunderclouds heavy with rain, and follows this up by evoking the "ocean"—a calm, sparkling sea under a clear blue sky, he has told a little story in pictures. It's like a strip of film-montage:

Wintry landscape
*dissolve to*
summer landscape;
*cut to*
rolling thunderclouds
*dissolve to*
calm sky and seascape

The reader will have guessed that we are talking about the opening of *Richard III:*

Now is the winter of our discontent
Made glorious summer by this sun of York,

And all the clouds that lour'd about our house
In the deep bosom of the ocean buried.

The audience is not *informed* of the change from winter to summer; they are shown it, they share it. The actor is not throwing emotions at us, but building up a picture, image by image, moment by moment.

Shakespeare was an extraordinarily visual writer. The poet Thomas Gray said of him, "Every word with him is a picture." One of the features of his writing is to show the audience things that are not there, by feeding the mind's eye.

Think—

says the Chorus in *Henry V*

when we talk of horses that you see them

and to give our imagination a nudge, he adds a very precise image:

Printing their proud hooves in the receiving earth—

but if Chorus himself doesn't "see" the horses, the audience won't either. Shakespeare's words alone cannot make the audience see images in their minds; the actors must see them too.

Macbeth, on the night of the murder he dreads to commit, has an hallucination:

Is this a dagger which I see before me,
The handle towards my hand?

There is no dagger; but the audience will not understand the scene unless the Macbeth-actor sees it (and many don't). As Ralph Richardson said—and his Macbeth was *not* one of his most successful roles, and he had trouble with this scene—"Well, if *I* can't see the dagger, Cocky, (Cocky being Sir John Gielgud, the director), do you wonder the audience can't, either?"[1]

> Let us (it is Chorus speaking again)
> On your imaginary forces work.

Today we'd say "the forces of your imagination." Shakespeare and the actors gathered up the audience into a giant game of make-believe. With words he conjured up a communal hallucination. But the actors had to work on their own forces. Indeed, one of the titles once suggested for this little volume was "Workbook for Imaginary Forces."

☾    ☾    ☾

Not only are horses to be imagined in Shakespeare, but a whole panoply of things that would test the most ingenious stage designer—shipwrecks, haunted castles, storms on sea and land, armies in full array, battlefield graveyards, ghosts, will o' the wisps, and magic forests. The weather, too, has its part to play. How many sunsets and sunrises there are! In how many plays does darkness play a role!

Yet Shakespeare had at his disposal no more than a troupe of talented actors and musicians and a bare stage with a few pillars and a balcony. Performances took place under the open sky, in broad daylight. They started at about two in the afternoon, so in the opening scene of *Hamlet,* where visibility was supposed to be nil, the actors had only their acting to create the gloom—that, and the author's secret weapon, the words.

And the words asked the audience to believe they were somewhere long ago and far away.

---

[1] Quoted from Garry O'Connor: *Ralph Richardson.*

In Troy, there lies the scene…

This is Illyria, lady…

So this is the forest of Arden.

> …our ships have touched upon
> The desarts of Bohemia?

Many a schoolmaster still tells his English Lit. class that the Elizabethan stage was so primitive, so lacking in scenic resources or artificial lighting, that Shakespeare was *forced* to use poetry to describe the setting and the weather. Oscar Wilde devoted a whole essay, called "Shakespeare and the Scenery" to tell us how Shakespeare was constantly apologizing for the poverty of his theater, as if the poet really wished he were Henry Irving, who could restage the whole coronation of Henry VIII (with an army of extras), or Beerbohm Tree, who rebuilt the Sphinx on stage for his *Antony and Cleopatra!*

According to this view of things, if Shakespeare had had a modern lighting panel, he wouldn't have needed to write,

> Look, where the morn in russet mantle clad
> Walks o'er the dew of yon high eastern hill…

But we do Shakespeare wrong if we assume that he is standing in the wings, ready to pop on at any time and shore up his play with props of poetry by telling us things that could not be shown otherwise. He was not a nineteenth-century novelist like Dickens, who relished writing virtuoso impressions of nature as the backcloth to the action.

When characters comment on the sunrise or the sunset, the visitations of the moon or the fading of the stars, they are generally not dropping out of character to play "the narrator" for two or three lines, they are reflecting their own change of mood.

The glow-worm shows the matin to be near
And 'gins to pale his ineffectual fire...

Night's candles are burned out, and jocund day
Stands tiptoe on the misty mountain tops

are certainly graphic descriptions of daybreak, but the poetry in them should not let us forget that for both these speakers (King Hamlet's ghost, and Romeo) dawn presents a threat to them at that moment: At first light, both must flee—that's what daybreak means to *them*.

Sunrises and nightfalls are not merely mentioned for their own sake—they are there to tell us something about the character who comments on them. And the actor needs to seize upon these manifestations of nature—these suns and drifting clouds and cold, chaste moons—to see what they reveal to him or her about the character being played.

Let us see how this works in practice.

((    ((    ((

In both *Romeo and Juliet* and *Macbeth,* night is important. Their most dramatic scenes take place at night, and even a cursory reading of the plays reveals that the word *night* is constantly recurring. But how different are the silver moonlight and the nightingales of Verona from the thick smoky phantasmagoric pall that hangs over Dunsinane! We might expect this, however, since one play is a romantic love story and the other a tragedy full of witchcraft and murder; and although there is no evidence that Shakespeare ever visited either Italy or Scotland, a dramatist would be missing a chance not to use the two different atmospheres.

Yet for both Juliet and the Macbeths, night is more than a mere background to their dramas. Shakespeare had a knack of getting inside the skins of his characters and of seeing the world through their eyes, and so "night" becomes a focal point for their emotions.

To Verona first. The lovers' first private meeting, the so-called "balcony scene," takes place at night—and all the images in the scene reflect this. To Romeo, Juliet is as radiant as a light shining in the darkness—he compares her to a sunrise, she is fairer than the moon, her eyes are like "two of the fairest stars in all the heavens," and her presence like an angel in the sky.

If this sounds corny and romantic, we should remember that Romeo is taking for his comparisons things he actually *sees* in that dark garden—the moon is up, the stars are out, and the sun will shortly rise. But he has time to dally, he need not fear her family, for "I have night's cloak to hide me from their eyes"; and Juliet can speak her real feelings without showing her blushes, "Thou know'st the mask of night is on my face." Night and the darkness act for each of them as a liberator. The same scene could not take place by daylight, for they could not face each other in the same way.

( ( (

How night works on Juliet's imagination we can see when we look at a later scene—to a speech of Juliet's that always causes difficulty, because in context, it seems too long, too wordy, and it threatens to hold up the action, and out of context it suffers from overexposure, appearing in innumerable anthologies, and as an audition piece, and frequently as material for Young Ladies' Elocution Contests. This is Act III scene 2.

It is the day after Romeo and Juliet swore their love. Already a secret marriage has been arranged, and Juliet's nurse (who's in on the secret) has set off to find a rope-ladder to facilitate Romeo's climb into Juliet's bedroom that night to consummate the marriage. Juliet is waiting for news. The afternoon sun beats down.

The Ancients imagined the sun as a chariot of fire driven across the skies by Phaeton, or Phoebus, the son of the sun god.

Juliet starts by addressing it.

> Gallop apace, you fiery footed steeds
> Toward Phoebus' lodging—

If the opening lines are somewhat over-literary we should remember that the author was still in his twenties. If his writing sounds a bit like Marlowe's here, it may be because he had seen *Edward II,* and absorbed the phrase, "Gallop apace, bright Phoebus, through the sky"…

Anyway, no girl of thirteen ever *spoke* like Juliet—which is one reason why no actress of thirteen can play her. But when we look into the words, and beyond the words, to discover Juliet's feelings (which is what we are doing here), we find emotions that every girl of her age would recognize, when she's in love for the first time.

"Gallop apace" Juliet cries to the horses of the sun:

> …And bring in cloudy *night* immediately.
> Spread thy close curtain, love-performing *night,*…

and later:

> Come, civil *night,*
> Thou sober-suited matron, all in black,…
> Come, *night!* Come, Romeo! come, thou *day-in-night!*
> Come, gentle *night;* come, loving, black-brow'd *night,*
> Give me my Romeo;…

All in the space of seventeen lines.

Repetitive? Deliberately so! To anyone who objects, as Polonius would, "This is too long," one can point out that this is not meant to be a neat little poem, and the length of the speech is a measure of her desperation.

If someone in Shakespeare speaks at great length about something, it is a sign that the matter is of enormous importance *to them.*

It is as repetitive as the throbbing of the blood in her veins, as repetitive as a church bell. "Night" has become for her, not merely darkness, but the act of love itself. She speaks to night as to a lover—more, a husband. Night means Romeo.

Come *night,* come Romeo…

It is not her mind speaking, but her body, her blood, her sex.

It is clear that her thoughts are on the act of love, for when she says:

> Give me my Romeo; and, when he shall die
> Take him and cut him out in little stars
> And he will make the face of heaven so fine
> That all the world will be in love with night
> And pay no worship to the garish sun.

She is not merely being fanciful-poetical, for to the Elizabethans *to die* was a euphemism for having an orgasm. (The French still call it *la petite mort.*) The word *come* also had, even in Shakespeare's day, a double entendre. In short, the whole speech is an erotic *cri de coeur* of an adolescent girl, ravenous for her new bridegroom—and her feelings are all channelled into the word "night."

To return to our classroom exercise: If Amy can say the word "night" three times, and convey to John that she is thirteen, and longing for her new husband's embrace, that will take place that very night, she is on the way to understanding how to play Juliet.

((    ((    ((

"Night" for the Macbeths, is quite another kettle of fish. They plan to kill King Duncan.

—My dearest love,
Duncan comes here tonight.
—And when goes hence?
—Tomorrow, as he purposes.
—O! never
Shall sun that morrow see.

The first thing he tells her, coming home from the wars, is that the King will be their guest that night. The word murder is not spoken, it is a tacit agreement. Have they spoken of it before?

While waiting for her husband, Lady Macbeth has already invoked the powers of darkness.

Come, thick *night,*
And pall thee in the dunnest smoke of hell
That my keen knife see not the wound it makes
Nor heaven peep through the blanket of the dark
To cry, "Hold, hold!"

For "heaven," of course, read "God," whose name was not to be taken "in vain" in Elizabethan theaters.

If this talk of heaven and hell is not mere rhetoric, if Lady Macbeth means what she says, then she acknowledges the existence of God—which suggests she has a conscience. She wants to use night as hell's smokescreen to take cover from God's sight. She stands at the crossroads between good and evil—and deliberately chooses the path to hell. If the Macbeths are believing Christians, their struggles of conscience are all the more painful.

And Macbeth? His qualms about committing the murder are greater:

> But in these cases
> We still have *judgment* here…

> His (Duncan's) virtues
> Will plead like *angels trumpet-tongu'd against*
> The *deep damnation* of his taking off

These Christian words are not accidental. Macbeth is a believer. Night, for him, is full of "nature's mischief."

> Now o'er the one half world
> Nature seems dead, and wicked dreams abuse
> The curtain'd sleep, witchcraft celebrates
> Pale Hecate's offerings, and wither'd murder,
> Alarum'd by his sentinel, the wolf,
> Whose howl's his watch, thus with his stealthy pace,
> With Tarquin's ravishing strides, towards his design
> Moves like a ghost.

In other world, daytime is heaven's time, night is hell's playground. He knows what awaits him if he murders Duncan—judgment and deep damnation—he too stands at the crossroads, and yet he, too, chooses to walk the path to hell, with eyes wide open; and he hopes nobody will notice!

> Thou sure and firm-set earth,
> Hear not my steps, which way they walk, for fear
> The very stones prate of my whereabout,…

The murder once committed, another must follow. Banquo suspects them and Banquo must die. Now Macbeth, who formerly abhorred night, calls it up like an accomplice.

> Come, seeling night,

(His words resemble his wife's—a sign that he is coming to resemble her.)

> Scarf up to the tender night of pitiful day
> And with thy bloody and invisible hand
> Cancel and tear to pieces that great bond
> Which keeps me pale.

And night begins to fall:

> Light thickens, and the crow
> Makes wing to th' rooky wood…
> Good things of day begin to droop and drowse,
> Whiles night's black agents to their preys do rouse.

But he has turned his back on "good things of day"; he has himself become one of "night's black agents."

His attitude toward night has shifted, an indication that his whole character has started to change and is beginning its downward slide toward mass murder, despair, and death.

If sentences have their key words, characters can be said to have their key words, too. They are easily spotted, since they recur again and again. They signal matters that preoccupy the characters. In *Macbeth*, "night" is one, "blood" is another.

Blood gushes out when the murder is committed, ("Who would have thought the old man to have had so much blood in him?"). Blood defiles the murderer:

> Will all great Neptune's ocean wash this blood
> Clean from my hand?

Blood leaves a stain that cannot be removed (Lady Macbeth, sleepwalking, "seems thus washing her hands"). Blood flows like a river:

> I am in blood
> Stepp'd in so far that, should I wade no more
> Returning were as tedious as go o'er.

Blood even turns the sea red:

> No, this my hand will rather
> The multitudinous seas incarnadine,
> Making the green one red.

The word "blood" absorbs many others—crime, murder, brutality, evil, damnation—and guilt. Not for nothing can it be called a key word, for it unlocks the characters' deepest and most complex feelings.

To examine the way Macbeth reacts to "night" and "blood" is to get a startling insight into his character. There are a hundred ways of playing Macbeth, but the actor who treats these two motifs as mere incidents on his path through life, instead of as the *center points of his mental landscape,* is ignoring the helping hand that Shakespeare offers him.

☾    ☾    ☾

Many roles in Shakespeare seem at first sight so complex and wordy that an actor may be forgiven if he does not know at once where to find the entry door. Finding the key word to the character will help to focus his searchings.

The key word to a character often proves to be the key word to the play as a whole.

The great cycle of plays that Shakespeare wrote about English history from the time of Richard II (early fourteenth century) up to his own time Henry VIII (late sixteenth century) carry the names of the kings, but the thread that runs through the whole cycle is the problem of kingship: what it means to govern one's fellow men.

In our own days, kings have become little more than rubber stamps, but the same problems that confronted Shakespeare's kings now face presidents and prime ministers.

Kingship is symbolized by the crown. In each play the crown of England is present—a physical object. The word itself echoes through the plays like a leitmotif. To each wearer it represents something different. It can be a gift of God, a jewel to be coveted, and a ring of gold that eats away its bearer, or even a hollow golden "O."

Actors playing the kings often begin by reading up on their character in a biography, or by consulting effigies and contemporary portraits. But Shakespeare was not out to make historically accurate portraits of these men, and frequently he deliberately alters the known facts. He was basically using these figures to illustrate the different prototypes of leader—dictators, demagogues, usurpers, tyrants: those who are up to the job, and those who are not. He that plays the king will stimulate his own imagination more by asking himself, "What is *my character's attitude to the crown?*", than by reading a handful of biographies.

For those who know their historical Shakespeare, a good classroom exercise would center round the word *crown*. The speaker says the word in character, three times, and the rest of the class guess which king is speaking—and at which stage in his life.

❲    ❲    ❲

As we have seen previously, Shakespeare possessed an arsenal of some 30,000 words. But just as a sculptor portraying a dancer in movement can make a mass of bronze balance on two small "pointes," so he could make a whole character, or play, balance on one or two simple, important words.

One simple word can carry the weight of dozens. Repeat it, and its density increases. In moments of crisis, repetition and simplicity can wring the heart. Perhaps he learned this from the Bible he heard in church as a boy.

Babylon is fallen, is fallen that great city.

Oh my son Absalom, my son, my son, Absalom!
Would God I had died for thee, O Absalom,
my son, my son!

And here is Shakespeare, using repetition in moments of passion...

O Lord! my boy, my Arthur, my fair son!
My life, my joy, my food, my all-the world.

O Iago, the pity of it! the pity of it, Iago!

Tomorrow and tomorrow and tomorrow...

I am dying, Egypt, dying...

—What do you read, my lord?
—Words, words, words.

O let me not be mad, not mad, sweet Heaven!
Keep me in temper; I would not be mad.

At certain high moments, it looks as if the poet is handing over the reins to the actor; as if saying, "You can say 'dying' in a way that is more moving than half a dozen lines of my poetry." Often this occurs when a character is in the grip of an emotion so over-whelming that coherent words no longer suffice.

Othello, maddened by jealousy, loses his customary eloquence and cries like a savage beast: "O! blood, blood, blood!" He is no longer master of himself,

Juliet's nurse, not usually at a loss for words, has none when she sees her beloved mistress (supposedly) dead:

O woe! O woeful, woeful, woeful day!
Most lamentable day, most woeful day
That ever, ever I did yet behold!
O day! O day! O day! O hateful day!
Never was seen so black a day as this!
O woeful day! O woeful day!

What other poet would dare to be so *unliterary?* Not Racine or Corneille, certainly! And it is interesting that in foreign versions of the play the translator frequently "corrects" Shakespeare by reducing the speech to two or three lines! Thus, in the name of "good taste" robbing the actor of some acting material.

Certainly it puts an actor's gifts to the test to ask him or her to convey such huge emotion without the support of eloquent words, or when a simple word is repeated.

One of the most terrible moments in *King Lear* is when the aged monarch enters carrying the body of his beloved daughter Cordelia, whom he has seen being hanged. He cries to the mute, assembled soldiers:

Howl, howl, howl, howl! O you are men of stone....

"Howl" is a command: The men are hiding their emotion. It is also, by its onomatopoeic "ow" sound, the king's own cry of anguish. He is himself howling, like a wounded wolf. The word does not merely describe his pain, it *expresses* it. No one who has heard John Gielgud's recording of this speech can easily forget this cry.

To appreciate the double use of this cry, one has only to imagine it in another language. A French King Lear cries, "Hurlez!"— which is simply the command. In Swedish, the king cries "Krik, krik, krik, krik!"—which only goes to support Robert Frost's definition of poetry as "that which gets lost in translation."

And Lear again, facing the fact that Cordelia is no more, whispers to her limp body:

Thou'lt come no more,
Never, never, never, never, never.

He seems to be describing the abyss of eternity. He is wringing the word "never" of its last drop of meaning. No rich poetry could be so eloquent at this moment than this simple word.

((    ((    ((

So we have seen that, in speaking Shakespeare, the actor needs to concentrate his thoughts on the word he is saying, not before or after, but at the moment of uttering it; and to use the word to convey its implications for him/for his character. This applies as much when he is playing a simple messenger (announcing to King Macbeth for instance, "The queen, my lord, is dead") as when he is given the responsibility of playing the hardest parts in the canon; when he has to channel a lifetime of feelings through one simple word: "Pity," or "howl!" or "never," or even, "oh!"

# VI

# VERSE AND PROSE

~

British actor on tour in the Netherlands met a distinguished man of letters, who told him: "I've just finished
my new translation of *Measure for Measure*. And, what's
more, I've got it all into blank verse—and that's something *even
Shakespeare himself couldn't manage!*"

Evidently the conscientious man thought that verse was in
some way superior to prose; and since twenty-eight percent of
the material in the plays is in prose, would have considered that
Shakespeare left more than a quarter of his work unfinished. It's
amusing to think of Shakespeare, having written a scene in prose,
putting it away among his rhyming dictionary and his book of
synonyms and thinking "I'll turn that into verse when I have the
time." (As a translator might.)

Why did he use verse at all? When modern poets (Eliot,
Auden, Fry) write plays in verse, the results are apt to seem self-
conscious and bookish, and the plays date very quickly—or as
Tom Stoppard would say of old plays, they "go off, like ripe fruit,"
but with Shakespeare, verse seems perfectly natural. Again, nowadays verse in the theater slows everything up, and it takes a long

time to say a simple thing, yet Shakespeare's best verse is tighter—he crams more meaning in fewer words.

To understand this, we must turn back to that heady afternoon in 1587—according to one historian "the most important date in English drama"—when Christopher Marlowe's *Tamburlaine* burst upon the English stage. Until then the theater had been a simple form of popular entertainment, all "clowning and grocers' plays" someone called it, and hardly the place for a respectable writer. But Marlowe showed what could happen when a poet joined the ranks of the playwrights.

Tamburlaine was the great ruler of Samarkand who in the fourteenth century swept through the Middle East conquering Persians, Syrians, Tartars, and Turks. In his prologue Marlowe promised:

> ...you shall hear the Scythian Tamburlaine
> Threatening the world in high astounding terms
> And scourging kingdoms with his conquering sword.

And "high astounding terms" was what he gave Tamburlaine (and everyone else) to speak. The audience was given a banquet of fine language; they left the theater inebriated with the rolling verses they had heard. For fellow poets it was like the discovery of America—the doors of the theater had suddenly been flung open for poetry, too. The great star actor of the Rose Theatre, Edward Alleyn, must have been gifted with a miraculous voice to be entrusted with such verbal music as this:

> Now walk the angels on the walls of heaven,
> As sentinels to warn th' immortal souls
> To entertain divine Zenocrate:
> Apollo, Cynthia, and the ceaseless lamps
> That gently look'd upon this loathsome earth,
> Shine downwards now no more, but deck the heavens
> To entertain divine Zenocrate:

The crystal springs, whose taste illuminates
Refined eyes with an eternal sight,
Like tried silver run through Paradise
To entertain divine Zenocrate:
The cherubins and holy seraphins,
That sing and play before the King of Kings,
Use all their voices and their instruments
To entertain divine Zenocrate:

(Part Two: Act II. 4.)

If Shakespeare was there that afternoon, (let us suppose he was), the performance would have been a blinding revelation. At twenty-three, this young man would already have some ideas for plays trotting round in his head, and might have been reading the new *Chronicles of English History* by Raphael Holinshed, published that very year, 1587; at the same time he was no doubt penning his first attempts at writing poetry, and finding he had a fluency with words. Suddenly, when he heard Tamburlaine, the two interests fused into one. If Tamburlaine could be treated like that, why not the great English warrior, Talbot? Why not England's scourge, Richard III? And furthermore, now he knew how to make these figures talk! Marlowe had helped him to find his voice.

Kings, emperors, and historical figures needed a sonorous, elevated way of speaking, and Marlowe's verse gave them just that.

And yet we might further imagine that when his head cleared, Shakespeare went into an alehouse to think over—and even make some notes upon what he had seen and heard. His ambition was fired: to write something like that! And yet…

1) Tamburlaine is more a dramatic poem, than a poetic drama. Action there is in plenty; but drama—very little.

There was certainly spectacle, and striking images. A king being strung up on a tree and shot at, made a marvellous effect. (At a later performance, an eyewitness tells us, one of the guns "swerved" and shot a member of the audience.) And then there was the scene of two captive kings yoked, and harnessed like oxen, to draw great Tamburlaine's chariot, he cracking his whip and crying:

Holla, ye pamper'd jades of Asia!

This phrase would turn up years later in Shakespeare's work, when he created the character of a loud-mouthed swaggering soldier who loved the playhouse not wisely but too well, and who burst into taverns drunkenly trying to imitate Alleyn's Tamburlaine (much as young people today imitate Hollywood idols), and who bore the explosive name of Pistol.

Young Will's reservations about the play he saw, continued:

2) Many people in the play are speaking, but they have only one voice: the author's. You could take a speech from one character and give it to another, and nobody would notice. In theory, the speech about "divine Zenocrate" could have been given to anybody.

3) Since they all talk the same way, where are the characters' individualities?

4) There is no humor in the play (but Kit Marlowe is renowned for his lack of a sense of humor).

5) The verse is certainly high and astounding, but how regular it all is, like hoofbeats. Each thought is contained in one line or two—the verse is constantly end-stopped. The verse form dictates the emotions—shouldn't it be the other way around?

6) Isn't it all rather literary?

Shakespeare, brought up in the country, and hearing the dialogue of Marlowe, the university scholar, must often have been nagged by the unreality of it all: "But people don't talk like that!"

Marlowe, who was the same age as Shakespeare, might have developed as a writer and grown out of these youthful defects, if only he had not been murdered six years later, stabbed in the eye at Deptford as he waited for the boat to carry him on a dubious mission to France.

He did not invent blank verse—that had been in use for some thirty years, ever since the Earl of Surrey chose the five-beat line for his translation of Virgil's *Eclogues*—but he gave the kick-start to English poetic drama, empowering countless young writers to discover their talents. "Marlowe," said Granville Barker, "sowed, but he was not to reap." It was left to Shakespeare, who took over where Marlowe left off, to do the reaping.

In his early years as a playwright he was to be influenced by Marlowe, yet we can feel him fighting to be free of him. Richard III is a Marlovian figure, though gifted with an impish humour that Tamburlaine never possessed:

> Was ever woman in this humour wooed?
> Was ever woman in this humour won?
> I'll have her, but I will not keep her long.

But the lines often have the same end-stopped, rhetorical, marching-on-the-spot character:

> Poor key-cold figure of a holy king!
> Pale ashes of the House of Lancaster!
> Thou bloodless remnant of that royal blood!

And Shakespeare must have had this Marlowe verse in his head:

> Gallop apace, bright Phoebus, through the sky,
> And dusky night in rusty iron car...   (*Edward II* )

when he gave Juliet a speech beginning:

> Gallop apace, you fiery-footed steeds
> Towards Phoebus' lodging; such a waggoner
> As Phaeton would whip you to the west
> And bring in cloudy night immediately...

Yet in the same play he invents a character—and how much more freely his imagination runs when he does not have to conform to characters his audience knows—who talks like a living person: Juliet's Nurse. In her you can hear the chatter of thousands of good-hearted, simple, motherly women down the ages.

> NURSE: Even or odd, of all days in the year,
> Come Lammas-eve at night shall she be fourteen.
> Susan and she God rest all Christian souls!—
> Were of an age. Well, Susan is with God;
> She was too good for me. But, as I said,
> On Lammas-eve at night shall she be fourteen
> That shall she, marry; I remember it well.
> 'Tis since the earthquake now eleven years;
> And she was wean'd, I never shall forget it,
> Of all the days of the year, upon that day;...

Is it verse or prose? Shakespeare's first printer did not know, and printed the passage as prose. Listening to it, you would hardly know either. As Granville Barker points out, "...the lines are to be scanned—and can only be scanned—dramatically and characteristically" and he goes on to say:

> We shall hardly exaggerate if we say that in the writing
> of the Nurse Shakespeare solves at a stroke all the essen-
> tial problems of the dramatic use of blank verse.[1]

By "characteristically" he infers that the Nurse's lines could not be given to anyone else.

Marlowe wrote in verse, and it sounded like it. It also sounded like a good translation from some Latin or Greek playwright, which was what Marlowe was reared on. Evidently Shakespeare admired this, up to a point. But he was not so soaked in classical literature. He had probably "heard" the Nurse, standing chattering

---

[1] H. Granville Barker, *Upon Dramatic Method*, 1956.

at a street corner or in a pie shop at Stratford, and he brought her into Verona. In the same way he would later bring Falstaff and Mistress Quickly, and even the Marlowe-quoting Pistol,—pure Elizabethans—into a play about *Henry IV* who reigned nearly two centuries before, without any fear of anachronism.

So we see Shakespeare divided between what he feels he ought to do and what he really wants to do. He writes in verse, because that's what Marlowe did, and that's what the public expects, and because it gives a certain structure to the thoughts; yet he refuses to let the verse form dominate him. He pulls it about, stretching it, chopping it up, kicking it around, because the character's thought processes are more important than some literary rules.

> That it should come to this! But two months dead: nay, not so much, not two: so excellent a king, that was, to this, Hyperion to a satyr; so loving to my mother that he might not beteem the winds of heaven visit her face too roughly. Heaven and earth! Must I remember? why, she would hang on him, as if increase of appetite had grown by what it fed on; and yet within a month, let me not think on't, Frailty thy name is woman! a little month—or ere those shoes were old with which she follow'd my poor father's body, like Niobe, all tears; why she, even she,—O God! a beast, that wants discourse of reason, would have mourned longer,—married with my uncle, my father's brother, but no more like my father than I to Hercules: within a month, ere yet the salt of most unrighteous tears had left the flushing of her galled eyes, she married.
>
> (*Hamlet*: I.2)

Prose, or verse?

In all editions of Shakespeare this is printed as verse: Which of course it is, but the listener's not to know. For whatever shape it takes on the page, the text of Shakespeare's plays is written in the first place to be heard.

Verse, or prose—need the distinction bother us then? Is it not a matter of more interest for scholars and printers than for actors? The actor's task is to make the role come to life, the words are there—does it make a difference in what form?

I think it is of primary importance. These changes of form are the playwright's signals to the actor. He wrote few stage directions, or direct indications of mood and character (compare Eugene O'Neill, who prefaces nearly every line with bracketed notes, like "(bizarrely)" or "(in a strange voice)," and unlike a composer Shakespeare does not write *allegro, andante, vivace,* and so on, on the script: But it is in the swings from verse to prose, and in the varieties of verse used, that we find Shakespeare's hidden score markings.

It is worthwhile to see if we can decipher them. This is, of course, not simply a matter of speaking, it is also a matter of character drawing. How a person speaks reflects how he thinks, and this embodies what he feels. Unlike Marlowe, Shakespeare tries to give every personage his own voice (or voices), each as individual as his fingerprint.

Why then, sometimes verse, sometimes prose? Because Shakespeare is not one to abide by any rules, there seems to be no system, no formula. All we can do is to watch him at work, see when he does it—and try to draw what conclusions we can.

Schoolmasters sometimes tell us that he gave highborn people verse to speak, and let lowborn simple people express themselves in prose. It certainly seems this way in *A Midsummer Night's Dream,* where Bottom and his fellow tradesmen are the only ones to talk in prose, and only move to verse (horrible verse) when they present the playlet about Pyramus and Thisbe.

It is true that his great gallery of portraits of unlettered men, the comic servants, earthy gravediggers, pompous policemen, country yokels, all speak prose. But this does not explain why Juliet's Nurse often speaks verse, nor the old gardener in Richard

II, nor those two romantic shepherds in *As You Like It,* Sylvius and Phebe.

Nor does it explain why some comedies (*Much Ado About Nothing, The Merry Wives of Windsor,* and a great deal of *As You Like It*) are primarily written in prose. It is too easy to think that Shakespeare was writing quickly, and prose was easier; I doubt that he found verse more difficult to write, and for actors it's much more easy to learn. This is a practical point that would not be beneath his consideration. His company produced some fifteen plays a year which left them no more than about three weeks' rehearsal for each play. An actor needed to be a quick "study."

The comedies were, however, written "in holiday mood," so there may be a clue there. Namely, that prose is relaxed and spontaneous.

Rosalind and Orlando (in *As You Like It*) are very much in love, and enjoying each other's company—and they talk in prose; while Sylvius and Phebe are under a strain all the time, she giving herself airs, and he forcing himself to play the lover—and they are discovered speaking in verse. What a difference in spontaneity there is between Sylvius' verse,

> Sweet Phebe, do not scorn me; do not, Phebe:
> Say that you love me not, but say not so
> In bitterness. The common executioner
> Whose heart the accustom'd sight of death makes hard,
> Falls not the axe upon the humbled neck
> But first begs pardon: will you sterner be
> Than he that dies and lives by bloody drops?

(poor lad!) and Rosalind's outburst in prose:

> O coz, coz, coz, my pretty little coz, that thou didst know how many fathom deep I am in love! But it cannot be sounded: my affection hath an unknown bottom, like the bay of Portugal.

We cannot imagine Sylvius, in that mood, expressing himself in prose, nor Rosalind, so free and gay, saying the same thing in verse.

In the same way, if we think of simple people like Launcelot Gobbo, Dogberry the constable, Costard, or Mistress Quickly expressing themselves in verse, it wouldn't fit them at all. Corin, another old shepherd in *As You Like It,* is no fool, he has a certain dignity—listen how beautifully and simply he expresses his view of life:

> Sir, I am a true labourer; I earn that I eat, get that I wear, owe no man hate, envy no man's happiness, glad of other men's good, content with my harm; and the greatest of my pride is to see my ewes graze and my lambs suck.

Unlettered he may be, but he could not express himself better. Quiller-Couch said that the first requirement of writing is that it be "appropriate" and how appropriate this is, to Corin.

Verse, then, is not in any way "superior" to prose—as our Dutch man of letters may have thought—it is merely another means of expression. And prose is not a sign of stupidity or lack of education or grace.

We might be tempted to think that verse is limited to people with a certain nobility who would mind their language—who would, in life, take pains to express themselves as well as possible—except that Hamlet frequently speaks prose, and even when he speaks verse, we have seen how unverselike it is. His advice to the Players, ("Speak the speech, I pray you, trippingly on the tongue…") is written in a light way, and indeed, trippingly. He is at ease with the Players, they are his old friends. The mood changes when he starts to quote a "passionate speech" from an old play in their repertoire:

The rugged Pyrrhus, he, whose sable arm
Black as his purpose, did the night resemble
When he lay couched in the ominous horse,
Hath now this dread and black complexion smear'd
With heraldry more dismal;...

(Fragment of an unused play of his? or Shakespeare parodying himself?)

What is important is the contrast: Hamlet's light familiar style of speaking set against the orotund rolling cadences of an out-dated theater style. Shakespeare juxtaposes verse and prose like a painter using light and shade, the one giving value to the other.

When Brutus addresses the Roman crowd after Caesar's death, he uses prose. Brutus normally talks in verse, so this may be a touch of demagogy, Brutus signalling "I'm just an ordinary chap like you":

Romans, countrymen, and lovers! hear me for my cause; and
be silent, that you may hear: believe me for mine honour, and
have respect to mine honour, that you may believe...

Marc Antony, two minutes later, will have no qualms about using more resounding rhetoric, and verse:

Friends, Romans, countrymen, lend me your ears;
I come to bury Caesar, not to praise him.
The evil that men do lives after them,
The good is oft interred with their bones;
So let it be with Caesar.

The contrast is breathtaking—and which of the two speeches will *civis romanus* remember? And which of the two speakers is the more tensed up?

*King Henry IV* is a play full of such contrasts. Up in the Palace of Westminster is the sick insomniac pious king, expressing himself with lofty formality:

> So shaken as we are, so wan with care,
> Find we a time for frighted peace to pant
> And breathe short-winded accents of new broils
> To be commenc'd in stronds afar remote.
> No more the thirsty entrance of this soil
> Shall daub her lips with her own children's blood...

This is a high-flown way of saying, let us be done with civil war, and make war against others, abroad. And down in the Boar's Head Tavern there is impious life-loving Gargantuan Falstaff, expressing himself with no formality at all. The following scene begins in plain, no-nonsense prose:

> Now, Hal, what time of day is it, lad?

We are in a different world. And the Crown Prince, Hal, when in Falstaff's company speaks Falstaff's language:

> Thou art so fat-witted, with drinking of old sack, and unbut-toning thee after supper, and sleeping upon benches after noon, that thou hast forgotten to demand that truly which thou wouldst truly know...

but when called up before his father, the Prince speaks with a different tongue:

> I will redeem all this on Percy's head,
> And in the closing of some glorious day
> Be bold to tell you that I am your son;
> When I will wear a garment all of blood
> And stain my favours in a bloody mask,
> Which, wash'd away, shall scour my shame with it...

And the play goes on switching from the high austere cadenced language of the Court, the formal verses relentlessly rolling on, to the loose shapeless gossipy game-playing prose of the tavern, with the Prince adjusting his diction according to whether he's at court or on a spree.

Falstaff would never speak in verse, he is too devil-may-care, and nobody would speak verse to him, he would soon take them down a peg or two! "I am not only witty in myself, but the cause that wit is in other men" he boasts—and blank verse is not a style to be witty in. In his presence, Prince Hal is also "in holiday mood," his jacket unbuttoned and his tie loosened; he is off-duty.

Thus prose is unbuttoned, unrestricted, off-duty language; while verse is language in formal attire, its hair brushed, its shoes polished—language on duty.

Besides, with verse there is a tension in the air. Hamlet is unbuttoned when he talks to the Players, or to his friend Horatio in the churchyard—he is at ease with them; or when he mocks Polonius or banters with Rosencrantz and Guildenstern—these scenes are in prose. But confronted with his detested uncle, or his father's spirit, and even with his own mother, with all of whom relations are more strained, then he speaks in verse. The soliloquies, of course, are also verse, for then he's at his most "uptight" —and the emotional stress is almost exploding the verse.

Lear and Othello are both rather distant, high and mighty people: Verse is their natural utterance. But when the one goes mad, and the other suffers an epileptic fit, their language goes into meltdown. Their thoughts are all disjointed, they are no longer in charge of them—and they go over into prose. Recovered, their speech regains its former formality and they revert to verse.

So the question we should most profitably ask ourselves, as actors, is not *why* Shakespeare uses sometimes verse, sometimes prose (which is his own affair)—but *when*. And we should try to avoid a generalized answer, because he rejects generalizations.

What are the circumstances, and who is talking to whom? What has come before, and what goes after?

Very often the style switches from one to the other in the middle of a scene: Hamlet greets Ophelia gently in verse ("Nymph, in thy orisons / Be all my sins remembered") and when she returns his gifts ("remembrances"), he suddenly switches into prose ("Ha, ha! are you honest?") and starts railing at her. There is a change of key. Is it at this moment that he apprehends the eavesdropping presence of her father and the king?

In *Julius Caesar,* Brutus and Cassius watch Caesar in procession return from the games. He is in a fury ("The angry spot doth glow on Caesar's brow") and when he has passed, they ask Casca what the matter is. In the ensuing scene, Brutus and Cassius speak verse, while Casca replies in prose, telling how Caesar had an epileptic fit in public.

> CASSIUS: But soft, I pray you: what! did Caesar swound?
> CASCA: He fell down in the market place, and foamed
> at mouth, and was speechless.
> BRUTUS: 'Tis very like; he hath the falling sickness.
> CASSIUS: No, Caesar hath it not; but you, and I,
> And honest Casca, we have the falling sickness,
> CASCA: I know not what you mean by that; but I am
> sure Caesar fell down. If the tag-rag people
> did not clap him and hiss him, according as
> he pleased and displeased them, as they use
> to do players in a theatre, I am no true man.

Casca is "a blunt fellow," and his words have the breathlessness and urgency of someone who has just witnessed an event that has shaken him to the core; this contrasts with the reflective, withdrawn patrician dignity of Brutus and Cassius. The prose blasts a hole in the middle of a scene that has been, up to then and thereafter, in measured verse.

Prose is, of course, best for comedy. It has looser rhythms, and the shape is not disturbed when interrupted by laughs from the audience. There is a element of comedy in the Casca scene:

CASSIUS: Did Cicero say anything?
CASCA: Ay, he spoke Greek.
CASSIUS: To what effect?
CASCA: Nay, an I can tell you that, I'll ne'er look
you i' the face again; but those that under-
stood him smiled at one another and shook their
heads; but, for mine own part, it was Greek to me.
(I.2)

This may be why in *The Tempest,* Caliban, the creature half-man half-monster, who has only learned language from his master Prospero, speaks verse, even in the scene with the jester Trinculo, and the idiotic drunken butler Stephano, who talk prose. (II.1) It is primarily a comic scene—but Shakespeare knew how to stop the laughter when he needed to, and verse has a way of stilling the audience. It is a further proof of his ability to make the public laugh and tremble at the same time.

Passing, often imperceptibly, from verse to prose, and back again, Shakespeare is indicating to the actors that *at that moment* there is a change of key, a modulation of mood, a passing from formality to informality. As we have seen this has less to do with the social status or intelligence or literacy of the character, and mostly to do with his relationship to the people he is with, and with the heightening or lessening of tension.

As actors, we should not be misled into thinking that the prose is easier to speak than the verse—any more than we should assume that Shakespeare wrote more carelessly or effortlessly in prose. Indeed, it may have been more difficult, since there are no guiding lines, and verse has its rules. It has been said that actors cannot speak his prose until they have first learned to speak his verse.

ROSALIND: Love is merely a madness, and I tell you deserves as well a dark house and a whip as madmen do: and the reason why they are not so punished and cured is, that the lunacy is so ordinary that the whippers are in love too…Yet I profess curing it by counsel.

ORLANDO: Did you ever cure any so?

ROSALIND: Yes, one, and in this manner. He was to imagine me his love, his mistress; and set him every day to woo me: at which time would I, being but a moonish youth, grieve, be effeminate, changeable, longing and liking, proud, fantastical, apish, shallow, inconstant, full of tears, full of smiles; for every passion something, and for no passion truly any thing, as boys and women are for the most part cattle of this colour: would now like him, now loath him; then entertain him, then forswear him; now weep for him, then spit at him; that I drave my suitor from his mad humour of love to a living humour of madness—which was, to forswear the full stream of the world and to live in a nook merely monastic…And thus I cured him, and this way will I take upon me to wash your liver as clean as a sound sheep's heart, that there shall not be one spot of love in't.

(*As You Like It:* III.2)

This is just as rhythmic and cadenced as any verse. And precision pays off. Punctuation is important—I know a lady director who frequently remarks to her actors, "Sorry—but the Boss has put in a semicolon there—would you please respect it?" This is not said out of overdue reverence for the Boss, but in the interests of clarity.

We have seen how, in speaking verse, it's important to point up the oppositions, the Black vs. White elements. They are here again in

Rosalind: tears/smiles, every passion something/no passion anything, like/loathe, entertain/forswear, weep/spit, Full stream of the world/nook merely monastic.

And again, the key words are important, like signposts on the way, to keep the argument clear. Rosalind is both trying to prove a point (that love is a madness that can be cured) and telling a story. If the key words aren't pointed up, the result is a verbal log-jam, and the audience loses the sense.

Vanessa Redgrave, one of the great Rosalinds of this century, had this to say about Shakespeare's prose:

> I had read a lot of Elizabethan literature and poems, at a time which was very vivid sensually and physically for me... (All I was trying to explain was that) Shakespeare's speech was totally familiar to me, although it's a special speech, a very meticulous prose, with very difficult phrasing, lengthy strings of words which you have to treat as you would a phrase of music—begin, follow through and *not let it drop*...[2]

The final words should be italicized: *"not let it drop."* The sentences are longer than we are used to in modern plays, the thoughts express themselves in long arcs of words. Nowadays we tend to chop everything up. Our impulses to speak come in short, sharp bursts. We stop frequently to search for the next word. But Rosalind is not like this, when she starts a sentence she knows where she is going, at least until the next colon or semicolon, for she thinks in "lengthy strings of words."

So breath control is as important as it is for a singer, and the moments of taking breath should not be left to chance but planned ahead, otherwise the player will be left in mid-sentence gasping like a fish stranded on dry land. (Older Shakespearean actors—I have heard it told of Laurence Olivier and Lewis Casson—used to compete with each other: "How many lines of verse can you say without drawing breath?")

Tied up with this is a question of energy. It is not simply

---

2 Interview with Ronald Bryden on BBC-TV; reprinted in *Acting in the Sixties,* ed. Hal Burton, (BBC).

because this is a classical play, and the Elizabethans used longer sentences, that Rosalind talks this way. She is a woman of great energy and wit, and this is how her energy expresses itself, bubbling over like a mountain spring, so the actress playing her needs to find the energy of her vivacity and gaiety, and keep it up till the end, otherwise, not only the speech, but also Rosalind herself, vanishes: "begin, follow through, and not let it drop."

The key words in prose (as you can see) are farther apart; in verse they are often two to a line. This means that prose can be played faster than verse—it's lighter, swifter, more fun, and less emphatic.

In verse, it's often the underlying rhythms that keep the actor going; in prose, the rhythms have to be discovered for themselves; and a different kind of energy has to be found. Prose is not half so easy as it looks.

# VII

# WHAT IS POETICAL?

TOUCHSTONE:
Truly, I would the gods had made thee poetical.
AUDREY:
I do not know what "poetical" is: Is it
honest in deed and word? Is it a true thing?
*(As You Like It:* III.3)

The word "poetry" has scarcely raised its head in our discussion of Shakespeare's verse and prose. This is because it's a word that needs to be handled with care, as it leads to many misunderstandings. It can cause actors to adopt a strange singsong delivery, which they think appropriate to poetic drama, and which is not appropriate at all. So it is worth looking at the role poetry plays in these poetic dramas.

Nobody, it is hoped, will confuse poetry with verse, and think that because a passage is written in iambic pentameters it is therefore poetry, and, conversely, a passage written in prose is not. For instance, Rosalind's speech (chapter 5) —like many of her utterances—can be qualified as poetry; as can Mistress Quickly's account of the death of Falstaff:

...A' made a finer end and went away an it had been any chris-tom child; a' parted even just between twelve and one, even at the turning o' the tide: for after I saw him fumble with the sheets and play with flowers and smile upon his fingers' ends, I knew there was but one way; for his nose was as sharp as a pen, and a' babbled of green fields. "How now, Sir John!" quoth I: "what, man! Be of good cheer." So a' cried out "God, God, God!" three or four times; now I, to comfort him, bid him a' should not think of God. I hoped there was no need to trou-ble himself with any such thoughts yet. So 'a bade me lay more clothes on his feet: I put my hand into the bed and felt them, and they were as cold as any stone; then I felt to his Knees, and so upward, and upward, as all was cold as any stone.

(*H.V.:* II.3)

and Hamlet's reunion with his old friend Yorick, the king's jester—dead these three and twenty years and now a skull:

Alas! poor Yorick. I knew him, Horatio; a fellow of infinite jest, of most excellent fancy; he had borne me on his back a thou-sand times; and now, how abhorred in my imagination it is! My gorge rises at it. Here hung those lips that I have kissed I know not how oft. Where be your gibes now? your gambols? your songs? your flashes of merriment, that were wont to set the table on a roar? Not one, now, to mock your own grin-ning? quite chapfallen? Now get you to my lady's chamber, and tell her, let her paint an inch thick, to this favour she must come; make her laugh at that.

(V.1)

On the other hand, "poetry" is hardly an apt description for this, though it is written in blank verse:

Besides, these writers say,
King Pepin, which deposed Childeric,
Did, as heir general being descended

Of Blithild, who was daughter to King Clothair,
Make claim and title to the crown of France.
Hugh Capet also, who usurp'd the crown
Of Charles the Duke of Lorraine, sole heir male
Of the true line and stock of Charles the Great,
To find his title with some shows of truth—
Though in pure truth it was corrupt and naught—
Convey'd himself as heir to the lady Lingare
Daughter to Charlemain, who was the son
To Lewis the emperor, and Lewis the son
Of Charles the Great. Also King Lewis the Tenth,
Who was sole heir to the usurper Capet,
Could not keep quiet in his conscience
Wearing the Crown of France, till satisfied
The fair Queen Isabel, his grandmother,
Was lineal of the Lady Ermengare,
Daughter to Charles the aforesaid Duke of Lorraine:
By the which marriage the line of Charles the Great
Was re-united with the Crown of France....

(*H.V.:* I.2)

Of course this is dreadful—and most readers will already have skipped it—but we must not take it seriously. The Archbishop of Canterbury is proving to the sabre-rattling Henry V that historically he can make a claim to the French crown. Shakespeare here is writing deliberately badly and jarringly to mock the bumbling old divine—whose next line is "So that, as clear as is the summer's sun..." and to show that, if a King wants to go to war, the most minuscule excuse will serve his purpose. (Those who saw Olivier's film of *Henry V* will not easily forget the hilarity of this scene, with the prissy old Archbishop, Felix Aylmer, constantly dropping his papers, getting them out of order, and totally losing the thread of what he had to say.)

This speech is not "bad Shakespeare" but Shakespeare, impishly, setting out to write badly—which is a different matter.

Most of his leading characters have a poetic turn of mind—that is, most of what they say can be recognized as poetry. One has only to think of Hamlet, Richard II, Othello, Antony, Cleopatra, Timon of Athens, Berowne—to name but a few. The writer is often praised for being "inspired" when he wrote their lines, and told off for being less inspired when he created many minor characters. It is true that there are a number of dull parts, and sometimes he did nod off. He cannot have been trying very hard, for instance, when he gave Northumberland (in *Richard II*) the following Christmas-card verse to speak:

> The next news is: I have to London sent
> The heads of Salisbury, Spencer, Blunt and Kent.
> The manner of their taking may appear
> At large discoursed in this paper here.

and a minute later to ask Bolingbroke to say:

> Thy pains, Fitzwater, shall not be forgot;
> Right noble is thy merit, well I wot.

Only William McGonagall could find any merit in this, and most critics kindly surmise that Shakespeare was adapting an old play by someone else, and some clods of the other writer had not yet been scraped away.

But Shakespeare's accusers are mistaken if they think that because he is writing poetic drama, all the characters should speak poetry: that Horatio should talk as brilliantly as Hamlet, that Bolingbroke's language should blaze as Richard's does, or that Enobarbus should be as trumpet-tongued as Antony. That they do not do so is not Shakespeare's failure, but Shakespeare's artistry. An orchestra needs trumpets and drums as well as violins.

Before going further we should ask, like Audrey, "What is poetical?" There would seem to be three kinds of poetry concerned.

Jean Cocteau said that there was a distinction between "poetry *in* the theater" and "poetry *of* the theatre." We call these plays poetic dramas, not because they contain poetry, but because they work on many different levels of meaning. Richard II is not merely a historical biography of a fourteenth-century monarch, it is a picture of all rulers who think they are, if not God himself, at least God's protected, and who butt their heads against reality. The poetry is not the icing on the cake, but the cake itself.

Then there is the poetry of character. When we say that this or that character is poetical, we do not mean they live in a dream-world, like Don Quixote, and speak in a flowery way, like Don Armado. On the contrary, they are those who react to the world around them in a particularly sensitive way, and translate their feelings into words and images. Usually they are the central character—people so exceptional that they deserve to have a play written around them. They are the exception, rather than the norm. Shakespeare didn't write a play about prosaic people like Horatio or Enobarbus, and when dull Bolingbroke moved into top place and became Henry IV, he had to share the stage with the more exciting characters Falstaff and Prince Hal.

Enobarbus is a blunt, nonpoetical soldier—but his language rises to poetry when he sees, and describes, how Cleopatra's barge, "like a burnish'd throne, Burn'd on the water..." (*Antony and Cleopatra:* II.3)

Finally (as this is what concerns us here), there is verbal poetry. This is the most difficult to define, although many poets and scholars have tried.

It is not a matter of writing about roses and violets, stars and moons, winds and waves (although a lot of Shakespeare's poetry does contain these things). It is not a matter of using rare and pleasant-sounding words, like *myriad, dulcet, pellucid, welkin,* or *blazon.* It is not a matter of bringing in figures from ancient legends, like Diana, Jove, or Apollo. Nor is it a convoluted way of saying simple things, like calling the moon a "silver orb" or the sun a "fiery chariot."

These are the mere appendages of poetry, fashionable in his day, like ruffs and hats and kid gloves. Many a poet used them—Shakespeare too. But mere mention of them does not turn verse into poetry. Poetry can also call a spade a spade.

Poetry—and he was writing dramatic poetry—occurred when high emotions were so graphically expressed that the language attained the condition of music.

Any Shakespeare anthology presents us with nuggets of golden language, passages in verse and prose that take the breath away with their beauty:

> Eros!—I come my queen.—Eros!—Stay for me
> Where souls do couch on flowers, we'll hand in hand
> And with our sprightly port, make the ghosts gaze;
> Dido and her Aeneas shall want troops,
> And all the haunt be ours.

> The odds is gone,
> And there is nothing left remarkable
> Beneath the visiting moon.

> Let Rome in Tiber melt, and the wide arch
> Of the ranged empire fall! Here is my space.
> Kingdoms are clay; our dungy earth alike
> Feeds beast as man. The nobleness of life
> Is to do thus (embracing).

These three quotations are from *Antony and Cleopatra* alone. That they are sublime poetry cannot be doubted. We need no proof that Shakespeare was a poet—indeed, as George Rylands points out, "Shakespeare was a poet before he was a dramatist."

An anthology, however, shows only the peaks of his writing, like those recordings that gather together "Highlights" from operas. The pieces are taken out of their contexts and admired for themselves alone. Whole plays are not written in this tone.

When characters express themselves in these sublime terms, it is because their feelings are being stretched to breaking point, and because their imaginations are capable of articulating their cries of pain or, in the last example, ecstasy. Thus poetry emerges.

In the eighteenth century Shakespeare was thought of as "barbaric," his writing like a lump of rock in which precious gems were embedded. What was not sublime was dross. They wanted to keep Shakespeare the poet, and throw out Shakespeare the dramatist.

Nowadays the dramatist is more appreciated, and as actors our concern is more with him. After all, the dramatist was the breadwinner, and the poet his servant. Poetry was not an indulgence, it had to earn its keep.

To adjust the balance, it is interesting to look where he is *not* being overtly poetic; a great deal of the lines, however well expressed, do not deserve the name of poetry.

It is surprising how many of the great speeches—even the well-known ones, which have deservedly become highlights—begin very simply, in a quite conversational tone:

If it were done, when 'tis done, then 'twere well
It were done quickly...

> (*Macbeth*)

My liege, I did deny no prisoners...

> (Hotspur, *Henry IV*)

O! I have passed a miserable night...

> (Clarence, *Richard III*)

Most potent, grave, and reverend signiors,
My very noble and approv'd good masters,
That I have ta'en away this old man's daughter
It is most true, true I have married her: ...

> (Othello, to the senate)

I cannot tell what you and other men
Think of this life; but, for my single self,
I had as lief not be as live to be
In awe of such a thing as I myself....

(Cassius, in Julius Caesar: I.2)

O! what a rogue and peasant slave am I!

How all occasions do inform against me
And spur my dull revenge!

O! my offence is rank, it smells to heaven...

Look here, upon this picture, and on this;
The counterfeit presentment of two brothers.

(Hamlet)

There is nothing extravagant or overwritten here. They are the tones of people talking, and they use expressions that are not far from those any one of us would use today. Yet these characters are in highly charged emotional situations, fighting for their career, facing death, or eaten up with some obsession. Later, as the speaker goes on, and more complicated ideas and images crowd his or her mind, and the emotional temperature rises, the language will become denser and more highly charged.

Macbeth will talk of:

...Pity, like a naked new-born babe
Striding the blast, or heaven's cherubim, hors'd
Upon the sightless couriers of the air...

Clarence, telling his dream of being drowned, describes:

Wedges of gold, great anchors, heaps of pearl,
Inestimable stones, unvalu'd jewels,
All scatter'd in the bottom of the sea.
Some lay in dead men's skulls; and in those holes

Where eyes did once inhabit, there were crept,
As 'twere in scorn of eyes, reflecting gems,
That woo'd the slimy bottom of the deep,
And mock'd the dead bones that lay scatter'd by.

Hamlet will go on to shame his mother:

Rebellious hell,
If thou canst mutine in a matron's bones,
To flaming youth let virtue be as wax,
And melt in its own fire...

The point is, the poetry comes later. The speeches begin simply and limpidly, and then as the emotional voltage rises, it puts such pressure upon the language that the language glows red-hot, and changes its nature—it can even border on incoherence. Macbeth's vision of mounted cherubim, and Hamlet's metaphor of melting wax, are difficult to make sense of, but they are visionary, musical, and pictorial. They express a mind in torment. And the actor's task at that moment is perhaps not to understand, but to be in tune with a character who sees such a vision in his mind's eye, and bring it across that the audience may see it too.

A glance at the opening lines of many of his plays will reveal a similar pattern. Their starting point is everyday life; the poetry and the passion will follow. The plays can be said to rise, like bread baking in the oven.

It is true that some, like *Titus Andronicus,* and the first two parts of *Henry VI, Richard II,* and *Henry IV,* begin with a ceremonial scene, where we are straightaway plunged into an event where people are speaking formally and even grandiloquently. Others, however, open with characters speaking normal, workaday language. We have already seen how *Hamlet* starts with two soldiers on duty, and *Othello* with two men quarrelling in a street. *King Lear* begins with gossip:

I thought the king had more affected the Duke
of Albany than Cornwall...

as does *Antony and Cleopatra*:

Nay, but this dotage of our general's
O'erflows the measure...

*Julius Caesar* and *Coriolanus* both open with an unruly Roman
mob: in one, the tribunes speak—

Hence! home, you idle creatures, get you home:
Is this a holiday? What! know you not
Being mechanical, you ought not to walk
Upon a labouring day without the sign
Of your profession? Speak, what trade art thou?

in the other, the mutinous citizens have the word:

—Before we proceed any further, hear me speak.
—Speak, speak.

The opening of *Timon of Athens*:

—Good day, sir.
—I'm glad you're well.
—I have not seen you long. How goes the world?
—It wears, sir, as it grows.
—Ay, that's well known...

resembles the first scene (after the Chorus) of *Henry VIII*:

—Good morrow, and well met. How have you done
Since last we saw in France?
—I thank your Grace,
Healthful; and ever since a fresh admirer
Of what I saw there.

—An untimely ague
Stay'd me a prisoner in my chamber, when
Those suns of glory, those two lights of men,
Met in the vale of Andren.

All this indicates that Shakespeare's plays do not take place in an artificial world where everybody speaks nobly, loftily, and even poetically—though anthologies may give this impression. On the contrary, the *lingua franca* is colloquial everyday, unliterary speech. (He was more a listener than a reader.)

However, in this world, many people are under emotional pressure, or caught in circumstances where they need to express themselves more formally—and here Shakespeare, rather than imitating what they *did* say, lends them words that they *might* have said if they had suddenly been given the gift of tongues. The real Henry IV, for example, could never have spoken as he does in the play; but Shakespeare invents a Henry IV—an amalgam of all unimaginative, guilt-ridden, self-deluding, second-rate men who have found themselves in positions of power—and lends him a certain eloquence.

Further there are exceptional people, characters of great sensitivity and visionary imaginations, who are trapped in ineluctable predicaments, often through a weakness in their own character— Hamlet, Richard II, Othello, Macbeth, Lear, Coriolanus, Antony, Cleopatra, Timon—and they express their visions and their torments in complex pictorial language that perfectly depicts the workings of their minds.

We call this poetry because its expression is so beautiful— but poetry is the by-product, not the end. When Antony calls to the dead Cleopatra to join him in the afterlife ("where souls do couch on flowers") and walk there hand in hand, "make the ghosts gaze" and outdo even Dido and Aeneas—this is exactly what he "sees."

When Othello, shattered with remorse at the realization that he killed Desdemona unjustly, cries:

Whip me, ye devils
From the possession of this heavenly sight!
Blow me about in winds! roast me in sulphur!
Wash me in steep-down gulfs of liquid fire!
(V.2)

He is not being merely rhetorical, he is begging demons—however incredible it may seem to our literal minds—for just such a punishment, his fevered imagination being fuelled by medieval visions of hell.

To say this is far from "the way people talk" is to be reminded that it is far, too, from the down-to-earth opening of the play ("Tush! never tell me…"), the angry squabble between an embittered soldier and a rich nitwit. It shows how cosmic Othello's imagination is, and how anguished his suffering.

Yet even this speech begins "unpoetically":

Look in upon me, then, and speak with me
Or naked as I am I will assault thee.
—What is the matter?
—Behold! I have a weapon;
A better never did itself sustain
Upon a soldier's thigh: I have seen the day
That with this little arm, and this good sword
I have made my way through more impediment
Than twenty times your stop:…

Again, the speech will "rise" to poetry.

We know that Shakespeare disliked false poetry: The Sonnets prove it. "Shall I compare thee to a summer's day?" is asked ironically—because it was the cliché to compare one's beloved to something in nature. "My mistress' eyes are nothing like the sun" begins another, reacting to those poets or poetasters who would have said they were, or who compared their mistress to a goddess; Shakespeare says bluntly:

> I grant I never saw a goddess go;
> My mistress, when she walks, walks on the ground.

We can surmise, too, that he disliked overacting. We can overhear him speaking in Hamlet's voice when he says:

> O! it offends me to the soul to hear a robustious periwig-pated fellow tear a passion to tatters, to very rags, to split the ears of the groundlings...

Shakespeare, too, "walked on the ground." He wanted acting to be "natural" ("to hold a mirror up to nature," "that you o'erstep not the modesty of nature"), and he wanted to keep "mincing poetry" at bay.

If then, poetry got into his mature plays, he did not seek it, it forced itself in. He did not set out to write "poetic drama," but often he had no choice—his characters had no other way of expressing themselves in moments of passion and predicament. Like an airplane they sped along the runway with such force that, at a certain moment, the winds took hold of them, and they flew.

We have said that the word "poetry" needs to be handled with care. We might go further and suggest to the actor that it need not bother him. He should simply believe in what his character says. He should imagine that, not Shakespeare, but each character has written his own script and that the visions they see and describe, however fanciful to us, are real to them. Then the poetry will take care of itself.

# VIII

## SOLILOQUIES:
## PLAYING FOR YOUR PARTNER

~

Few of us spend much time talking to ourselves—and when we do, our utterances are unlikely to be more self-revealing than "Now where did I put the car keys?" or the occasional expletive when things go wrong. When we wish to formulate our innermost thoughts on important matters such as, "Am I in love with that person?" or, "Is dying nobler than living?" or, "Should I murder my boss?," we tend to do it in our heads.

Yet Shakespeare's plays are peppered with eloquent soliloquies on these, and other, subjects; and these can be a stumbling block to the actor, who asks—with reason—"Who am I talking to?" and when told he's supposed to be thinking out loud, finds it hard to believe that he's thinking out loud enough to be heard by a whole theater full of people.

Soliloquies are an essential feature of Shakespeare's plays. He is passionately interested in exploring what goes on inside people's heads when they are alone. For many people the word "Shakespearean" suggests historical pageantry, battle scenes with flags flying and soldiers fighting, ceremonial set pieces with kings in ermine, and golden crowns lying on cushions, and leather-coated soldiers with halbards guarding the doors—pomp and circumstance. Certainly this is what his audience expected, and this is what he often gave them. But what his audience did not expect, but what he gave them nevertheless, was the drama going on inside the king's head when the tumult and the shouting had died; when the stage had cleared and the king was left alone. And four centuries later, it is these private moments that interest us most.

If we were asked to say what the word "Shakespearean" brings to mind—what is typically, essentially Shakespearean—we would point to just these solitary moments. For him the crown and ermine were just trappings—but who was the man within? What secrets did he whisper to his pillow? He noted the widow's weeds, the Cardinal's red robe, the general's uniform—but what did the human being inside them think when alone? He was fascinated by "great" people's secret lives.

He took renowned characters from history—Cleopatra, Marc Antony, Coriolanus, and a line of kings of England—and imagined their private thoughts. He went further than any biographer would dare. He took characters from legend and showed that they were not as simple as their stories made them out to be.

This is "typically Shakespearean" because he was one of the first who revealed that appearances are misleading. Marlowe's Tamburlaine and Ben Jonson's Volpone have no secret life—they are all of a piece.

Nobody should be taken at face value. The private face often contradicts the public mask. "I am not what I am." "Look like the innocent flower, / But be the serpent under 't." "Through tatter'd clothes small vices may appear, / Robes and furr'd gowns hide all." A king may be a murderer, a Puritan, a lecher, a faithful servant a double-dealing viper. To seem is not to be.

Yet when they are alone, they do not lie to themselves. (This is a convention not borne out by examples from real life.) Shakespeare gives them soliloquies wherein they reveal thoughts more private than those they would admit to their psychiatrist or confess to their priest. Understandably the conscientious actor wonders how to speak them aloud, and where to direct them.

In cinema and on TV, the problem is less acute. The voice-over enables us to hear his thoughts; or the camera can come impertinently close to the actor's face. But the theater demands projection.

It seems as if Shakespeare foresaw this problem and found several solutions for it. When a character arrives at a crisis in his life, and his thoughts are at their most private so that no one must know them, Shakespeare gives the actor reason to project, by providing him with an inanimate "partner" to direct his words to. It might be simply a stage prop, which has been part of the scene—a light, perhaps, or a weapon:

> Out, out, brief candle!
> Life's but a walking shadow, a poor player
> That struts and frets his hour upon the stage...
> (Macbeth: IV.5)

(the candle throws the actor's shadow on the wall behind him)

> Put out the light, and then put out the light.
> If I quench thee, thou flaming minister,
> I can again thy former light restore
> Should I repent me...
> (Othello: V.1)

> Is this a dagger which I see before me,
> The handle toward my hand? Come, let me clutch thee:
> I have thee not, and yet I see thee still.
> (Macbeth: II.1)

or a king's crown, which gives its bearer sleepless nights:

> O polish'd perturbation! golden care!
> Thou keep'st the port of slumber open wide
> To many a watchful night!
> (Henry IV Part 2: IV.5)

(Crown Prince Hal is addressing the crown he will shortly inherit.)

Lovers address their partners in their absence, Lady Macbeth apostrophizes her husband before he comes home: "Glamis thou art, and Cawdor…" and Romeo overhears Juliet addressing her memory of him ("O Romeo, Romeo! Wherefore art thou Romeo?")

Sometimes characters left alone with a dead body, share their intimate thoughts with the corpse:

> O! Pardon me, thou bleeding piece of earth,
> That I am meek and gentle with these butchers.
> (Julius Caesar: III.1)

demands Marc Antony of Caesar's corpse. And in *Richard III* (I.2) Lady Anne holds quite a long discourse with the cadaver of her murdered father-in-law, Henry VI:

> Pale ashes of the house of Lancaster!
> Thou bloodless remnant of that royal blood,
> Be it lawful that I invocate thy ghost,
> To hear the lamentations of poor Anne,
> Wife to thy Edward, to thy slaughter'd son,
> Stabb'd by the self-same hand that made these wounds!

Some characters see their major problems rise up before them like living beings. King Henry IV, like Macbeth and Hamlet (and perhaps Shakespeare himself?) suffers from insomnia. Alone, in the watches of the night, in his palace of Westminster, while all his subjects slumber, he is talking to sleep as to a friend—

> O sleep! O gentle sleep!
> Nature's soft nurse, how have I frighted thee,
> That thou no more wilt weigh mine eyelids down,
> And steep my senses in forgetfulness?

Most frequently of all, characters address their soliloquies to Nature, and to natural phenomena:

Thou, Nature, art my goddess; to thy law
My services are bound.

(King Lear: I.2)

Come, night! come, loving black brow'd night!

(Romeo and Juliet: III.1)

Then I defy you, stars!

(Romeo and Juliet: V.1)

Timon of Athens arraigns the sun as a force that brings forth putrefaction:

O blessed breeding sun! draw from the earth
Rotten humidity; below thy sister's orb
Infect the air!

(IV.3)

Others invoke supernatural phenomena, like Lady Macbeth:

Come, you spirits
That tend on mortal thoughts, unsex me here,
And fill me from the crown to the toe top full
Of direst cruelty; make thick my blood,
Stop up the access and the passage to remorse,
That no compunctious visitings of nature
Shake my fell purpose, nor keep peace between
The effect and it! Come to my woman's breasts
And take my milk for gall, you murdering ministers,
Wherever in your sightless substances
You wait on nature's mischief.        (I.5)

or Prospero, calling on gentler spirits:

Ye elves of hills, brooks, standing lakes, and groves;
And ye, that on the sands with printless foot

Do chase the ebbing Neptune and do fly him
When he comes back;...

(The Tempest: V.1)

Hamlet, after seeing the Ghost, shoots out in all directions:

O all you host of heaven! O earth! What else?
And shall I couple hell? O fie!

(his limbs have turned to jelly:)

Hold, hold, my head!
And you, my sinews, grow not instant old,
But bear me stiffly up!

then he turns to the departed spirit:

Remember thee!
Ay, thou poor ghost, while memory holds a seat
In this distracted globe. Remember thee!...

(Hamlet: I.5)

Marc Antony takes leave of his life by talking to the sun as to a companion in arms:

O sun! thy uprise shall I see no more;
Fortune and Antony part here; even here
Do we shake hands.

And when he is dead, Cleopatra is so aggrieved that she begs the sun to burn itself out and leave the world in darkness:

O sun!
Burn the great sphere thou mov'dst in; darkling stand
The varying star o' the world.

The most blinding example is that of King Lear haranguing the storm:

Blow, winds, and crack your cheeks! rage! blow!
Your cataracts and hurricanoes, spout
Till you have drench'd our steeples, drown'd the cocks!
You sulphurous and thought-executing fires
Vaunt-couriers to oak-cleaving thunderbolts,
Singe my white head!

(King Lear: III.2)

We have piled up these quotations for a very good reason: to show how Shakespeare helps the actor.

All the objects addressed are an extension of the character addressing them. It is normal that a young girl in love begs the sun to go down and pleads with night to fall, and a murderer-to-be speaks to an imaginary dagger. But when Lady Macbeth summons up thick night made thicker by the smoke of hell, and evokes evil spirits, something else is happening. The author is creating an aura of evil around her that no actress, however charming she may be, will be able to shake off. A woman who communes with evil spirits is herself an evil person.

Antony, on the other hand, addresses the sun. The play abounds in metaphors about the sun and the moon, and Antony's grandeur, generosity, and importance in the world are often compared to the sun's. In the end, the author has so worked on the audience's imagination that they cannot see one without thinking of the other. However much charisma and power the actor brings to the part, Shakespeare gives him more.

As to Lear, it is a cliché to say that the storm on the heath reflects the storm in his mind as it cracks up and madness sets in. But what a backup Shakespeare gives the actor, with this storm! The audience, hearing Lear challenging it to blow harder, understands that it's a metaphor for what is going on in Lear's head, and so projects on to the actor, playing "madness," more madness than he actually plays.

By associating, in our mind's eye, Lady Macbeth with hell and spirits, Antony with the sun, and Lear with a tempest bringing chaos, Shakespeare is, in fact, doing a lot of the actor's work for him. In the audience's mind he superimposes on what it sees— the actor—a picture of something it can only imagine—a metaphor of the role.

All this has also a very practical advantage. An actor needs a point at which to direct his energy when playing. In a scene, between two or three people he has his partners, and one calls to mind Stanislavski's advice to the players, "Play for your partner!" Note that he said, not "play to your partner" or "at your partner" but "*for* your partner"—meaning, no doubt, "play so that your partner can act better"—and one of the paradoxes of acting is, that the more one plays for the other actors on the stage, the more convincing one becomes; while the narcissistic actor—who plays for himself—or the charm actor, who plays overtly for the audience—seldom achieves the effect he desires. The audience is seldom duped: They feel it when one actor is trying to take all the bedclothes.

But when you see duos like Iago and Othello, or Katherina and Petruchio, or Beatrice and Benedick, playing *for* each other, it can be like the white fire that crackles between two elements of an arc light.

Partner can mean two or three people, or a hundred: It can also be the army that Henry V drives on to victory, or the Roman crowd that Marc Antony manipulates and urges on to rebellion.

So it is a master stroke to provide an actor in soliloquy with an inanimate, mute partner, like a candle, or Night, or even an abstraction personified, like Sleep, or Majesty (Kingship) that many Shakespeare monarchs address.

Otherwise the soliloquy would be spoken to the empty air, and the actor's energy get dispersed, like water from a garden sprinkler—whereas, given a object to direct it to, a focus, the same energy can be concentrated like a jet of water from a hose.

And there's the question of projection. Young actors are often told that they must "project to the back of the gallery" if they want to be heard, and this can lead to some forced speaking—but when Juliet summons the night to fall, and Antony says farewell to the sun, they have something to project to. The author did not give them to say "I wish it were night" or "That's the last time I see the sun," but "Come, night!" and "O sun!" There is a distance to be covered between the speaker and the object addressed. And since the sun and the night cannot actually *hear*, the actor is at liberty to "place" them where he will, whether it's a point on the second balcony, or a place on the stage as if the night and the sun were imaginary actors. In sum, the actor has a "partner" to share his feelings with; and paradoxically, just at those moments when the character's thoughts are at their most private.

The audience, then, is in the same position as when one character is talking to another: They are eavesdroppers, they overhear the conversation. In many other soliloquies, notably Hamlet's, the audience themselves becomes the "partner."

☾    ☾    ☾

If we were watching a play by Chekhov, set on a Russian country estate in the 1890s, we should be disconcerted if one of the characters stepped forward and began asking us what he should do next. This is because, when we settled into our seats, we made a tacit agreement with the actors that they would pretend they were the family and friends of a Russian landowner, a hundred years ago, and we would pretend we weren't there. We are just peeping through the keyhole. Besides, Chekhov's avowed aim was to "present life as it is."

Just so, when Shakespeare was produced in pictorial decors, and the designer had set up a handsome Italian garden, or a gloomy haunted Scandinavian castle, audiences were disconcerted when a character in doublet-and-hose stepped out of the action and began addressing them.

Perhaps it reminded them too much that they were watching a play. Actors and directors, too, had problems with addressing the audience. Some thought it cheap, others found it arty. The proscenium arch that separated players from spectators was very comforting. So Shakespeare was levelled down to become a cosy dramatist who wrote plays about people long ago and far away.

But he didn't set out to present "life as it is." He didn't want an audience of voyeurs, and he certainly made no attempt to pretend they "weren't there." When Hamlet talked of the theater "holding a mirror up to nature," he was simply encouraging a group of barnstorming actors to act more naturally. And a mirror in Elizabethan times was broadly used to mean "a critical view." (A popular book of the 1580s was called *A Mirror for Magistrates*.) The mirror was not supposed to reflect *exactly*, but to show people who they were—as when a mother says to a child who has come in from the garden covered in mud, "What a state you're in—go and look in the mirror!"

Shakespeare is not supposed to be "real" in the way that Chekhov is "real." Stanislavski said he didn't want his audience to say "Let's go and see *Three Sisters*"; he'd rather they said, "Let's go and spend an evening at the Prozorovs'." Nobody, however, would think of saying "Let's go and spend an evening at the Macbeths'."

A Shakespeare play makes no bones about being a *performance*, just as a musical comedy or a ballet is a performance. And the characters represent both themselves, and narrators of their own stories.

Sometimes they pop out of the action to tell us their plans: "I will go tell him of fair Hermia's flight"—"I'll to the Friar, to know his remedy." Sometimes they stop the action simply to amuse us, music-hall style, like Launce in *Two Gentlemen* with his hilarious stories of his "stony-hearted" dog. (*2G.V.:* II.3)

As his talent matured, so Shakespeare saw that he could give more depth to the soliloquy, spoken to the audience. More than simply amusing them, he could confuse them too.

Falstaff, for instance, finding himself alone with the public, entertains them with gossip about the other characters ("I do see the bottom of Justice Shallow. Lord, Lord! How subject we old men are to this vice of lying...") and also about how he has misused the Exchequer, and sent a whole army of half-starved recruits to their deaths: "food for powder, food for powder; they'll fill a pit as well as another." Now few people could approve anything that Falstaff does: He scrounges, steals, tells lies, eats too much, drinks too much, talks too much; he is a toady, a coward, and a parasite. His life is a catalogue of dishonest actions.

Yet this is the character who most frequently steps out of *King Henry IV* to entertain us and to win our sympathy. Irresistible he must be, since not only his band of layabouts commends his charm, but also the Crown Prince of England is for a long time under his spell. He wins the public's sympathy, too: Falstaff is looked upon as Shakespeare's greatest comic creation, and many a tear is shed when the Prince finally rejects him.

In the theater he disarms all criticism, because he makes us laugh. Yet when we get home, and look again at the way he behaves, we start to wonder whether he really is a laughing matter. The distinction between what he seems to be and what he is (and does) is alarming.

It is a perverse stroke to give the best soliloquies to the villain of the piece: and this Shakespeare often does—with Iago and Richard Crookback—and even in *Troilus and Cressida* to that pox-ridden old go-between Pandarus.

We can see how Shakespeare is teasing our sense of morality. When Iago takes us into his confidence and starts telling us his horrid plans, he gets us on his side. We start thinking "Will he succeed?" and later, "Yes, it's turning out as he said it would" and even "He's winning!" We start to sympathize, and even identify with him. It's only at the end, when we see what a fearful result his machinations have had—the awful tableau of the credulous Othello and the innocent Desdemona, both slaughtered—that we, too, start to feel guilty. For we were accessories before the crime, and so we are partly responsible.

Robert Bolt once told us in a private conversation, how, when *A Man for All Seasons* was first produced, the audience took the role of the Common Man to its heart. *He,* too, constantly addresses the public and wins its confidence—becomes as it were their friend. But when, at the end, the Common Man deserted Sir Thomas More and went off to find securer employment elsewhere, before Sir Thomas was executed, a shock of unease went through the audience. They felt guilty—because most of them, in similar circumstances, would probably have done likewise.

In the same way Shakespeare disconcerts us, by making wicked and immoral characters, like Falstaff, Iago, and Richard Crookback, into immensely likeable people, villains we have no desire to boo…until, that is, the tide suddenly turns.

When they step out of the action, and involve us in their malefactions, this effect is multiplied.

((        ((        ((

On the other hand there is Hamlet (no villain, he), whose name has become almost synonymous with soliloquy. In fact, Hamlet's solo speeches represent half the play—not in length, but in importance.

The play shows the happenings at Elsinore subsequent to the death of the old king, and the rapid marriage of his wife with his own brother. But in the foreground, Hamlet stands, giving us his reflections on these events.

The Hamlet we see in the scenes with other people is like an unfinished portrait. In society he is only half himself—only when he is alone is he complete. When behaving socially, he cannot express his feelings (except by feigning insanity). "But break, my heart, for I must hold my tongue!" sums up the tension he feels in company. Only when he is by himself—and how he longs to be!—"Now I am alone" is not telling the audience what it can see for themselves, but a cry full of emotion—then his pent-up feelings burst forth. Look how the soliloquies begin with a cry:

> O! that this too, too solid flesh would melt...

> O! all you host of heaven!...

> O! what a rogue and peasant slave am I!...

and his last one ends:

> O! from this time forth
> My thoughts be bloody, or be nothing worth!

The soliloquies allow us to see a side of Hamlet that nobody else sees—the secret Hamlet. No wonder most of the other characters, who do not know this side of him—think he's mad.

There is evidence that before the *Hamlet* play that we know (1603) there existed another play of the same name, based on the Icelandic saga of *Amleth;* whether it was by Shakespeare or by another writer is not known—all trace of it has disappeared. Shakespeare took this old play about fratricide and revenge, and rewrote it—and the story goes that his major contribution was to give the Prince soliloquies.

If we imagine *Hamlet* without them, we can suppose it was a fast-moving melodrama full of ghostly visitations and poison plots and madness and sword fights—probably worth any playgoer's money. But to stop the action time and again, so that we can tune into the Prince's mind—this is an idea of genius. The secret human being at the center of the confusion, this was what Shakespeare liked to explore.

> But I have that within which passeth show:
> These but the trappings and the suits of woe  (I,2)

says Hamlet of his own mourning clothes—and the soliloquies explore that "that within."

And what interests us chiefly in the play in this century is not the thriller aspect of spies and murder and duels with poisoned swords, but Hamlet's private thoughts. The soliloquies are the life-preserving fluid that has made the play immortal.

It is blindingly obvious that these speeches were written to be played with the audience as "partner"—played not simply *to* the audience, but *with* them. Lately however we are used to seeing Hamlet thinking aloud, talking to himself, addressing the air around him—anything except the public. Talking to the audience would, for a long time, have been considered cheap. It broke the convention that we the audience were peeping through the keyhole.

However, the lines show us that Hamlet was inviting the audience to participate. He harangues us:

> That it should come to this!
> But two months dead: nay, not so much, not two;
> So excellent a king;

He continually asks us questions: "Who would bear the whips and scorns of time…? Who would fardels bear…?" and, especially, "Is it not monstrous that this player here…could force his soul so to his own conceit / That from her working all his visage wann'd…?…What's Hecuba to him, or he to Hecuba / That he should weep for her?"

Such direct questioning could, of course, provoke unwanted replies. Charles Dickens, in *Great Expectations,* shows what happened when Hamlet was played by a rather talentless actor called Mr Wopsle:

> Whenever that undecided Prince had to ask a question or state a doubt, the public helped him out with it. As for example; on the question whether "twas nobler in the mind to suffer," some roared yes, and some no, and some inclining to both opinions said "toss up for it"; and quite a Debating Society arose. When he asked what should such fellows as he do crawling between earth and heaven, he was encouraged with loud cries of "hear, hear"…When he recommended the player not to saw the air thus, the sulky man said, "And don't *you* do it neither; you're a deal worse than *him!*" And I grieve to add that peals of laughter greeted Mr Wopsle on every one of these occasions."

Richard Burbage, the original Hamlet, evidently possessed a superior talent to Mr Wopsle's, in being able to challenge an audience and to dominate it at the same time. But when we read (II.2):

> Am I a coward?
> Who calls me villain? breaks my pate across
> Plucks off my beard and blows it in my face
> Tweaks me my the nose? gives me the lie i' the throat,
> As deep as to the lungs? Who does me this?
> Ha!
> 'Swounds, I should take it, for it cannot be
> But I am pigeon-liver'd…

we see, at "Ha!" that Shakespeare has foreseen the possibility that a disgruntled spectator might seize the chance to heckle Hamlet with a cry of "I do!"—so that Hamlet's " 'Swounds, I should take it" comes like a spontaneous reply.

A few lines later, he tells us that he has heard:

That guilty creatures sitting at a play
Have by the very cunning of the scene
Been struck so to the soul that presently
They have proclaim'd their malefactions...

(such an incident is known to have occurred in the Elizabethan theater; one day a woman watching a murder scene cried out that she had done likewise), and he plans to devise a play that will provoke a confession from his uncle. This only adds to the certainty that Hamlet is playing *with* the audience.

There is no compunction, of course, upon modern Hamlets to do the same; the frame of the production must decide this.

Any actor who tries, however, to share his soliloquies with the spectators (even if it's only with a group of watchers in a rehearsal room or a drama class) will find how his energies are released. The fact of having someone to act *upon* (to shock, to challenge, to question, to defy, even) summons up in him more passionate and fervid emotions (because the brake has been released) than if Hamlet is simply reflecting upon his condition, and rehearsing his thoughts—simply being *overheard.*

I once had the occasion to mount *Hamlet* on a replica of the Elizabethan stage. There was no decor (as such) and the houselights were left on. When Hamlet came to the soliloquies, he stepped forward and played them with the spectators—and it was noticeable how the audience's attention quickened. The soliloquies were the high point of the show. The other scenes they watched raptly, but at the soliloquies they felt concerned.

The French director Louis Jouvet once said that "Comedy is a conversation with the audience." The English playwright had proved this centuries before—and not only comedy, but tragedy and history plays as well.

For on the Elizabethan stage, it was impossible to pretend that the audience was "not there." Playing on an open platform with spectators on three sides, and in broad daylight, the actor was surrounded by a sea of faces. He could see them as clearly as they could see him. He had no choice but to address them, and Shakespeare, always adept at making a virtue of necessity, ensured that he used them, and harnessed the energy they had.

And if anybody finds it illogical that a medieval Prince in a castle in Denmark can be talking to (even asking the advice of) an audience in Elizabethan London (or for that matter, in twentieth-century New York or Tokyo or Moscow, or wherever *Hamlet* is played), then it will be worthwhile looking at the theater for which Shakespeare originally wrote, and which he undoubtedly helped to design.

IX

# SHAKESPEARE'S PLAYHOUSE:
# THIS UNWORTHY SCAFFOLD

~

Shakespeare was eleven years old when the very first London theater was built. He was in his early twenties when he first entered it by the stage door, probably as a small part player with a knack for writing verse. While he was writing his early plays, five more theaters sprang up around the same area. Playgoing was suddenly "in"—London had acquired a voracious appetite for it; scores of poets, men of letters, hack writers and even actors suddenly discovered a talent for playwriting to satisfy the demand, and businessmen saw the theater as an investment as profitable as bearbaiting or cockfighting. He was in his thirties when the company moved to more luxurious premises, and in his forties when they acquired in addition a smaller private theater for more experimental work. At fifty he retired a wealthy man.

Just as Charlie Chaplin's career coincided with the early days and sudden flowering of the commercial cinema, so Shakespeare discovered the Elizabethan theater in its infancy, espoused it early, and grew up with it. He inspired it and was inspired by it. Their union brought about a Golden Age.

There is a tide in the affairs of men
Which, taken at the flood, leads on to  fortune…
                                        (Julius Caesar)

In his youth the tide was in, and he had taken it at the flood.
Fortune followed.

☾   ☾   ☾

Previously the players had been itinerant, setting up their stages
where they could, often in the yards of coaching inns—square,
enclosed courtyards with an upper gallery running round them
that led to the bedrooms. In 1576 an actor called James Burbage,
who was also a trained carpenter, decided to make a permanent
home for his company, the Earl of Leicester's Men, and for the
price of £600  built in Shoreditch a playhouse he simply called
The Theatre.

Shakespeare had seen the Earl of Leicester's Men perform
when they were on tour at Stratford-upon-Avon during his childhood. Records show that they played there in 1573, 1576, and
1583. (Other companies performed there, too—the visit of the
players was an annual occurrence.) They performed in the Guild
Hall and were welcomed—and paid off—by Stratford's High
Bailiff, who in the early days was John Shakespeare, Will's father.
No doubt the boy Will met James Burbage, and his sons Richard
and Cuthbert on these occasions.

He was to spend the rest of his professional life with the
Burbage family. In 1591 he had his first known success as a play-
wright at The Theatre, and later became a shareholder. Richard
Burbage was to become one of the two greatest Elizabethan actors,
and the first ever to play Richard III, Hamlet, Lear, Othello, and
Macbeth.

The Earl of Leicester's Men, later, after Leicester's death in
1588, the Lord Chamberlain's Men, played The Theatre for

twenty-two years. In 1598 the lease of the land was up for renewal, and the landlord, Giles Allen, made such outrageous demands that the Burbages were cornered. Obviously Allen wanted the land and the building for himself. So the Burbages found a new site on very marshy land in Maid Lane, on Bankside. But they had no theater.

Then an unheard-of thing happened. They found a clause in the original contract that stated that the building erected upon Allen's land was the property of the builders, providing it were removed before the lease expired. Time was running out. So one night the Burbages arrived with a team of demolition men and simply dismantled The Theatre. They made a lot of noise about it, too, behaving "in verye outragious violent and riotous sort," according to Allen, though his view was probably prejudiced. It was a bitterly cold December, and the river Thames was frozen over. The timber was piled up on carts and driven across the ice to the other side of the river, where it was stacked up on the new site. Allen went to law, and lost.

Evidently it was only the timber that was transported—the fittings, the lathe, and the thatch would have been left as a pile of rubble on Allen's empty plot. The operation was made easier because of Burbage's original carpentry, the way the timbers were slotted and pegged together.

On Bankside, The Theatre was rebuilt, this time at a cost of £1400—double the original price. A new master builder took over, and considerable modifications were made. As dramatist-cum-producer of the company's most successful plays over the previous eight years, Shakespeare would certainly have had a big hand in suggesting improvements that would facilitate the staging, not only of his existent plays, but the plays he had in mind to write.

In 1599 a glorious new theater was opened that dared to call itself nothing less than The Globe. Its logo was an image of Hercules with the globe on his shoulders (in which some saw a reference to the strong men who lugged the theater across the Thames).

The new theater released Shakespeare's imagination. In the next few years he was to write the four tragedies that show his imagination working at its highest voltage: *Hamlet, Othello, King Lear,* and *Macbeth.* There would also come the great "Roman" plays—*Julius Caesar, Coriolanus,* and *Antony and Cleopatra,* though it's not sure if this last was ever produced.

Shakespeare continued to write for The Globe for the next fourteen years.

In 1608, the company acquired the lease of an old children's theater in Blackfriars, close to where the railway station now stands. This was a smaller theater (it seated seven hundred) and was situated in the Great Chamber. It was an indoor theater, and would serve for performances in winter and the evenings. They put the seat prices up, to make it more exclusive. If Shakespeare's last plays—*Cymbeline, The Winter's Tale,* and *The Tempest*—are more difficult to understand, this is because they were written primarily for the more elite public of the Blackfriars.

In 1613 a disaster happened that ended Shakespeare's career. He had been persuaded to round off his cycle of plays about English kings by bringing it up to date with a play about *Henry VIII,* subtitled *All Is True.* It was a return to his more popular, Globe Theatre style, with pageantry and masques and cannons going off, and it was produced at the Globe. An eyewitness tells us what happened:

> Now, King Henry making a masque at Cardinal Wolsey's House, and certain cannons being shot off at his entry, some of the paper, or other stuff wherewith one of them was stopped, did light on the thatch, where being thought at first but an idle smoke, and their eyes more attentive to the show, it kindled inwardly, and ran round like a train, consuming within less than an hour the whole House to the very grounds.[1]

---

[1] Sir Henry Wotton, poet and diplomat, in a letter to Sir Edmund Bacon, (2 July 1613) three days after the fire.

"See the world's ruins" wrote Ben Jonson, who witnessed the fire. It was said to be the most spectacular conflagration in London since the burning of St Paul's.

Within a year the Globe Theatre was rebuilt, "the finest that ever was in England." But Shakespeare was no longer part of it. He had three years left to live, but he wrote no more.

Thirty years later, the Puritans, who had long railed at the theaters for being dens of vice, "Venus pallace and Sathans synagogue," got their way, and in 1642 all London theaters were closed; and they were to stay closed for another eighteen years. "The Globe, the Glory of the Bank" (Ben Jonson's words) served for a while as a cowshed, and in 1644 it was demolished.

A generation went by, and in that time many of the secrets and traditions of Shakespearean acting and staging and verse-speaking, were lost for ever.

((     ((     ((

The entrance fee was cheap. To go in the building cost one penny, dropped into a money box held by a "Collector." This gave you the right to standing room in the yard of the theater, under the open sky. If you wanted a seat, and a roof over your head, you paid another penny to climb up to the galleries. For three pennies you had the best seats, nearer the stage, when you could see and—which was important for some—be seen. There was also a Lords' Room, the equivalent of our boxes, which was exclusive, and cost a whole shilling (twelve pennies). In those days an artisan could earn for a seventy-hour week between six and eight shillings. Clearly the Globe was a commercial theater, run at popular prices.

The spectator in the yard, looking up at the galleries surrounding this open amphitheater, would see a cross-section of London society, from members of the Court, aristocrats, judges, philosophers, admirals, in the better seats, while surrounding him in the standing room area were apprentices who'd taken the day off, simple artisans, as well as thieves (pickpockets had a field day) and prostitutes (many of them also looking for work). Upstairs were those who appreciated a well-turned phrase, a joke in Latin, or a gracefully executed dance, while downstairs were many whose tastes were more for blood-and-thunder, gory deaths, a wrestling match, or low-comedy fooling. ("He's for a tale of bawdry, or he sleeps," remarked Hamlet, rather unjustly, of Polonius' tastes as a playgoer.)

In each play, Shakespeare had to find entertainment for them all. This explains the glorious mixture of genres in his plays—how sublime poetry is intermingled with fights and songs and bloodshed and comedy, it explains why he is at once earthy and airy. To please at once a cross-section of society he frequently portrayed a society at all its levels.

We remember how *A Midsummer Night's Dream* shows us how the King and Queen of the fairies, Duke Theseus and his court, four ill-assorted lovers, and a party of rude mechanicals, all cross each other's paths in the same wood—and how he even contrives a meeting between the ethereal Titania and the down-to-earth Bottom; and how *Henry IV* depicts life in the Palace of Westminster, and its effects on life in the stews and inn-yards of Cheapside, as well as country life in the gardens of Gloucestershire—a panoramic view that led Kenneth Tynan to acclaim the two parts of *Henry IV* as "the twin summits of Shakespeare's achievement…great public plays in which a whole nation is under scrutiny and on trial."

Performances began at two in the afternoon—the Elizabethans rose earlier than we do, they lived by daylight, and daylight was obligatory to illuminate these open-air performances: A flag was hoisted on the tower of the theater, to tell London that the show was beginning, and flourishes of trumpets called the audience to their places, and chivvied along latecomers. This, too, annoyed the Puritans, jealous that the playhouse attracted more comers than the church:

> Wyll not a fylthye playe, wyth the blast of a Trumpette, sooner call thyther a thousande, than an houres tolling of a Bell, bring to the Sermon a hundred?[2]

The preacher miscalculated. More than a thousand came to see "fylthye playes"—the Globe Theatre had a capacity for three thousand spectators: an undoubted proof of its popularity in a city whose population was about 25,000. The spectators must have been crowded together, as in a train at rush hour: For the present replica of the Globe Theatre on London's Bankside, whose measurements are exactly the same as those of Shakespeare's Globe, is only allowed by the fire brigade to accommodate 1,500.

Yet it is a tribute to the audience's discipline that when the old Globe burned down, although there were only two exits, nobody was hurt, and everyone got out in time—although there was one slight accident, as Sir Henry Wotton tells:

> …nothing did perish but wood and straw, and a few forsaken cloaks; only one man had his breeches set on fire, that would perhaps have broiled him if he had not by the benefit of a provident wit, put it out with a bottle of ale.

The great fear in those days was not fire, but germs. If someone among those three thousand closely jammed spectators had caught the plague, the sickness could spread like…wildfire. If the plague appeared, the authorities were quick to shut the theaters down, once the number of deaths from the plague exceeded forty. Just at the moment when Shakespeare was achieving fame, in 1592 and 1593, the theaters were closed, and it is in these years that he composed his two long narrative poems *Venus and Adonis* and *The Rape of Lucrece*. Both were best-sellers. Both he had carefully

---

[2]John Stockwood, preaching at St. Paul's Cross, 1578.

prepared for publication—something he never did with his plays. Did he, one wonders, consider poetry his real profession—and the writing of plays only a sideline?

He wrote disparagingly of the Globe Theatre as "this unworthy scaffold," "this cockpit" (an arena for cockfights), and "this wooden O"; and "O" referred not only to its circular shape, but suggested that it was a thing of "nought"—and nought, or naught, had in those days sexual connotations—a brothel was called a "naughty house." Was he joking?

Let us look more closely to see how unworthy his scaffold was.

《　　《　　《

The spectator in the yard sees the stage jutting out like a peninsula, and taking up about half the amphitheater. So the audience (in the galleries at least) surrounds it on three sides.

For an actor, alone on this stage—doing a soliloquy, say, or a prologue to introduce the play—this shape presents special problems. On the one hand he knows he is seen from all round, so every small movement he makes must be meaningful from all sides; at the same time he has to keep the attention of a large public, a third of which at any one time are behind him and cannot see his face, nor—what is more—his lips.

How the actor solved this problem we do not know. One thing he probably did not do was to swing his head constantly from left to right and left to right, as though he were watching a slow tennis match.

I once saw Sir Tyrone Guthrie—who had a long experience of open stages—demonstrate his solution, (using a monologue of Hamlet's), which was that the actor performed a slow imperceptible pivot over 270°, starting facing left and ending facing right, so that all the spectators got a fair slice, and everybody imagined he had seen more of the face than he thought he had.

Anyway, Shakespeare must have taken account of this problem when he composed the soliloquies and monologues: which may account for the apparent repetitions in them and the passages where images pile up on one another—a way of ensuring that everybody gets the point, even if they miss some of the words.

This may sound commonplace, and an underestimation of the writing, but we should never forget that his relationship with his theater was a two-way traffic. If he was writing for this great instrument, the instrument was giving him feedback and suggesting to him ways of writing that made his output more effective. Purely practical problems—like allowing an actor time for a costume change, or a breathing space, or finding ways of clearing dead bodies off the stage— (problems that might have been overlooked if the writer Shakespeare were not a practical man of the theater) often pushed him to use his imagination in unexpected ways. (I think it was Donald Wolfit who pointed out how often "our Master Poet-Dramatist" gives his leading actor—Macbeth, Lear, Hamlet—time off during the fourth act to gather strength for the final explosion of energy in Act V.)

The front part of the stage was open to the sky. Over the back part hung a roof, supported by two fairly massive pillars, on cubic column bases, half way up the stage. The ceiling of this roof was painted like the sky and decorated with golden stars and signs of the Zodiac. This was known as the "Heavens."

Below the roof were one (or two) balconies, overhanging the stage; and at the back of the stage a large alcove, known as the "Inner Stage." It would be hidden from view by a painted curtain—which could be drawn aside—or by an arras, a kind of heavy tapestry that could not be drawn.

On either side of this Inner Stage were two doors, symmetrically placed, and above each door was a window. This whole structure at the back of the stage was called the Tiring House; the actors' dressing rooms were behind it.

In the "Heavens" was a trapdoor, and on the stage itself another, leading to the space beneath the stage known as the cellarage, or "Hell."

The whole was sumptuously decorated, with gilding and woodcarvings. The poet Spenser mentioned "the painted theatres," and the wooden columns supporting the roof were "painted in such an excellent imitation of marble that it might deceive the most prying observer." This was noted by a Dutch traveller, Johannes de Witt, who left us the only known contemporary drawing of the inside of an Elizabethan theater, The Swan. It appears in all books on Shakespeare's theater, but it was probably quite inaccurate as it seems to have been drawn from memory, and to this day experts disagree about its reliability. De Witt's drawing, together with his Latin description of the theater only came to light in 1888, found in the university of Utrecht. Until then nobody knew what the Elizabethan stage looked like.

The Tiring House building with its large open stage in front stood facing our spectator when he entered the theater. Emphatically it should be said that it was a piece of architecture and not a "decor," (stage set) and it served for every play. The Elizabethan playgoer no more expected to see what we call a stage set than a modern concertgoer would expect the orchestra playing the Pastoral Symphony to perform in a setting of trees and haystacks.

The stage with its structure of balconies, doors and windows was simply what the Swiss designer Adolphe Appia called "a machine for acting on." It represented nothing, except itself— the stage of the Globe Theatre. It was there to set off the actors— to enable them to make entrances, exits, appear above, peep out of windows, or pop out of the ground.

The modern picture-frame stage needs decors as a background for the actors, since the spectator's eye is drawn to what's behind them. Very often the decor is a work of art in its own right. Years ago the public would often applaud the decor before it had even been used. The Shakespearean stage, on the other hand, meant nothing unless there were actors on it. The performance should be imagined not as a picture, but as a piece of sculpture that stands in space and can be viewed from all round.

Nowadays we say we go "to see a play," but in Shakespeare's time it was "We'll hear a play." The audiences were like those of radio drama, they saw the setting in their mind's eye. The words told them where they were.

In Troy there lies the scene…

Two households, both alike in dignity,
In fair Verona, where we lay our scene…

Unto Southampton do we shift our scene…

— What country, friends, is this?
— This is Illyria, lady…

Well, this is the forest of Arden…

Thou art perfect, then, our ships have touched upon
The desarts of Bohemia?…

— How far is it, my lord, to Berkeley now?
— Believe me, noble lord,
I am a stranger here in Gloucestershire:
These high wild hills and rough uneven ways
Draw out our miles and make them wearisome…

The plays are made up of dozens of short scenes, and the location switches constantly from one place to another. The audience was trained to pick up signals in the opening lines of the scene, if they wanted to know where the characters were supposed to be:

— Who's there?
— Nay, answer me: stand and unfold yourself.

Obviously they are on sentry duty (But which speaker is the sentry?)

KING:
Go, call the Earls of Surrey and of Warwick.
But, ere they come, bid them o'er read these letters,
And we'll consider of them. Make good speed.
*(Exit Page.)*
How many thousand of my poorest subjects
Are at this hour asleep!

Where else would the King be working so late at night but in the palace?

The theater had no need to erect a battlements decor for the one extract, or a palace decor for the other (as the Victorians did)— the audience had its wits about it and could guess.

The characters bring their environment with them. As a general rule, characters in Shakespeare are where you would expect them to be—unless otherwise stated. The king is in his palace, the drunkard is in the tavern. If Lady Macbeth enters "reading a letter," we can assume that she's at home.

Sometimes the location doesn't become clear until half way through the scene. *Othello* opens with Iago and Roderigo quarrelling. Where are they? The opening lines give no clue. Not until the scene is well advanced do we hear: "Here is her father's house; I'll call aloud." For it's only at this point that Brabantio's house becomes important in the scene, and not before.

Frequently the dialogue gives no indication at all of where a scene is taking place. If Shakespeare doesn't tell us, then it doesn't matter. What counts is what the characters are saying to each other, not where they are. For these scenes, the Globe's bare stage was ideal. It served for everywhere, and nowhere.

The major drawback of a bare stage—as any director or drama teacher know—is that there is nothing to keep the actors apart from each other—no barriers. Shakespeare's characters are frequently eavesdropping on each other, talking out of balconies to people below, addressing rebel armies from battlements and towers, watching plays or processions, hiding behind bushes and trees, or seeing visions. Ghosts need to appear as if from nowhere, and visions vanish into thin air.

The major function of the Globe architecture was to provide these possibilities of separation. It broke up the space, giving actors the opportunity of acting at different levels, thus creating a spatial tension—such as when Romeo below, and Juliet above, declare their love without being able to touch, or when Buckingham publicly "begs" Richard of Gloucester (appearing above) to accept the crown.

Let us take the Globe Theatre stage apart, and see how each element functions, and in which plays.

THE BALCONY It would stand for the battlements where Hamlet, Horatio, and Marcellus come to watch for the Ghost (who'd materialize on the main stage). The walls of besieged Harfleur (*Henry V*): "The Governor and some citizens on the Walls; the English forces below. Flint Castle, where *Richard II* faces the rebel army ("Enter on the Walls King Richard, the Bishop of Carlisle, Aumerle, Scroop and Salisbury"). Northampton Castle *(King John)* from which little Arthur tries to escape from being blinded: ("The wall is high, and yet I will leap down..."—but the walls are too high, and he dies in the attempt). "The Gallery above" where Gloucester *(Richard III)* makes a show of piety by appearing "between two Bishops."

THE WINDOWS We hear a lot about "the balcony scene" in *Romeo and Juliet,* but a look at the script indicates that "Juliet appears above at a window," and in the garden below Romeo asks "What light through yonder window breaks?" Evidently it is theatrical tradition that gave Juliet a balcony.

Other people appearing at windows include Desdemona's

father, woken to hear the shocking news that his daughter and Othello are "making the beast with two backs;" and Shylock's daughter Jessica, who appears "in the lovely garnish of a boy" and tosses down a casket of jewels to Lorenzo before quitting the family home *(Merchant of Venice)*.

A window is a window: It rarely stands for something else.

THE DOORS There is, in *A Midsummer Night's Dream*, the surprising stage direction: "Enter Oberon, the King of Fairies, at one door, with his train; and Titania, the Queen, at another, with hers." Since it is hard to imagine doors in "a wood near Athens," it is clear that the author is writing these notes for the actors, not for readers.

The opposing doors were an important way of indicating a change of location. In many plays the action swings between two opposing camps—the French and the English, or the Trojans and the Greeks; or between distant towns, like Rome and Alexandria, Venice and Belmont, London and Gloucester, and it was sufficient for, say, the English army to exit by one door, and the French army to enter by the other, for the audience to understand that the scene had shifted.

Indeed it is quite possible that the scenes overlapped: Tension could be kept up, and time saved, if while the English were rounding off their scene with the usual rhyming couplets, the opposing camp were already taking up their positions and setting down their stools, or whatever they needed, ready to take up the next scene.

Shakespeare's plays had the fluency of films. They were written so that one scene faded, or "cut," into another. We know now that in films, sharp editing can make or break a movie, and that the previous image still remains on the retina when the next shot has already begun. As Eisenstein put it, and he made a study of the dramatic shock that occurs when you cut from, say a distant line of approaching soldiers to a huge close-up of Ivan the Terrible,

"Editing is conflict." Shakespeare knew this: From the frightened whispering murderers, Macbeth and his wife, he "cut" to the eruption on stage of a drunken porter; from the tender description of Ophelia's death by drowning, he "cut" to the boisterous entrance of two comic gravediggers.

The Victorians never understood this. They thought Shakespeare's plays were about scenery. They would bring down their curtain at the end of a scene and spend minutes humping heavy scenery about in order to amaze the audience, when the curtain rose again, by the transformation from the Forum at Rome to the Sphinx in Egypt. They would have thought Shakespeare primitive if they knew he established this transition by the mere shutting of a door.

THE PILLARS A number of the plays take place in woods and gardens—as we might expect from this country-born playwright. The audience would have no difficulty in "seeing" these marble-painted pillars as tree trunks (which is the material they originally were made of). Orlando could pin his love-sick verses to them as he drifts through the Forest of Arden, and, in "a wood near Athens," Oberon—who was as prone to eavesdropping as any government agent—could conceal himself behind one and listen. The square pedestals were an advantage. If they protruded enough, characters could sit or perch upon them, a place to sit being another thing lacking on a bare stage; and they could even climb upon them if they needed to address a crowd. Perhaps Henry V used one as a dais to urge his army to go "Once more into the breach," and Mark Antony, too, when addressing his "Friends, Romans, countrymen!"

THE INNER STAGE OR STUDY This feature really has the scholars quarrelling. Evidently there hung before it the arras through which Hamlet stabbed the prying Polonius. Falstaff, too, (in *The Merry Wives*) "ensconces himself" behind it to avoid Mistress

Page, and in *Henry IV, 1* he is discovered asleep there when the Sheriff raids the tavern. "No stage business was more common in our early drama" observes John Cranford Adams "than this of hiding behind the arras."[3] It was evidently an early form of bugging.

What sets the scholars at odds is the traditional idea that the Inner Stage was used for certain interior scenes. One older school of thought concludes that it served for Friar Laurence's cell, and for the Capulets' tomb *(Romeo and Juliet),* for Portia's casket collection *(Merchant of Venice),* for Prospero's cell *(The Tempest),* and even for the Queen's bedroom *(Hamlet).* Others aver that for this "there is no evidence whatsoever."[4]

A mere look at the sight lines seems to settle the matter. In a circular amphitheater, the interior of the Inner Stage would be visible to no more than half the audience. It is inconceivable that such important scenes be played there. Actors are quick to know when they are out of sight, and quicker than they are is the Manager, with his eye on box-office takings. Besides, the focal point of the Elizabethan theater is not upstage center (as in a proscenium theater) but, on the contrary, downstage center, where all eyes converge like spokes on the hub of a bicycle wheel.

What misled the older academics was the idea that the alcove at the back was a "stage within a stage," that the opening was a sort of proscenium arch, and the platform in front a kind of forestage. Perhaps they thought that the modern proscenium stage was the acme of theatrical architecture, and in Shakespeare's playhouse it was an embryo struggling to be born.

They were deluded in assuming that interior scenes would *necessarily* be played in a room, and exterior scenes—streets, fields, battlegrounds—outside, on the open platform. They thought that if Hamlet confronted his mother on the forestage, under open sky, the public would wonder why the Queen had an open-air bedroom. Of course the public thought no such thing. Told "He

---

3 John Cranford Adams, *The Globe Playhouse—Its Design and Equipment,* 1961.

4 Robert Speaight, *Shakespeare on the Stage,* 1973.

is going to his mother's closet," (the play doesn't mention bed-rooms), they knew, when the Queen came on, where she was—they didn't need to examine the furnishings.

Besides, Shakespeare is very free in his uses of inside and out-doors. Consider the famous exchange between Hamlet and Polonius.

> POL: … Will you walk out of the air, my lord?
> HAM: Into my grave?
> POL: Indeed, that is out o' the air. *(Aside.)* How pregnant his replies are!

This scene is "supposed to take place" in a room in the castle, not on the battlements or in the royal gardens. So where is Polo-nius inviting him to walk that's "out o' the air"? It seems evident that Hamlet is walking on the forestage, and Polonius is saying "Come inside"—that is, under the roofed part of the stage, if not "within," i.e., offstage. (Elizabethan actors didn't "go off," they "went in"; trumpets were heard "within"; props were "brought out" not "on.")

Now this is not a mistake on Shakespeare's part. It's not as if he's thinking of the staging while writing the play, and forgetting that his characters are indoors. On the contrary it signals a spe-cial way, essential to understanding Shakespeare, of regarding the theater. It can best be summed up this way: *The play takes place both in Elsinore, and also on the stage of the Globe Theatre, at the same time.*

The architecture and platform are that of the Globe, and the actors are actors; but the action of the play they are performing takes place in another country and another time,

Frequently the two overlap. Hamlet's Gravedigger sends out his mate to an alehouse close by the theater (Yaughan's); and while Henry IV is reigning over fifteenth-century England, Falstaff is ruling the roost in a tavern in a sixteenth-century Cheapside. A contemporary drawing of *Titus Andronicus* in performance shows the principals wearing Roman costume, and the extras in Elizabethan dress.

Audiences today play a game of make-believe, whereby they (in the dark) are in the theater and the actors (in the light) are in Ancient Rome, Denmark, or wherever.

The Elizabethan audience is sharing the same space and the same light as the actors. They know they are not "in Scotland" and that Lady Macbeth is really a boy. This gives the characters leave to make remarks, in character, which refer to the performance itself. When Macbeth says "Out, out brief candle!" to illustrate the fragility of life, he is referring to a candle that has been brought on (or brought out) to light the performance; and when he says "Life's but a walking shadow, a poor player, that struts and frets his hour upon the stage And then is heard no more," he (Macbeth) is referring, with false modesty, to himself (Burbage, the actor). As Sir Ian McKellen pointed out, how many travelling companies had "played" Dunsinane in the reign of Macbeth?

When Hamlet refers to "Hercules and all his load," he's drawing the public's attention to the figure on the Globe Theatre flag of Hercules carrying the world (or globe) on his shoulders, over the legend *Totus mundus agit histrionem,* or, "All the world's a stage." The play is referring to itself, as a play—rather like that Marx Brothers film in which Groucho turns to the camera and says (something like) "This gets better in the second reel."

Such a way of thinking absolves Shakespeare from criticisms about the anachronisms frequently found in his plays—clocks in Ancient Rome, ancient Britons wearing spectacles, and references to the Earl of Essex in *Henry V.*[5]

One of the most extraordinary uses of this double view (the action taking place both in the theater and in the play's location)

---

[5] Act V. Chorus. 29–34

leaps out of *The Winter's Tale*. Leontes, jealous of his wife's close relationship with Polixenes, says:

There have been,
Or I am much deceiv'd, cuckolds ere now;
And many a man there is even at this present,
Now, while I speak this, holds his wife by the arm,
That little thinks she has been sluic'd in's absence,
And his pond fish'd by his next neighbour, by
Sir Smile, his neighbour...

Leontes, in the play, is alone in his palace of Sicilia, but the man "even at this present" is there in the audience, John Citizen of London. Can we not imagine John's embarrassment as he slowly turns to look at the wife he "holds by the arm" wondering if she too has been "sluic'd," and looking beyond her to his best friend, maybe his neighbor, who has come with them to the playhouse, and who, on hearing this, puts on an innocent smile, as if he's thinking "What an amusing expression 'sluic'd'!"—a smile that freezes when he hears Leontes utter the next words, "Sir Smile, his neighbour..." And with what added attention are John and Mary Citizen, and Sir Smile, going to follow henceforth the story of Leontes, Hermione, and Polixenes! They will watch with the same bated breath as the guilty King Claudius watched the *Murder of Gonzago*.

THE HEAVENS "Hung be the heavens with black!" is the opening line of *Henry VI, 1,* for King Henry V is dead, and the speaker is not only referring to the world being in mourning but to the custom of draping the theater with black for tragedies, the "heavens" being the ceiling of the stage, beautifully adorned with stars, Zodiac signs, clouds, the moon, and the sun. Was this painted sun the one that Juliet adjured to "Gallop apace"? and this the "envious moon" that Romeo saw "sick and pale with grief" in envy of Juliet's beauty? Were these the disintegrating clouds that Antony likened to his own dissolution?

The painted sky was certainly the one referred to by Othello when he swore vengeance on Desdemona for betraying him: "Now by yond marble heaven…" and it was this ceiling that Hamlet meant when he talked of—

> this most excellent canopy, the air, look you, this brave o'er-hanging firmament, this majestical roof fretted with golden fire
> (II.2)

The words "canopy," "o'erhanging," "roof" make it clear.

The roof also carried some elaborate flying machinery. The heavens could open and, through the trapdoor, gods could descend—

> Jupiter descends in thunder and lightning,
> sitting on an eagle: he throws a thunderbolt.

reads a direction in *Cymbeline*. Puck might be flown in; as well as the Witches in *Macbeth*, who are said to "hover." And Ariel:

> Thunder and lightning. Enter Ariel, like a
> harpy; claps his wings upon the table; and,
> with a quaint device, the banquet vanishes.
>
> *(The Tempest)*

He probably wore giant wings perhaps that enveloped the table, hiding it from our view. The quaint device must have been…

THE TRAP DOOR TO HELL This was centrally placed on the platform, and when not in use, fitted flush with the stage surface. It must have been equipped with a lift, and mechanism for raising and lowering several people at once. Since the stage was only five feet from the ground, a cellar must have been excavated in the area beneath the stage to allow a place for the machinery and anything that had to appear (a tree, or a throne) that exceeded five feet in height. However, the land on which the Globe was built was marshy, which would have limited excavation. There was no question of going down for several stories under the ground, as the Paris Opéra does, and De Bourla Theater in Antwerp.

Mostly what appeared were manifestations of the supernatural. Probably the Ghost of Hamlet's father made his first entrance rising from it, and its possibilities evidently inspired Shakespeare when he came to imagine the Apparitions in *Macbeth,* arising through the steam of the witches' cauldron; while a minute later ("Why sinks that cauldron? and what noise is this?" [Hautboys]) there is presented:

A show of Eight kings; the last with a glass
in his hand: Banquo's ghost following.

It is possible, of course, that these ghostly Kings appeared through other traps. Other plays of the period note the existence of four smaller traps, at each corner of the stage, each suitable for one person to enter from—but whether these were already built into the first Globe Theatre is not known. (Perhaps Shakespeare had them specially installed for *Macbeth?*)

The large central trap was known as the "Grave trap." Evidently it was used for the churchyard scene in *Hamlet,* with the singing gravedigger tossing bones and skulls on to the stage, and Hamlet later leaping in to fight with Laertes, crying "I loved Ophelia!"

THE CELLARAGE Below the stage was the cellarage. "Well said, old mole, canst work i' the earth so fast?" cries Hamlet to his father, down below, whose voice commanding "Swear!" would be heard as a muffled boom in the enclosed space. Music, too, played there, would achieve a ghostly boxed-in sound. It certainly frightened Caliban, inspiring that unforgettable line:

This music crept by me on the waters.

ABOVE THE STAGE  The musicians usually played in the second balcony above the stage, whether sounding the braying trumpets that followed the stage direction "alarums and excursions," calling soldiers to arms, or the dulcet "food of love" music that was intended to calm Orsino's frayed nerves or soothe Richard II in prison. From this high position the sound would fly upwards, and not get between the actor and the audience, as in musical comedy theaters today.

In the tower above the stage was housed the great alarum bell that evidently made a most striking effect when sounding an alarm: Othello cries, during the riot in Cyprus, "Silence that dreadful bell, it frights the isle!" Up there, too, was probably the magnificent thunder effect that is cued so specifically in *Macbeth*, *King Lear*, and *The Tempest*. When Othello cries "Are there no stones in heaven / But what serve for the thunder?" (V.2) he was talking, in the first place, about thunderbolts, but perhaps he was also referring to the thunder machine that could have been (this is only guesswork) great stones, or cannonballs, in revolving iron drums, even rolling down a chute built into the walls that surrounded the audience, to give a Dolby-Stereo effect.

The acoustics of the theater must have been finely tuned, otherwise Shakespeare would not, in play after play, have provided his actors with such finely wrought and complex language. The high circular walls would insulate it from the noise of carts and horses outside, so that the actors' voices, even the boys', could ring out in the still air, caught between the walls of wood and lathe. Frances A. Yates was surely right when she called it a "sounding box."[6] It was a Stradivarius among theaters.

Such was the theater for which Shakespeare wrote, peopling its doors and balconies and traps with the creatures of his imagination. Far from being a primitive building that lacked the modern advantages of artificial lighting, scenery, revolving stages, and hydraulic lifts, as later generations have imagined, it turns

---

[6] See *Theatre of the World*, 1969.

out on inspection to be one of the most adaptable theaters ever designed, and its architecture a feast for the eye—"the gorgeous playing-place erected in the fields" a contemporary called it.

Indeed, its very structure must have provided him with the mold into which he could pour the molten ideas of his plays, just as the fixed form of the Sonnet, with its fourteen lines and preset rhyme scheme, gave him a framework for his feelings about Love and Time passing.

One can imagine him, when the idea for a new play was just starting to boil in his mind, standing there one morning when the theater was empty, gazing at the stage, and letting the building itself suggest to him the dramatic shape of the new work:

> The King's party comes on from the left—so later, the rebel conspirators enter from the right—in the Uprising scene, the people will surge on through the middle entrance,—the demagogues stand on the pillars—the King addresses them from the balcony—bring chairs on centre for the scene of the Queen Mother and the Princesses—for the woodland scene, a clump of trees arises from the grave trap—Then the night before the battle— (King's tent left, rebels' tent right) —the ghosts that appear to the king appear through the trap; Battle scene on forestage—maybe the Herald comes in through the audience on a horse?—the Cynical Observer of the battle watches and comments from the balcony—trumpets to call the retreat (musicians' gallery)—wheel on bed centre for King's deathbed scene—while bed carried off, three lords appear on balcony to discuss consequence of King's death and the state of the nation—trap open for King's burial scene (use Bell!) —rebel leader announces new order from balcony to people below— all stay on stage while Cynical Observer emerges from crowd and speaks the epilogue down stage center—everyone ready for final dance...

And lo! the new play (it is an imaginary one) has fallen into place, and it only remains for him to write the dialogue.

The Globe Theatre, besides its practical effectiveness, had another aspect that is often overlooked—a mystical one. We have seen that the canopy over the stage was called the "Heavens," and the trapdoor to the cellarage the "Hell." It follows then that the acting platform represented the earth. Hamlet says (II.2) "this goodly frame, the earth, seems to me a sterile promontory"—and the platform was indeed promontory-shaped, projecting into the auditorium like a tongue of land.

In religious terms, Mankind lives on earth, aspiring to Heaven ("What a piece of work is a man!"—Hamlet again—"…in action, how like an angel!") but being pulled down to the condition of a beast by the forces of Hell (by characters like Iago and Lady Macbeth) and often destroyed by them. Birth and death are for men and women "their exits and their entrances." It was not merely for its circular shape that it was called The Globe. If all the world is a stage, then all the stage is the world. The Idea was built into the architecture.

For a long time, historians thought the shape of the theater was based on the enclosed yards of the coaching inns, with their surrounding galleries, where the travelling players erected their temporary stages. But these were rectangular in shape; the Globe, however, was circular, and seen in plan form, bears a surprizing resemblance to the antique theaters of Greece and Rome, which were well known for their excellent acoustics.

Frances A. Yates tells us that a hundred years before the Globe, Leonardo da Vinci was working on improving the acoustical properties of churches, and that he studied the ancient theaters for guidance. On his plans he called these churches *teatri*. There was such a traffic of ideas between Italy and England, that the builders of the Elizabethan theaters could well have known this.

In her book on Renaissance architecture, *Theatre of the World*, Dr. Yates goes further in her search for the Idea behind the Elizabethan theater. She quotes Dr. Johnson's friend, Mrs. Thrale, who one day in the eighteenth century looked out of her window at some tenements that her husband had had demolished on Bankside and saw on the desolate ground under the debris some ruins, which she recognized as the foundations of the old Globe Playhouse. She observed that they were "hexagonal in form without but round within." She had seen the bases of the supports for the galleries and the foundations of the outer walls; the wooden stage had gone.

To support a hexagonal building, the pillars—circularly placed—numbered twelve; and Dr. Yates recognized the geometrical basis of classical temples, which were built to express both the Cosmos, the twelve columns reflecting the signs of the Zodiac, and Man's central place in the Cosmos—the image of a man standing with arms and legs outstretched within a circle, which was the subject of a famous drawing by Leonardo. Thus the very shape of the building contained a symbolic meaning—just as certain Christian churches are built in the form of a cross.

Vertically the building embodied the way the Elizabethans saw the universe, from hell below to heaven above, and horizontally it was a symbol of Man's central place in that universe. Thus the Elizabethan theater was more than a mere playing place—it was also, secretly, a sort of temple.

Why, then, did Shakespeare shrug it off as "this unworthy scaffold"? "this wooden O"?

The phrases should first be seen in their context. Many a commentator has been misled by them.

It is 1599. Burbage's company is opening the new theater, the Globe, a rebuilding of their previous playhouse, The Theatre. Perhaps after twenty-two years, the old theater was beginning to show its age, and now they have had the opportunity to implement all the improvements they dreamed of.

The opening production is *Henry V*—almost the last link in the chain of history plays with which Shakespeare first made his name in London, with the trilogy of *Henry VI*, at the beginning of the decade. Since then he has given us *King John, Richard III,*

*Richard II,* and two parts of *Henry IV* (where the actor playing Falstaff had an overnight success). In this play we saw the future Henry V already, when he was the Crown Prince.

Fashionable London arrives for the first night, partly to see the new theater, and partly to see if *Henry V* is the national, patriotic play everyone expects.

The flag is hoisted, the trumpets sound, and the play begins. A Chorus figure enters (though he had never used this device for his other historical plays). The Chorus is played perhaps by Shakespeare himself—an attentive touch, the favorite playwright and shareholder of the theater acting as our host for this opening of the new theater.

If he had begun on a low key, as he did with *Richard II* and *Henry IV,* he would not have caught the public, distracted by the occasion, immediately. He begins on a high key: "O! for a Muse of Fire…"

But let us not take everything he says at face value: Often there is irony behind what he says.

> O! for a Muse of Fire, that would ascend
> The brightest heaven of invention;
> A kingdom for a stage, princes to act
> And monarchs to behold the swelling scene.
> Then should the war-like Harry, like himself,
> Assume the port of Mars; and, at his heels,
> Leash'd in like hounds, should famine, sword, and fire,
> Crouch for employment.

He reassures those who feared he would belittle Harry, a national hero. Moreover, he raises him to the level of the god of war. This is what the public wants to hear!

It's a flamboyant start, with rousing talk of kingdoms, princes, monarchs, Mars—a signal that it should be played broadly. Then the tone changes. Suddenly he becomes apologetic—even over-apologetic. The "but" element appears:

But pardon, gentles all,
The flat unraised spirits that hath dar'd
On this unworthy scaffold to bring forth
So great an object: can this cockpit hold
The vasty fields of France? or may we cram
Within this wooden O the very casques
That did affright the air at Agincourt?

This block starts in low gear, and builds and builds to the word "AGINCOURT"—it was a famous victory, the very name set English hearts beating faster, made English patriots hold their heads high, just like mention of El Alamein after the last war.

Of course these wooden trestles, this scaffold, are unworthy of it, and compared to a French battlefield the Globe is no more than a cockpit! "Don't expect anything spectacular tonight" says this prudent Chorus, but in fact he and his company have prepared the *most* spectacular show they can imagine, showing off all the possibilities of the new theater, and laying on all the special effects they have—gunfire, smoke, explosions, hangings, soldiers scaling the balcony with ladders, battle scenes, and a full choir singing the Te Deum. We can take Chorus' modesty with a pinch of salt.

He has the best actors in London, and he's the most popular playwright—"flat unraised spirits" indeed!

O pardon! since a crooked figure may
Attest in little place a million;
And let us, ciphers to this great accompt
On your imaginary forces work.

(The figures in a book of accounts take up little space but can stand for vast sums of money.)

Having minimized the theater's contribution to the performance to the utmost, he now goes on to tell the public—his "partner" in this speech—that they have their role to play—they must *imagine what is not there.* The words of command will recur: "Suppose…," "Piece out…," "Divide…," "Think…" Nowadays, instead of "imaginary forces" we'd say "the force of your imagination."

> *Suppose* within the girdle of these walls
> Are now confin'd two mighty monarchies,
> Whose high upreared and abutting fronts
> The narrow perilous ocean parts asunder:
> *Piece out* our imperfections with your thoughts:
> Into a thousand parts *divide* one man,
> And make imaginary puissance;
> *Think* when we talk of horses that you see them,
> Printing their proud hooves i' the receiving earth,
> For 'tis your thoughts that now must deck our kings, …

This passage is often taken as Shakespeare's credo, and quoted widely as if it "explained" the Elizabethan theater—"We are poor players, we have nothing to show: You, the audience must imagine everything."

But there is something odd about the timing. If this prologue had appeared eight years before, when he first presented the huge trilogy on *Henry VI* (in about 1591), and he was inaugurating a new form of drama, it might have been timely. Since then he has written and staged *Titus Andronicus, The Comedy of Errors, The Taming of the Shrew, Richard III, Two Gentlemen of Verona, Love's Labour's Lost, Romeo and Juliet, A Midsummer Night's Dream, The Merchant of Venice, King John, Richard II,* and two parts of *Henry IV,* all in an old theater built a quarter of a century before, a far less "worthy" scaffold, where the company's "imperfections" were certainly more evident.

In all those eight years the public has done nothing else than imagine, suppose, and think they saw not merely horses that were not there, but palaces, gardens, forests, castles, armies, whole cities even. Isn't it a bit late now to say "Pardon, gentles all" for the theater's inadequacy?"

It's hardly likely that Shakespeare's company has suddenly taken a vow of poverty—especially as this first performance of *Henry V* was a gala night, celebrating the opening of the new theater.

Besides, by all accounts, the theater was anything but poor. We have seen how luxuriously the stage structure was adorned, with fine finishings and painted marble. Costumes, too, were rich and gorgeous: Noble families would hand on to the players clothes they had no more use for, and a brief glance at any contemporary portraits will show how elaborate and beautiful these were. Officially, too, the players were in a nobleman's employ—the Earl of Leicester's Men had now become the Lord Chamberlain's Men. And as a commercial theater, the Globe could not afford to be less spectacular than its competitors—the Swan, the Rose, the Fortune, or the Curtain.

And this was an age of pageantry and show—Queen Elizabeth's barge, when she sailed in state down the Thames was no less splendid than Cleopatra's, in Enobarbus's description of it. And although there was no decor, we can be sure that if a bed was rolled on, or a throne, a canopy erected, or the crown of England represented, it would be an exquisite piece of workmanship. The theater would not dare to be poor.

Shakespeare was no purist, no Grotowski. He would not refuse anything that added to the luster of his performances or the pleasure of his audiences. And though Chorus says "Think when we talk of horses that you see them," this does not mean no horses would appear. Probably Mountjoy, the French herald, entered on horseback through the audience (Henry, and the English camp, being on the stage, facing him). Shakespeare was too much of a showman to miss a trick like that.

For although Shakespeare was speaking the lines, it was not Shakespeare himself speaking. Again he is playing a part, the humble spokesman for the company. And Chorus has his tongue in his cheek, just as he has in the Epilogue, deprecating himself: "Thus far, with rough and all unable pen / Our bending author hath pursu'd the story; / In little room confining mighty men / Mangling by starts the full course of their glory."

So this idea about the austerity of the Elizabethan stage, which is quite current nowadays, is most likely a myth. The published plays are not complete blueprints for performances; they are simply dialogue scripts to tell the actors what to say. By all accounts he wrote swiftly, his imagination racing ahead, and no doubt could not be bothered to write any more than minimal stage directions. After all, he would be there directing rehearsals, and creating the spectacle. In *Henry V,* for instance, there is hardly anything about the battle of Agincourt itself, yet given the story and the circumstances this was probably the high point of the performance.

So he's playing to the gallery when he invents a Chorus figure, who begins by overpraising Henry—"so great an object"—and saying that if anything looks less than glorious, it's the players, mere "ciphers," who should take the blame. He is disarming those patriots who don't want to hear a word against their national hero.

And he goes on to write a play about a King who involves the church in searching for the tiniest excuse for going to war with France, and uses the gift of tennis balls as a pretext; who in anger, massacres French boy soldiers; who has his old drinking crony Bardolph hanged; who, despite his Churchillian rhetoric to the troops, adopts an "I'm a simple guy" language to woo the Princess of France, and who marries her for political reasons simply so that the two countries be united.

Within the framework of this spectacular, patriotic, national play about a King who was supposedly above criticism, he is writing another, secret play, which shows the trouble with Harry—that he was just as calculating and opportunistic as King as he was when he was Prince Hal.

The idea that within a Shakespeare play there is often hidden a "secret play," that gives the whole another meaning, is one that has yet to be explored in full.

Chorus finishes:

> For 'tis your thoughts that now must deck our kings,
> Carry them here and there, jumping o'er time,
> Turning the accomplishments of many years
> Into an hour-glass:

This is a brilliant image to describe the swiftness and the concentration of time in epic plays, but again, nothing new here, it's the tacit contract he had always had with his audience; and he signs off with a rhymed flourish (you can almost hear the actors in the next scene shuffling in the wings, waiting to come on):

> for the which supply,
> Admit me Chorus to this history;
> Who prologue-like your humble patience pray,
> Gently to hear, kindly to judge, our play.

Chorus certainly wants to please.

"Sweet Mr Shakespeare" often seems torn between the plays he knows the public wants him to write (which led him, according to Shaw, to choose such shrugging-off titles as *As You Like It,* and *What You Will*), and the plays that he himself needs to write—plays that express a view of life more penetrating, more ahead of his time, than those of other men.

For centuries, those who have overlooked Chorus' irony have thought that *Henry V* was merely one of the first kind, written "by public demand."

We have looked at the architecture of the Globe and we have guessed how it was used. We look at the two levels (stage and balcony), and at the pillars and the door and the traps, and project upon them our own ideas of production. We imagine that they were always used the same way. But is this not rather systematic?

There is no reason why Shakespeare, whose imagination as a writer was boundless, should be limited in his fantasy when he arranges the staging of his plays. We know that he liked to work spatially— did he never change the spatial shape of his theater?

The question occurred to me when directing *Richard II.* The King appears on the walls of Pomfret Castle; beneath him is the rebel army, begging him to surrender. Normally "on the walls" suggests that he is on the balcony, and the rebels on the stage below. But his monologues are of such intimacy

> What must the King do now? Must he submit? ...
>
> (III.3)

that it seems unreasonable that he should be so far from the audience. The speeches are written (to my mind) in "close-up."

Again, when the King finally agrees to descend from the balcony:

> Down, down I come, like glistering Phaeton,
> Wanting the manage of unruly jades

the rebel's lines do not give him time to disappear from view above, descend a hidden staircase, and appear on the main stage:

> — What says his majesty?
> — Sorrow and grief of heart
> Makes him speak fondly like a frantic man:
> Yet he is come.

That is all. Nobody can come down a staircase in that time, and it is unlikely he is using a fireman's greasy pole.

Suppose however, the king were on the main stage (where his monologues could be at the center of the audience's attention) and the rebels were in the pit, the yard where the groundlings stand—to which a small temporary ladder has been fixed—then the timing fits. Besides he calls the place "the base court." A cat-walk may have been erected among the standing public leading to the stage, without too much ado or loss of space.

I have never seen any evidence that the "yard" was used for acting, yet it is not improbable—providing everybody can see the actors.

In *Henry IV,* the action switches between the Court and the Tavern: Prince Hal, at home in both, is the link. Normally it is assumed that both are played on the main stage; stagehands whip away chairs and tables and replace them with a throne, to make the transition from one location to the other.

But supposing, in the yard, another rostrum were to be erected, lower than the mainstage, on which the tavern scenes were played? The Prince, and the popular Falstaff, would indeed be "among the people"; while at the same time, above them, the sleepless King at Westminster, is always present. Falstaff has a scene where he parodies the interview that the King is to have with the Crown Prince—and in a following scene the real interview (dramatic and moving, nothing like the parody) takes place. Would it not be interesting to see the two parallel scenes done on different levels?

Practically, it is possible. It cannot be ruled out that temporary fixtures—staircases, rostra—were added for certain productions. It is always assumed that the groundlings stood all the time—but perhaps they sat on the ground, on hired cushions, or on temporary benches?

The problem is, we know nothing about Elizabethan staging. The contractors' plans tell only of the permanent fixtures; the few eyewitnesses (of Globe performances after Shakespeare's time) record nothing. On the one hand we have the playscripts; on the other we have the theater. We can only guess at how the one was performed in the other.

# X

# RUNNING A RELAY RACE

~

Before we started rehearsals for *As You Like It,* the stage manager came up with a worried look. "I think we're in trouble," he said. "I've been through the play and made a list of the scenes. There are twenty-one scene changes—and once you get to the Forest of Arden, there are fourteen scenes marked 'Another Part of the Forest.'" He looked skeptical when I told him we'd be doing it "differently," and astonished when I tried to reassure him that "Anyway, those markings are not Shakespeare's."

At another theater, the Director was proud as a peacock of his current production of *Hamlet.* "We have thirty-five different scene changes," he boasted, "and we never return to the same one twice! I managed that, by cutting the first Battlement scene."

Both these productions happened within the last ten years. Both these good men had been working from respectable scholarly editions of Shakespeare where every scene has its location marked at the head of the scene—probably in those volumes called the Complete Works—and both had assumed that these indications were part and parcel of Shakespeare's play, and indicated his desires.

Yet as we saw in our brief look at the Elizabethan theater, half the scenes are not localized. When Shakespeare needs the audience to know where a scene is taking place, he slips it into the dialogue. Otherwise, the place is irrelevant. Shakespeare never wrote "Another Part of the Forest," nor in *Hamlet* "A Platform before the Castle" nor "Another Part of the Same," yet these indications have wriggled their way into most editions of the Complete Works like woodworm. Their insertion deserves to be called the Great Interference. It has blocked the understanding of Shakespeare for nearly two hundred and fifty years.

Some of the plays were published during his lifetime, not always in authorized editions. Unscrupulous printers would send scribes into the audience to note the text down in a kind of primitive shorthand, and hurriedly publish what they had written up (whereby Hamlet's famous monologue was printed in the First Quarto as, "To live, or to die—aye, there's a point"[1]). Or actors were paid off to sell their memory of a certain play—the actor who played Marcellus in Hamlet (doubling Voltemand and Luciano) was one such, since in one early edition his scenes are faithfully reproduced, while the rest of the text is pretty approximate, even down to the characters' names (e.g., Rossencraft and Gilderstone).[2]

It is no wonder that when John Heminges and Henry Condell, seven years after Shakespeare's death, brought out the Complete Works for the first time, in an edition called the First Folio, they wrote:

> where (before) you were abused with divers stolen and surreptitious copies, maimed and deformed by the frauds and stealths of injurious impostors…those are now offered to your view cured and perfect of their limbs, and all the rest, absolute in their numbers as he conceived them.

---

[1] See Anthony Burgess, *Shakespeare,* Ch.9, 1970.
[2] Introduction to the Arden Shakespeare, *Hamlet,* ed. by Harold Jenkins.

Heminges and Condell were working from direct transcripts of Shakespeare's manuscripts, and from the prompt books of The Globe Theatre—happily not destroyed in the fire.

They were the first to number the scenes (it is apparent that the plays fell into a five-act form) but provided no headings.

The Great Interference began nearly a hundred years later when in 1709 Nicholas Rowe published the first biography of Shakespeare—evidently the public up to then was less avid to know about the lives of famous men than nowadays—together with a new edition of the plays. Between Rowe and Shakespeare there was a great gulf fix'd. After the Puritans' closure of the theaters, those who reopened them had had to invent the theater anew. The proscenium stage came into fashion, performances took place indoors, and painted decors were the fashion. Rowe judged Shakespeare by the theater of his own time, and found him wanting. Rowe was himself a bit of a playwright, he'd studied Aristotle, and was rather sorry for Shakespeare who had no knowledge of those "written precepts," for it led to "a great many faults."

> We are to consider him as a man that liv'd in a state of almost universal licence and ignorance.

In other words, Shakespeare did not know the rules.

What Rowe did not realize was that Shakespeare refused to be dictated to by the written precept of a Greek who lived three hundred years before Christ, and that he couldn't give a damn for "rules." His only criterion was, "Does it work?" He had been on the stage for some years as an actor, all his senses alert to the audience's reactions. He had "stood at the back," during performances, watching how this or that scene went down with the public. He knew those moments when three thousand people are agog at what is happening, holding their breath like one man, and he knew those moments when their attention wanders, when they start coughing and fidgeting:

As in a theatre, the eyes of men,
After a well grac'd actor leaves the stage,
Are idly bent on him that enters next,
Thinking his prattle to be tedious...                    (*R.* II)

The public, too, is not concerned with rules, it wants its interest kept alive. And if, to achieve that, you tell three stories at once,
juggling them like balls, switch from one place to another, alter-
nate comedy and tragedy, poetry and melodrama, jump two months
or sixteen years, it doesn't matter—so long as they are not bored.
As Peter Brook would say later, "Boredom is the devil." It's not
that Shakespeare was "ignorant" of the rules, as Rowe thought,
it's simply that he blew them sky high.

For men of Rowe's generation, though, those who lived before
the Restoration (1660) lived in the Dark Ages, and so he set about
editing Shakespeare.

And the Great Interference began when he assiduously
assigned locations to all the scenes in Shakespeare. He went
through each scene, and decided where it might take place. Polonius charges Reynaldo with a spying job, and later Ophelia comes
in: It must be "A room in Polonius's House." Rosalind and Celia
converse; later the Duke and his court come on to watch a
wrestling match: so this scene takes place on "A Lawn before the
Duke's Palace." Occasionally he suggests unlikelihoods, like having
Roderigo wandering about in Othello's "castle" (*Othello:* II.3)

And when it came to the battle scenes of *Antony and Cleopatra* (as Harley Granville Barker pointed out) the action is chopped
up into twenty-two scenes of which ten are from only four to
twenty-two lines long, yet each carefully designated: "A plain near
Actium…" "Another part of the plain…" "Between the camps…" But

what is Shakespeare trying to do? To give us, in terms of drama,
a sense of the effect of this three days' battle upon the lives and
fortunes of his characters.[3]

---

[3] "Shakespeare's Dramatic Art." In *A Companion to Shakespeare Studies,* (Cambridge, 1934).

There we have it in a nutshell. It's not the battle itself that interests Shakespeare, but its *effect* on the participants.

The effect of Rowe's Great Interference was to put directors and designers and actors on the wrong tack, and this went on for a couple of centuries. When he added to the first scene of *Othello,* "A Street in Venice," theater practitioners started imagining canals and bridges and Venetian architecture, and local residents at their daily occupations—and so his stage direction took on a life of its own that, when realized, distracted the spectator from what was really happening—when all Shakespeare required was Brabantio's window.

Besides, these constant scene changes upset the flow of the action, setting each scene apart from its fellows (even causing some directors to drop the curtain between them) whereas the play, in Granville Barker's words

> …is like the running of a relay race; as each scene ends the thread of the story is promptly picked up to be carried on into the next.

Certainly, Rowe's interfering markings make for more comfortable reading—they put us into the mood for the next scene and help us to guess who will come on; but if followed in performance they are as irritating as those inserted titles in old silent films, "Meanwhile, back at the ranch…"

The actor would do better to ignore them; or to use a modern edition of the plays (like the Penguin, or the New Arden) in which they no longer appear.

((    ((    ((

A young director recently came up with a real problem:

"I'm rehearsing my first Shakespeare play. We did every scene separately, allowing a lot of time for each. We went into every scene in depth—characters, mood, atmosphere. Finally I had each scene polished like a little gem. I couldn't wait to put it all together. Now the other day we had our first run-through. It was a disaster. It was heavy, boring, and fussy. It seemed it would never end. I don't know what's gone wrong."

The young director may have fallen into the following trap: Although each scene in Shakespeare is like a little playlet (each contains a little story), a performance of Shakespeare should not resemble an evening of one-act plays.

It's a pity each scene looked like a little gem, when it should have looked like a piece of mosaic, its worth only clear when set among its fellows.

Three things are important when examining the unit of a play we call a scene:
—the beginning
—the ending
—the turning point.


## THE BEGINNING

The scene proper begins with the first line spoken. With this line the actor captures the audience's attention. Nothing of importance to the scene happens before this line—Shakespeare's a master at starting a scene with a bang:

*Enter Lady Macbeth.*
That which hath made them drunk hath made me bold,
What hath quench'd them hath give me fire.
Hark!
Peace!
It was the owl that shriek'd, the fatal bellman
That gives the stern'st good night...

(II.2)

She's not bold at all, she's on edge, listening to every little sound. The two broken lines (indicating pauses) show this.

Or take this:

*Enter Roderigo and Iago.*
RODERIGO:
Tush! Never tell me; I take it much unkindly
That thou, Iago, who hast held my purse
As if the strings were thine, should tell me this.
IAGO:
'Sblood, but you'll not hear me:
If ever I did dream of such a matter,
Abhor me.
RODERIGO::
Thou told'st me thou didst hold him in thy hate.
IAGO:
Despise me if I do not.          (*Othello:* I.1)

A noisy, quarreling beginning. What is "this" and "such a matter"? And who is the hated "him"? Our attention is caught by the raised voices. Now Iago can calm down and tell what's biting him.

Three great ones of the city
In personal suit to make me his lieutenant
Off-capp'd to him;…

For the beginning of a scene, the advice to the players is: Get to the opening line as soon as possible.

This is a totally different matter in, say, a play by Chekhov. *Uncle Vanya* opens:

NURSE: Drink your tea up.
ASTROV: I don't feel like it.

We are in a garden. A table is set for tea. There is a guitar lying on a chair. Nurse is knitting. The audience needs the time to take in this information before the dialogue starts. Astrov is "walking up and down." This is a sign that he's restless. It's his restlessness that causes Nurse to say, "Drink your tea up." So something is certainly going on before the characters start talking.

Such a beginning would be impossible in a Shakespeare play. The rhythm is different, and mood is important. Besides, Chekhov is writing for a captive audience, who are settled comfortably in their seats, in the dark, expecting to watch an imitation of daily life.

Shakespeare's audiences, in the open air, many of them standing, were impatient for something to happen. He has to distract them from looking at the sky, at birds flying overhead, and at each other.

If "mood" is necessary in a scene—and there are Chekhov-like scenes in the plays, notably those concerning old Justice Shallow in his Gloucestershire garden (*Henry II:* I.V)—then it can be established *within* the scene, that is, after the first lines have been spoken.

## THE ENDING

Risking a generalization again, we observe that the real ending of a scene occurs three or four lines before the end: a promise is taken, a decision made, a rendezvous fixed—things that advance the story.

The actual final lines of the scene are frequently a formality, or a repetition of what has been said already: They can be spoken as the actors are going off. These scenes "end" at the slashes:

IAGO:
My friend is dead; 'tis done at your request:
But let her live.

OTHELLO:
Damn her, lewd minx, o damn her! //
Come, go with me apart: I will withdraw
To furnish me with some swift means of death
For the fair devil. Now art thou my lieutenant.

IAGO:
I am your own for ever.        (*Exeunt*)
                              (III.3)

HELENA:
...I will go tell him of fair Hermia's flight
Then to the wood will he tomorrow night
Pursue her; // and for this intelligence
If I have thanks, it is a dear expense:
But herein mean I to enrich my pain,
To have his sight thither and back again.
(*Exit*).
                    (*A Midsummer Night's Dream:* I.1)

ANTONIO:
...These griefs and losses have so bated me
That I shall hardly spare a pound of flesh
Tomorrow to my bloody creditor. //
Well, gaoler, on. Pray God Bassanio come
To see me pay his debt, and then I care not.
(*Exeunt*).
                    (*Merchant of Venice:* III.4)

As can be seen there is a notable drop in tension in the last
lines. Time would have been wasted if the actor finished his final
couplet in midstage, and then had to cross the stage to reach the
door. If he said it while exiting, the lines could be half heard: It
wouldn't matter if a stagehand had already appeared to "strike"
any props or chairs from the scene or to set up accessories for the next.
    The director today is of course at liberty to end the scene as

he thinks fit; but it is useful to know the way the plays were written, so as not to try and give a final flourish to lines that were deliberately weak.

## THE TURNING POINT

"Yes—oh dear yes—the novel tells a story," E.M. Forster was obliged to admit, in (he says) "a drooping regretful voice"[4] and yes, so does a play. It was not the philosophy or the poetry or the character exploration or the theme or the mood, but the story that kept those penny-paying Elizabethan artisans standing for two or three hours in the yard of the theater watching the stage. It was they, too, who must have wanted those upbeat, dream-come-true endings to the comedies, where lovers are reunited, wooers get married, enemies pardoned, long-lost daughters found, and dyed-in-the-wool villains become Born Again men of unassailable virtue, that even Shakespeare was forced to provide. "Yes—oh dear yes" (one hears him thinking) "a play tells a story and a story must have an ending."

Yet how often we actors and directors, confused by all the technical and artistic problems that cloud the air in rehearsal time, come to neglect the story, or take it for granted, so that the wood sometimes cannot be seen for the trees.

Like our young director, we have all known first run-throughs that have been shapeless and muddled, and often it's because of this. Sometimes it is profitable to sit down afterwards with the cast, and to suggest that we're all like painters with our nose too close to the canvas, and that it's worth stepping back a bit to get some distance—and to make sure that everyone is clear about the basic story that, as a group, they are telling. And if this proposition seems too insultingly simple, check through the time-sequence of the play.

---

[4] E.M. Forster, *Aspects of the Novel.*

Many an actor who has lost his way has been helped to focus his performance by being asked this: "Tell us the story of your character in the play."

Every scene in the play helps to push the story one step further, because every scene has its own little story to tell. Usually this means that one (or more) character undergoes a change, a Turning Point, after which *things are never the same again*. It's essential to find it, although often it's concealed.

An example is this short scene from *Macbeth:* which comes directly after the soliloquy spoken of earlier.

> *Enter* Lady Macbeth.
> How now! what news?
> LADY M: He has almost supp'd: why have you left the chamber?
> MACB: Hath he ask'd for me?
> LADY M:                          Know you not he has?
> MACB: We will proceed no further in this business:
> He hath honour'd me of late; and I have bought
> Golden opinions from all sorts of people,
> Which would be worn now in their newest gloss,
> Not cast aside so soon.
> LADY M: Was the hope drunk,
> Wherein you dress'd yourself? hath it slept since,
> And wakes it now, to look so green and pale
> At what it did so freely? From this time
> Such I account thy love. Art thou afeard
> To be the same in thine own act and valour
> As thou art in desire? Wouldst thou have that
> Which thou esteem'st the ornament of life,
> And live a coward in thine own esteem,
> Letting "I dare not" wait upon "I would,"
> Like the poor cat i' the adage?
> MACB:                          Prithee, peace.
> I dare do all that may become a man;
> Who dares do more is none.
> LADY M:                          What beast was't, then,

That made you break this enterprise to me?
When you durst do it then you were a man;
And, to be more than what you were, you would
Be so much more the man. Nor time nor place
Did then adhere, and yet you would make both:
They have made themselves, and that their fitness now
Does unmake you. I have given suck, and know
How tender 'tis to love the babe that milks me:
I would, while it was smiling in my face,
Have pluck'd my nipple from his boneless gums,
And dash'd the brains out, had I so sworn as you
Have done to this.
MACB: If we should fail,—
LADY M:                              We fail!
But screw your courage to the sticking-place,
And we'll not fail. When Duncan is asleep,
Whereto the rather shall his day's hard journey
Soundly invite him, his two chamberlains
Will I with wine and wassail so convince
That memory, the warder of the brain,
Shall be a fume, and the receipt of reason
A limbeck only, when in swinish sleep
Their drenched natures lie, as in a death,
What cannot you and I perform upon
The unguarded Duncan? what not put upon
His spongy officers, who shall bear the guilt
Of our great quell?
MACB: Bring forth men-children only;
For thy undaunted mettle should compose
Nothing but males. Will it not be receiv'd,
When we have mark'd with blood those sleepy two
Of his own chamber and us'd their very daggers
That they have done't?
LADY M: Who dares receive it other,
As we shall make our griefs and clamour roar
Upon his death?

MACB: I am settled, and bend up
Each corporal agent to this terrible feat.
Away, and mock the time with fairest show:
False face must hide what the false heart doth know.
*(Exeunt.)*

"This business" is the murder of the King. At the start, there are two opposing forces: Macbeth has dug his feet in, he knows if he goes on (the soliloquy has told us), damnation awaits him in the after-life, while Lady Macbeth is set upon this deed being done. At the end of the scene, however, he and she are united—two false hearts entwined. She has overcome his doubt. Macbeth has yielded: when, and why?

We notice at the start that he avoids sharing his deep fears of damnation with her—he bleats an excuse about "golden opinions." Spiritual talk would carry no weight with a practical woman like her.

Lady Macbeth makes three onslaughts on his reluctance. She goes for the jugular:

a) She withdraws her love: "From this time Such (with a gesture) I account thy love."

b) She withdraws her respect: calling him "coward" and not a "man,"

c) She shows how easy it is, done together, "What cannot you and I perform…?." No problems of conscience for her!

Macbeth weakens at "If we should fail,—" and he yields at "Bring forth: men-children only…" There's the Turning Point.

This sheds a blinding light upon their relationship. *He would rather give up his immortal soul than lose the love and respect of his wife.* This is his whole problem. It's not her arguments that convince him—he never says "You're right"—it's herself, her "undaunted mettle," her feminine manliness. "Bring forth men-children only…"

Looking for a simple, technical gear change in the scene, we have discovered what binds them; and what causes his downfall.

It's not merely a Turning Point in the scene, but one in Macbeth's whole existence, for from now on it's downhill all the way.

((    ((    ((

The Turning Point is a recurrent feature in the plays, but two other examples suggest themselves. They are in scenes too long to be quoted here but are worth mentioning since the scenes frequently appear out of context as auditions or set pieces in classwork.

One is in the famous duologue between Hamlet and his mother (III.4). Hamlet has been railing at her for not seeing the difference between her present husband

> A slave that is not twentieth part the tithe
> Of your precedent lord, a vice of kings,

and his own father. Gertrude will not hear—"No more!" she cries, three times. Both of them are at a fever pitch of emotion.

Then the father's Ghost appears. He has come to "whet" Hamlet's "almost blunted purpose"—for it seems that his son has forgotten the promise he made to him on the battlements. It's a Turning Point that is also a Turning-back Point. Hamlet realizes that his mother cannot even *see* the ghost of her "precedent lord": She sees only "vacancy" and "incorporal air" (an ironical use of words!). Her former husband no longer exists for her, even in her mind.

Gertrude concludes that Hamlet is mad:

> Mad as the sea and wind, when both contend
> Which is the mightier.

she will later tell Claudius, who will have him sent away.

A Turning Point in the scene; a Turning Point in the play.

Another happens when Richard of Gloucester woos Lady Anne (*Richard III:* I.2). In this scene the author has set himself an almost impossible task—and brought it off. The task is, to show how a lady who has lost her husband and her father-in-law can be seduced by the man who murdered these two, over the corpse of the father-in-law. Add to this the fact that the lady is highly pious, and the murderer monstrously ugly and deformed. Actresses are constantly puzzled over how to make this turnabout from bitter hate to sexual attraction.

In our opinion the wind changes at one particular word.

Lady Anne's is a language of vituperation: She constantly calls him "Devil," "Demon" "Minister of Hell" "Hedgehog," "Toad"…

He, on the other hand, ceaselessly praises her as a "Saint," an "Angel," "Divine perfection of a woman"…

(Everything she secretly wants to hear.)

Every insult of hers he ripostes with a compliment on her sanctity. Suddenly, to this beautiful but lonely, sex-starved widow he springs a word which is totally unexpected:

ANNE: And thou unfit for any place but hell.
RICH: Yes, one place else, if you will hear me name it.
ANNE: Some dungeon.
RICH: Your bedchamber.

Evidently the word troubles her: It upsets her, it's as if he's suddenly kissed her. Somewhere deep down it also excites her. The word is the Turning Point. Henceforth, Lady Anne is fighting a losing battle: Richard will win her.

Again, the language holds the key.

# XI

# BUILDING A CHARACTER

D efining a character in a play does not come easily. Many actors who ask their directors for bread are given a stone. Alec Guinness, cast as Richard II, consulted his director Ralph Richardson about how he wanted the part played. Sir Ralph picked up a pencil, and replied, "Like that. Sharp and slim. That's what we want."[1]

Peter Ustinov, while filming *Quo Vadis,* was summoned by the director Mervyn Leroy to hear his views on the character of Nero. He was told "Nero...? son of a bitch..." and after a few minutes, "plays with himself a' nights..."[2]

And it is surprizing to read Laurence Olivier's view of King Lear: "He's like all of us really, he's just a stupid old fart."[3]

When a director feels it necessary to give an actor a thumbnail sketch of a Shakespeare character, based on a personal, generalized, give-me-the-result outlook ("He's a saint"), or on a psychological understanding of the role ("He had an unhappy childhood"), the actor's only answer can be, "Thank you. On which page?"

---

[1] Garry O'Connor, *Ralph Richardson,* 1982.
[2] Peter Ustinov, *Dear Me.*
[3] Laurence Olivier, *On Acting.*

Reading a role in a modern play, the actor tries to reconstruct the character the author had in mind. Some older writers, like Shaw and O'Neill, furnish a portrait in the stage directions, not only telling us what the character looks like and what he wears, but how he will behave in certain situations: an asset to producers pressed for time, but a straitjacket for actors. Writers more actively associated with the theater, like Mamet and Pinter, will leave the dialogue and action to speak for themselves. So the actor combs the play for indications about the character's life. In fact he's fencing off the area within which he can function.

If he's to play Astrov in Uncle Vanya, for example, he will note his age (forty-seven), his profession—a country doctor in a provincial backwater, and vastly overworked and certain physical characteristics: It is said that he was handsome once, but now his good looks have faded, and even his moustache has grown unruly. Astrov has his weaknesses—he "likes a drop of vodka," says the nurse, probably understating the truth; and his strengths—he is passionately interested in trees, and is privately charting the gradual deforestation of the area, though whether this interest indicates vision or a mere bee in his bonnet, the actor will have to decide.

Astrov is attracted to the idle, languorous Yelena—he visits the house more and more frequently since she is in residence, but he has no eyes for the plain, industrious Sonya, and is unaware that she harbors passionate feelings about him. Although a kindred spirit of Vanya's ("In the whole district there were only two decent, intelligent men—you and I") and his coeval, he faces the midlife crisis totally differently. Vanya loses his head, attempts murder, and considers suicide, while Astrov is already convinced that life is "hopeless," for they are both putrefied by the dreary life in the provinces. He feels a certain nostalgia for a time when life was less tiring and complicated, for he says to the nurse, "I had a nurse like you when I was a child."

Undeniable facts like these will form the basis of the actor's interpretation of Astrov's character. What happens when he looks for like information in Shakespeare?

About age, Shakespeare is intermittently specific and rarely helpful. Nobody knows how old "old Gobbo" is, or Polonius, but "young Hamlet" is revealed in the last act to be all of thirty, which given the life expectancy of the Elizabethans, would then have been considered middle-aged. This hardly tallies with our mental impressions of Hamlet.

Juliet is still thirteen, "on Lammas-tide shall she be fourteen," and King Lear is "fourscore and upward." Here we come to the crux of the matter. When an actress has the emotional capacity to play Juliet, she is too old; and when an actor still has the physical strength to sustain the role of Lear, he is still too young. So what counts is not reality, but the acting of it. Shakespeare's first Juliet was an adolescent boy, and Lear was written for an actor (Burbage) in his mid-thirties. Evidently, Shakespeare's theater is based on a game of "Let's pretend" and asks of his audience a "willing suspension of disbelief." When he specifies a character's age, he is simply giving the audience information necessary for the purposes of his story, he is not writing instructions for casting directors.

Physical characteristics frequently go unmentioned. He does not help us to "see" Lady Macbeth or Rosalind or Iago or Hamlet—and when we think we see them, our memory is simply conjuring up images of well-known actors in the parts. Some producers have thought it obligatory that Hamlet, being Danish, should be blond: as if the existential problems he faces were only true of Scandinavians. It is true that Olivier dyed his hair blond for the film, but he has explained that he had a practical reason. Filming in black-and-white, he needed his hero to be immediately recognizable in the crowd scenes, among other dark-haired actors.

So it is quite a shock to hear Hamlet's mother describe her son, rather ungraciously, as "fat and scant of breath." We should be careful to separate our impressions of the characters from what is actually written.

We may imagine Lady Macbeth to be tall, dark, and satanic-looking, but the *play never says so*—she might equally well be small, plump, and angelic.

On the other hand, more earthy characters do have pronounced physical presences. Much play is made of Falstaff's sweatiness and obesity:

> a roasted Manningtree ox with a pudding in his belly

as of Justice Shallow's emaciation:

> when 'a was naked, he looked for all the world like a forked radish.

Mistress Quickly is seen fussing about her tavern like "Dame Partlet the Hen," and Bardolph's red drinker's-nose is frequently the subject of comment:

> (Falstaff) saw a flea stick upon Bardolph's nose, and 'a said it was a black soul burning in hell

It seems that the Comic Muse worked differently upon Shakespeare's imagination from the Tragic Muse.

Occasionally the cast list informs us of the character's profession. The rude mechanicals who prepare a performance for Theseus' wedding party are specified as a joiner, a weaver, a bellow's mender, but nothing further is made of this. An actor like Robert de Niro would not need to spend two months in a weaver's workshop as a preparation for playing Bully Bottom. Their jobs are noted simply to indicate where they stand on the social ladder—to indicate that they are all respectable artisans, and not a scratch company of actors, which would be even lower on the scale. Other characters are labelled "an executioner," "a murderer," a "schoolmaster." Doll Tearsheet is an aging whore. Her name suggests she plied her trade with vigor, but we do not expect to hear her expressing moral qualms about her work—it is simply the way she earns her living.

Most characters seem content with their lot. Hardly anyone is what is called "upwardly mobile"—except Macbeth, and the play relates what difficulties he faces because of it. People are not dominated nor exhausted by their work in the way that Dr. Astrov is, or Willy Loman. Only kings, wracked by the problems of how to govern their fellow men, have qualms about the way they do their work.

About some facts, Shakespeare even contradicts himself. Othello is called "the Moor," yet Iago speaks of his "thick lips" and "sooty bosom," and he himself says "I am black," which suggests that he is negroid. He is also "of royal blood." Probably we shall never know his country of origin: For Shakespeare it was enough that he was not white. And Lady Macbeth says that she "has given suck," while of Macbeth it is stated "he has no children." But we should be wasting our time if we conjectured what became of them. (One young director suggested that it meant that she was Macbeth's mother!—but the theory did not stand up.)

In short, about most of Shakespeare's characters we do not know enough even to fill in their passport form. Clearly, the approach that leads an actor to create a Dr. Astrov or a Willy Loman or a Blanche Dubois will not be fruitful when a Shakespeare character is in question. The actor must look elsewhere.

( ( (

To start work on a role, an actor needs some kind of a foothold. Simon Callow relates his difficulties when working on Shakespeare with director William Gaskill:

> We argued especially about character. It was my deep conviction that all acting is rooted in character. It was a semi-Stanislavskian point of view, but mainly derived from the misery I experienced as an actor until I had a firm grip on who I was in the play. Bill countered by saying that character was a bourgeois concept based on identification. He said that for him a character was of no interest, only what he did. If a play, says Brecht, is a report on an event, the audience only needs to know as much about the character in the play as makes the event clear.[4]

Many an actor will understand Callow's "misery" and his hunger for a "firm grip" on "who" he was supposed to be. Only "who" is too nebulous a word to get a "firm grip" on.

Suppose an actor asks a director, "Who is this character?" and the director replies, "Tell me first who you are." The actor would be hard put to reply in any but the most general terms. He might give his name, his position in the company, a brief account of the highlights of his career. But in reality he knows he's too complex a character to be summed up in a few words. Or he might say "Ask my agent." It is easier to say "who" someone else is, than to answer the question about oneself.

After *The Birthday Party*, Harold Pinter received a letter from a member of the public who was puzzled by the roles of the two intruders Goldberg and McCann. She asked the author three questions: "Who are these people? Where do they come from? Are they mad?" adding that without the answers to these questions, she could not understand his play. Pinter is said to have replied: "Who are you? Where do you come from? Are you mad? Without an answer to these questions, I cannot understand your letter."

---

[4] See *Being an Actor*, Chapter V, 1984.

"Who?" is clearly not a question that provokes a simple answer.

A biographer can tell us "who" Napoleon was, because his life is over and his achievements can be summed up. Tolstoy can tell us "who" Anna Karenina was—but it takes him over 1,000 pages.

And besides, both novelist and biographer are only writing from one point of view—that of an observer, after the event.

Shakespeare is not like that. He is presenting to us the event while it takes place. He is not the narrator—the characters play out their roles before us. Nor is he the observer—we are.

An Elizabethan actor did not ask "who" his character was. Bully Bottom, cast as Pyramus, says, "What is Pyramus,—a lover? Or a tyrant?" Nor did he use the word character—he said "part."

As an unperfect actor on the stage
Who with his fear is put beside his part...

was Shakespeare's way of describing stage fright.

Bottom (again) wanted to play "the lion's part." A part is, of course, a piece of a whole; it is also the word musicians in an orchestra use when referring to their individual scores. Often it is liberating to think of a Shakespeare play in terms of music.

☾   ☾   ☾

The word *character*, as John Barton has pointed out, was not used in Elizabethan times to denote fictional beings, it was simply a term of lettering. "'Tis Hamlet's character," says Claudius, recognizing his stepson's handwriting in a letter. The word as we know it in the modern sense came in some 150 years later, with the advent of the novel. Indeed, Shakespeare's contemporary dramatists, like Marlowe and Jonson, had fairly rudimentary ideas about character drawing.

Marlowe's *Tamburlaine* was first performed in 1597. In it, Tamburlaine always seems to be addressing a public meeting; it is pure oratory. We never catch him facing a doubt, or struggling with himself; arguing for "this" against "that," wondering which path to take—facing a choice; we never feel a conflict between the public man and the private man. Yet it is just these doubts and dilemmas that bring a Shakespeare role to life.

Even Ben Jonson did not recognize this. Ben was a friend. Shakespeare's company produced some of his plays, and Ben acted in them himself. He was the last friend Shakespeare saw before his death, and he wrote some of the tenderest tributes after it.

But Ben Jonson adhered to the then current theory that each man had a particular temperament, which was caused by the dominance of a particular liquid or "humour" in his body, of which there were four—black bile, phlegm, blood, and choler. So a man with too much black bile would have a melancholic temperament—and be melancholic through and through. He gave his characters explanatory names, like Sir Epicure Mammon, Sir Politick Would-be, Dame Pliant, Doll Common, Zeal-of-the-Land Busy (a Puritan), and set them off behaving according to their humors. And so the braggart is always bragging, the angry man is always angry, and the sensualist forever hunting the pleasures of the senses. Like little toy trains they were condemned to run endlessly along the set rails from which their author would not let them depart.

Shakespeare did the opposite. He gave his melancholic persons bursts of gaiety and action, his angry men he let weep, and his sensualist was frequently heard quoting the Bible and talking of God. Jonson would have thought this very disorderly. Far from being convinced by Shakespeare's portrayals of mankind, he published an attack on the "ill customs" of the current stage, desiring a theater showing:

> … deeds, and language, such as men do use:
> And persons, such as Comedy would choose.

In other words, Shakespeare's theater was not for Jonson "true to life."

When after his death, the London theaters were closed down, the kind of plays that Shakespeare was writing could never be written again.

Great writers turned more and more to the novel, to present their image of life. Tolstoy, Dickens, Balzac, and Chekhov brought character drawing to a fine art. They drew portraits of individuals from their most intimate thoughts to incidental details of their dress and their hair. They drew people we can "see," and whose thoughts had a certain coherence. They told us how they spent the day, how they walked and talked, and how they developed from the cradle to the grave.

A lot of what we look for, when we try to analyze a "character" in a play, comes from what novelists have accustomed us to expect.

This does not imply that Shakespeare, as a portrayer of human beings, is rough and primitive (as the eighteenth century thought him to be). Nor does it mean that since his time mankind has learned more about the workings of the human heart. On the contrary, it may have forgotten a lot. Shakespeare may be ahead of us. Perhaps we go wrong by looking for too much coherence. The realistic novel is not more "real" than the poetic drama, it is simply representing a different plane of reality.

A journalist interviewing Tom Stoppard put it this way: "Well, perhaps characters in a play are never *real*. Have you met anybody who's reminded you of Oedipus Rex lately?"

Yet compared with characters of Dickens and Tolstoy, Balzac and Chekhov, many of Shakespeare's creations appear incomplete, underwritten, "scarce half made up." Certainly the Malvolios, Falstaffs, and Hotspurs spring into life and seem to jump off the page, but others appear to be little more than a series of speeches. It is hard to discover the "person" who says them, or what drives him.

We can hear his voice but we cannot see his face. It is almost impossible to "reconstruct the character the author had in mind."

Even with major roles, we look in vain for Shakespeare's attitude to them. Does he approve, or disapprove of Falstaff? Bernard Shaw found Falstaff "a disgusting and besotted old wretch," while for Orson Welles he is "the greatest conception of a good man, the most completely good man, in all drama," and W.H. Auden went further, seeing him as "a comic symbol of Jesus Christ." Only Shakespeare withholds his opinion. Richard III (in the play) is certainly a bad king, and Henry V, "war-like Harry," seems to be a good one—but does Shakespeare approve of war? And what are we to make of Richard II? One scene suggests approval, another the opposite. Isn't there something missing?

《　　《　　《

If Shakespeare's characters seem incomplete, that is exactly what they are intended to be. He is not failing to produce a finished portrait, he is not even trying. He does not pretend to be, like a novelist, a godlike creator who knows everything about his creatures. He is—and it is salutary sometimes to underestimate him—a man of the theater writing material for actors, and leaving them space. Anna Karenina (for instance) is Tolstoy's and nobody else's; but Hamlet (for instance) is half Shakespeare's script, and half the actor's who will eventually play him.

We can imagine him laying down his pen and saying, "Well, I've done my work—the actor can fill in the rest, with *his* body, *his* personality, *his* voice, and *his* emotions." The roles are open-ended.

So he doesn't fuss us or nag us with matters that are not the concern of his story—whether Ophelia is dark-haired, or what gestures Claudius should make. He does tell us that Hamlet is accustomed to wear "suits of solemn black" because that's essential to the tale, and that Helena is tall and Hermia minute, because that is part of the fun. He tells us Ophelia goes mad, but he does not presume to explain why—perhaps the player will find a reason. He does not treat actors as his instruments, but as his colleagues. He opens the door, and points the way along the road, but he does not know the journey's end.

Such open-handed generosity can be disconcerting to an actor accustomed to being presented with a finished role, and asked to perform it. Today's author is tacitly saying, "I have an ideal image of my Blanche Dubois (or Anna Christie, or whoever): Miss Smith, see if you can become her." And Miss Smith sets off in quest of this fictional character, like a hunter in search of her prey. Her eventual success, or failure, in the role will be judged by how far she has realized "what the author intended." But the role remains the property of the author.

This is not Shakespeare's way. He does not postulate the existence of an imaginary being, and the player is not told to go off anywhere to find it. Miss Smith is being told by the author: "Ophelia could be you—in other circumstances. I will provide these: I will give you situations to play, the words to speak, the emotions to feel and express. Trust me, be convincing—and let's see where you end up."

Miss Smith is not being asked to leave herself behind and hunt for Ophelia somewhere else, but to be herself more fully: like a plant, to stay where she is and put down a taproot into her experience, her talent, and her imagination, and draw her sustenance from there. What Shakespeare is putting on the line is the player's sheer acting ability: Has Miss Smith (or Master Smith, in his day,) the emotional expressiveness and the voice to convey the love, bewilderment, innocence, distress, and ultimately the suicidal madness of this young unwilling victim of the moral disease that plagues the court of Elsinore?

Shakespeare is writing material that lies dormant until it is fertilized by the player—and depending on his, or her, personality and talent, the result will always be different. Miss Black's

Ophelia will be a different person from Miss Smith's. Time and place will contribute: Tomorrow's Ophelia will be otherwise than today's; a Polish actress will not portray her in the same way as an American actress. Nobody can say with certainty "what Shakespeare intended," but we may hazard a guess that this multiplicity of possibilities was something he, as a practical theater man, had in mind.

Certainly he was writing material for his Globe Theatre actors to put into rehearsal the following week. But he certainly had one eye on the future also; he knew what he wrote would last, and that his powerful plays would outlive the thatch-and-loam of his wooden theater, and be played by actors "yet unborn." Modesty forbade him from appointing himself their posthumous director.

((    ((    ((

We are now the future generation for whom he also wrote. He has handed us the plays, opened the door, and pointed the way. Turning round, we find that the author has disappeared, wordlessly:

> Leaving no intimate word or personal trace
> Of high design, outside the artistry
> Of thy penned dreams.            (Thomas Hardy)

We shall never know if he approved of Falstaff and applauded Richard. Leaving a "Don't Disturb" notice on his gravestone, he has left us to make of the plays what we can.

It is not surprising that he left behind no traces of his life, for in his work, too, he does his best to disappear. He keeps his own counsel. He sets two characters in opposition, but he refuses to take sides. He shows one imperfect ruler being replaced by another, but does not suggest that this means progress, only change. He may give one character a good deal more to say than another, but this does not mean that he "favors" him, any more than the scientist favors one of the two chemicals he pours into a test tube to record the resulting reaction. His personal opinions he keeps to himself. Poet Ted Hughes talks of his writing as "egoless."

To understand Shakespeare it is important to know this: to expect that any situation will be presented from two or more sides, and any character can provoke opposing views.

There is a danger for us actors of taking as authentic one character's view of another.

Hamlet is notably generous in giving his opinions of other characters in the story. Polonius is a "great baby…not yet out of his swaddling-clouts," a "rash, intruding fool"; Osric is a "waterfly"; Rosencrantz and Guildenstern are compared to "adders fang'd." Upon Claudius, the "Bloat King," he upsets a thesaurus of abuse, calling him a "Slave," a "Cut-Purse," a "King of Shreds and Patches," a "Vice of Kings"; while for his own father he ransacks the roll call of the Gods—Hyperion, Jove, Mercury, and Mars combine in him. And many directors and teachers assume that Shakespeare shared Hamlet's views.

Nearly a hundred years ago, Bernard Shaw spotted the error:

> Mr. Martin Harvey is the best Osric I have seen: he plays Osric from Osric's own point of view, which is, that Osric is a gallant and distinguished courtier, and not, as usual, from Hamlet's, which is that Osric is a "waterfly."

Many actors are tempted to play the other parts as Hamlet sees them. And so we get Claudiuses that out-Herod Herod, and Poloniuses that are no more than lean and slipper'd pantaloons. The assumption that "This is what Shakespeare intended" because "Look, it's in the text!" is a rash one. It ignores the fact that nobody else in the court of Elsinore suspects Claudius of murder, not even his wife—indeed, nobody else has a bad word to say about him, and Hamlet is alone in his opinion. And Polonius is, in his own eyes, the cleverest man in Elsinore; as Lord Chamberlain, and advisor to the royal family—and how generous he is with his advice!—he is, in fact, running the country. His constant spying, and employment of spies (what Hamlet calls his "intruding"), he himself would describe as "eternal vigilance."

One of the most extraordinary roles in the play is that of the Ghost of Hamlet's father. He is said to be dressed in armor and to go by "with martial stalk." He has lost all claim to humanity, for the sentinels refer to him as "this thing," this "horrid sight" that appears to their "oppress'd and fear-surprised eyes," so that they are "distill'd / Almost to jelly by the act of fear." Even Hamlet, on first sighting him, talks like a Gothic novel about bones, hearses, and sepulchres.

> What may this mean
> That thou, dead corse, again in complete steel,
> Revisit'st thus the glimpses of the moon
> Making night hideous?

(Since the first performances of *Hamlet* were matinees in an open-air theater, it was the words, not the stage lighting, that were designed to create an atmosphere of horror.) If an actor takes his lead from all this spooky talk, it is natural that he will try to play the bogeyman and make his aim that of the Fat Boy in *Pickwick Papers*—"I wants to make your flesh creep."

But if the role is played from the Ghost's own point of view, it can be seen that *to frighten* cannot be his intention. On the contrary, he must overcome Hamlet's fear of him, otherwise he cannot reveal his dreadful secret and convince Hamlet of his mission. He must try and be as human as he can, to reassure Hamlet that he is not an ill-intentioned goblin, or the devil who has assumed a pleasing shape. Alone with Hamlet, he need not even behave like a king. "I am thy father's spirit." More than a revenant talking to a haunted man, he is above all a father talking to his son.

Thus the role played from its own point of view turns out to be the very opposite from the way it is perceived by Hamlet.

It would be illuminating to gather together one afternoon all the characters in the play—excluding Hamlet and the Ghost, of course—simply ask each of them in turn what they think is going on in Elsinore, and how they view the crisis caused by the Prince's behavior. Since none of them was privy to Hamlet's conversation with his dead father, each of them would react to the situation differently. (To encourage actors to explore their roles from *their own point of view,* a similar exercise would be profitable among the characters of any Shakespeare play.)

The conventional, sentimental, view of the play *Hamlet* is that it shows one man in a corrupt society who alone has access to "the truth," and—poor guy!—is generally misunderstood. But Elsinore sees it otherwise, and the play takes on an extra dimension when it shows, at the same time, a basically normal, reasonable society, tragically disrupted by a father-obsessed young man who has—to all extents and purposes—gone mad.

This is what we mean when we say that Shakespeare has deliberately withdrawn himself without comment. His plays show a situation from every side, in all its contradictory complexity, and to offer anything so simple as an "opinion" would not clarify it, but simply belittle it.

So we should avoid putting Shakespeare's characters in glass bottles and sticking labels on them. The answer to Bottom's question "a lover, or a tyrant?" might be "both." In a book long out-of-print,[5] J.B. Priestley has described how creative writers seldom base a character on a single model. They take, say, the joviality of one person they know, the cowardice of another, the wit of a third, and the ingenuity of someone completely different, and amalgamate them all to create a new being.

---

[5] *English Comic Characters,* Chapter on Falstaff.

Shakespeare went even further. He would take two radically different characters—let's say, a man who loves company and a hermit—and fuse them into one person. He would create a character in which the one is housed within the other—and when push comes to shove, the inner man breaks out. Timon of Athens was such; a gregarious party-giver who suddenly turned misanthrope and went off to live alone "upon the beached verge of the salt flood," railing against Mankind.

Shakespeare would take a puritan ascetic like Angelo *(Measure for Measure)*, whose "blood is very snow-broth" and who orders the closure of Vienna's brothels—and show him eaten up with lechery.

He would create Cressida, a Trojan girl who eloquently swears to be forever faithful to her Troilus—otherwise let History say "as false as Cressid'"—and shows her presently betraying him with the opposing Greek army. Her declaration of fidelity is no less sincere, at the time—but within her is another Cressida. Hamlet, too, is equally sincere when he makes his unconditional promise to his ghostly father to avenge him:

> …thy commandment all alone shall live
> Within the book and volume of my brain
> Unmix'd with baser matter: yes, by heaven!

but there *is* other matter in his brain, and he postpones and postpones his vengeance.

Hamlet is generally thought of as an intellectual prince, paralyzed into inaction by "thinking too precisely on the event"— but look what a man of action he also is (though at the wrong times!). His uncle Claudius is a brother-murderer—but Shakespeare shows him kneeling down and trying to pray.

After their deaths the Macbeths are called "this dead butcher and his fiend-like queen"—but the author has showed Macbeth as, at base, a hell-fearing Christian, and his queen as a loving and self-effacing spouse.

So the actor who sets out to play Richard II as a "poet" will be ill-at-ease in the scenes where Richard is unfeeling and tyrannical, *unless* he starts out by accepting that Richard is both poet *and* tyrant.

Othello, the noble, eloquent general, houses within him a savage, grunting, murderous beast, more dangerous than Caliban.

The story goes of Burbage, the Globe Theatre's star actor, sitting together with Shakespeare in a tavern; and Burbage says, "Frankly, Will, there is nothing I cannot play. Whatever part you write, I can do it. I challenge you to write a part I cannot play!"—"'t is well" says Shakespeare—and goes away to write Othello.

The task of encompassing the opposite poles of human behavior—being both Christian *and* mass-murderer, or noble *and* savage, or puritan *and* lecher—is the challenge that Shakespeare sets up for his players, then as now, and often it is the one task that defeats them. Katherina is both shrew and docile housewife. King Lear is both aged tyrant and childish old man. What interests Shakespeare is the duality of Man, the Jekyll-and-Hyde syndrome. As Racine said, "There are two men within me." Most actors can play one extreme of a character, but not the other.

Stanislavski said, "When playing an evil character, look to see where he is good." When playing Shakespeare's three-dimensional characters, it is as well to look for both extremes together, co-existing. Like a coin that has two sides, they also have their heads and tails.

( ( (

## SMALL PARTS

When Charles Dickens died, an engraving was published showing the author daydreaming in his study, while the air around him swarms with tiny, fairy-sized drawings of some of the hordes of characters he created—they number, according to a recent calculation, some two thousand. A similar picture can be imagined of Shakespeare, at the end of his working life, dozing under the mulberry tree he planted in his Stratford garden (a tree that outlived him by one hundred forty years, and when cut down was chopped up into Shakespearean relics, the number of which—says Prof. S. Schoenbaum, was "little short of miraculous"), for in his plays he created also some eight hundred fifty characters, ranging over a whole cross-section of society, from kings to beggars, including a handful of supernatural creatures. His imagination, too, was little short of miraculous.

Few writers can move outside their own social level. Writing schools teach authors to "write about what they know," so most of them avoid dealing with princes and potentates, and rarely write convincingly about unlettered beggars or rustics without romanticizing them.

But Shakespeare, it seems, knew everybody. He could give lines to Kings and Queens that no monarch would be ashamed to speak, and two pages later he could furnish dialogue for tradesmen or pickpockets or country servants, with lines that do not patronize them, but leave them their dignity.

Many of these secondary roles are very short. Actors are often disappointed about how "little they have to say," confusing the length of the role with its importance. I once found an actor appearing in scenes in which he was not set down to appear (and in which he had not been requested to appear), claiming that it made his role "more interesting." He was playing Davy, Shallow's rustic servant, in *Henry IV Part Two*—and Davy's most telling line (in my view) is "I hope to see London once ere I die." Shakespeare never tells us whether he did or he didn't, and so one assumed he would die with his dream unfulfilled; but in the scene where Shallow arrived in London, there was Davy!

Far from making his part stronger, the actor had in fact weakened it; it was if Chekhov's Three Sisters were to arrive finally in Moscow. It is not the length of time an actor appears on the stage that is important, but what he does when he is on. It is surprizing to note how few scenes Ophelia has; while Sir Andrew Aguecheek, one of the most memorable parts in *Twelfth Night*, has less than forty lines.

Not all of Shakespeare's characters are three-dimensional. Many contain no "duality" at all, and scarcely any individuality. They have a name (some not even that), and a few lines to say, before they exit and are heard no more—or, since doubling and trebling are common in the plays, before the actor dons another costume and returns in another, and hopefully juicier, part.

Whoever said "There are no small parts, there are only small actors" was mistaken: There *are* small parts, and they have to be played. For many they are the first step in a career. John Gielgud's first professional role was a Herald in *Henry V;* his only line (to King Henry): "Here is the number of the slaughtered French." Little more than a walk-on part, many would say. But when we know that at the Battle of Agincourt, through Henry's leadership, the British lost only a hundred men, while the French lost a whole *six thousand,* then it can be seen that the Herald's announcement was of vital importance; and that Shakespeare had given the actor, even in the five seconds it takes to speak the line, something to act. (The reader who disbelieves this is invited to try it for himself.)

What is the actor to do when cast as, say, Old Man in *Macbeth:*

Three score and ten I can remember well;
Within the volume of which time I have seen
Hours dreadful and things strange, but this sore night
Hath trifled former knowings...

(II.4)

or as Philo (friend to Antony) who opens *Antony and Cleopatra:*

Nay, but this dotage of our general
O'erflows the measure; those his goodly eyes
That o'er the files and musters of the war
Have glow'd like plated Mars, now bend, now turn
The office and devotion of their view
Upon a tawny front; his captain's heart
Which in the scuffles of great fights hath burst
The buckles on his breast, reneges all temper
And is become the bellows and the fan
To cool a gipsy's lust. Look! where they come.
Take but good note, and you shall see in him
The triple pillar of the world transform'd
Into a strumpet's fool; behold and see.

(I.7)

and Philo's role is over.

Or what is he to make of the Doctor who is invited to observe Lady Macbeth sleepwalking? (V.1 and 3).

I'd call these roles "witnesses."

Let us imagine the central action of the play (Macbeth's regicide, or Antony's obsession with the Queen of Egypt) as a great fire: It scorches the people involved, but even those standing far off feel the heat on their faces, and are upset by it. Old Man and Philo are among these. The actor needs to look around not for a "character" to play, but for an *emotional reaction* toward the central action, or the "fire." (We have seen Old Man on television, when "senior citizens," pale and shaking, are interviewed after witnessing an earthquake; and many a Senator has been furiously indignant, like Philo, at seeing a world leader robbed of his dignity and charisma through too close involvement with a lecherous woman.)

As for Lady Macbeth's physician, he is simply called in to observe, but he overhears her talking in her sleep, and discovers something he would rather not know—that she helped to kill the previous King!—a secret that can only be a burden to him:

> More needs she the divine than the physician.
> God, God forgive us all!...
> I think, but dare not speak.
>
> (V.1)

He, too, is scorched by the fire. (One could write a whole short story about this doctor.)

Shakespeare's plays, it has been said, begin with discord and end in harmony. He takes an event—a murder, a marriage, a declaration of war, an abdication, a rebellion, a shipwreck—which upsets the natural order of things and throws it "out of joint"; and he shows how dozens of people are affected by this upheaval. The minor roles in a play are all these people. As actors, they are required to be re-acters.

Once I played the part of a Messenger in a Greek tragedy. My task was to come on and relate how King Oedipus died. I was trying out all kinds of physical and vocal ways of bringing home this event to the listeners, but I had forgotten one thing. The director stopped me. "But *you*," she said, "*you* have just witnessed this, with your own eyes. You! You are someone who has seen a miracle. You are in a state of shock. You are not a newspaper reporter, selling a story—you were perhaps the only witness. Tell us what *you* saw, from your point of view. Make it personal."

I gladly pass on this advice to all those who are cast in the small roles that we can call "witnesses." Make it personal...

# XII

# HOW DO YOU REMEMBER
# ALL THOSE LINES?

A well-trained memory is a kind of life insurance for an actor. In youth, the memory is alert. Working with child actors one is often amazed at the speed and accuracy with which they can learn, not only their own lines but everybody else's as well. Older actors have more difficulty. Often they are not even put up for important jobs because of a reputation for forgetfulness—"He'll never learn it!" Many talented old actors are limited to small parts in films and radio work because of fading memories.

The memory is not often put to the test in this age of pocket calculators, electronic diaries, computers, and, in our profession, cue cards. Yet the memory is like a muscle—if it is not exercized it will atrophy. Dancers regularly do classes between engagements to keep their bodies in trim, but fewer actors, when they have spare time on their hands, exercise their memories.

Yet every English actor knows the story of Dame Sybil Thorndike who, very early in her career, set herself the task of learning a new poem everyday, "before breakfast" she said, to keep her learning faculties in trim. The result was that at the age of eighty-two, when she was given a play to do that was simply a two-hour monologue, she learned it without exhaustion and played it with her customary aplomb.

In the days before printing was invented, memory was indispensable. Homer was written to be recited, not read, and the Greek orators had no notebooks to support them while delivering their great addresses.

Indeed, the Greeks called Memory "the Mother of the muses," and invented a mnemo-technique called the Art of Memory—Aristotle writes about it in *On Memory and Recollection*—which was passed on to the Romans, and later absorbed into the European tradition.

In Elizabethan times Francis Bacon was still referring to it. It worked by association. Since sight was supposed to be the most impressionable of the senses, the system proposed attaching things-to-be-remembered on to images of things-already-known, or to things visible. Thus an orator in a public square, with five topics to discuss, would mentally attach one topic each to five objects in his line of view—say, a temple, a statue, a villa, a government building, and an obelisk. While he was talking, these erections would act as reminders.

In the Renaissance, special buildings, full of images and decorations, were designed for such orators, and called "memory-theaters." Dr. Frances Yates has devoted a book to these creations, called *The Art of Memory*.[1] She argues that Shakespeare's Globe Theatre was one of the last of these, and that its architecture, (seen from the stage) contained a number of these visual "reminders."

It is certain that Elizabethan actors, who kept a repertory of some fifty plays in their heads, and had only three weeks rehearsal time to prepare a new production, must have been gifted with remarkable memories. It is true today that any actor embarking on Shakespeare needs a precise memory. Saying approximately what is set down is not acceptable—and Shakespearean language

---

[1] See *The Art of Memory*, 1966.

is not easy to improvise. (There was an old actor-laddie who learned off specially a chunk of Shakespearean verse that would fit any occasion—no doubt a passage about sunrise or flowers—and when he forgot his lines he would trot this out and hope the audience would not notice that he was, in Shakespeare's phrase, "beside his part.")

Oddly enough, however, Shakespeare is not difficult to learn, and once learned—as many an old actor will agree—it tends to stick in the mind, while many other author's writings swiftly get effaced. It is worthwhile trying to discover why this is.

Probably this has to do with music. The memory retains music more easily than words. Most of us, although we need to look up addresses and telephone numbers that we frequently use, can conjure up songs and melodies that we learned decades before. And it is notable that musicians have a longer working life than actors—Horowitz and Rubinstein were still giving concert performances in their old age, and I once saw Pierre Monteux conduct the *Rite of Spring* from memory at the age of eighty-nine; climbing on to the podium was for him a bigger problem than remembering the score.

To commit a passage to memory, it helps to plug into that chamber of the brain where sounds and rhythms are stored—to make contact with the musical part of the memory. As an example of how this works, here is a verse, not this time by Shakespeare, but by Lewis Carroll, which is remarkably easy to memorize. Indeed, one commentator on *Alice in Wonderland* has observed that many children know it without consciously having learned it:

'T was brillig; and the slithy toves
Did gyre and gimble in the wabe.
All mimsy were the borogroves
And the mome raths outgrabe.

This is pure sound. The words produce no images that we can cling on to, and although in the book Humpty Dumpty does give Alice a helpful explanation of it all ("Well, 'toves' are something like badgers—they're something like lizards—and they're something like corkscrews...also they make their nests under sundials—also they live on cheese."), most people have forgotten his interpretation while remembering quite clearly those verse.

It is the music of the language that makes it stick. Obviously the rhythm helps, and the rhymes—toves/borogroves, wabe/ outgrabe. But within the stanza there is a subtle play of echoing sounds (assonance and alliteration).

We can follow certain sounds through and see how they recur:

ĭ: brillig—gimble—mimsy
ī: slithy—gyre
br/gr: brillig—borogroves—outgrabe
m: gimble—mimsy—mome
o: toves—borogroves—mome

The mouth remembers the sound it has just made and finds it easy to make a similar sound soon afterwards: The -li- of *brillig* modulates easily into the -li- of *slithy;* when the mouth has said *mimsy* it can remember *mome*. The verse has no sense or images (it is rather like an abstract painting), but it is full of echoes: It is the sounds themselves that act as memory aids.

A great deal of Shakespeare works this way. There is in Hamlet's "To be, or not to be" monologue a particularly knotty passage that is hard to memorize.

> For who would bear the whips and scorns of time,
> The oppressor's wrong, the proud man's contumely,
> The pangs of dispriz'd love, the law's delay,
> The insolence of office, and the spurns
> That patient merit of the unworthy takes,
> When he himself might his quietus make
> With a bare bodkin.

The order of these calamities is hard to recall, and neither mental images nor logic can help us. The knot is easier to unravel if we follow the sounds through. The speaker, as he says *whips* knows that the next phrase contains a -p- also, and so the word *oppressor's* pops up on his mental screen, bringing in its train more -p-'s: p̲roud, p̲angs, disp̲riz'd.

Disp̲riz'd l̲ove links -p- and -l-, and there are four -l-s: l̲ove—l̲aw—del̲ay—insol̲ence. Back to -p- again: sp̲urns, p̲atient. Then the -ā- of *patient* echoes through t̲akes—qui̲etus—m̲ake; and -a- leads to -b-: *bare bodkin!*

Richard III opens with a dazzling display of alliterative pyrotechnics:

> Now are our b̲rows b̲ound with victorious wreaths;
> Our b̲ruised arm̲s hung up for m̲onum̲ents;
> Our stern al̲arums changed to m̲erry m̲eetings;
> Our d̲readful m̲arches to d̲elightful m̲easures.
> Grim̲-visag'd war[2] hath sm̲ooth'd his wrinkled front;
> And n̲ow, instead of m̲ounting barbed steeds,
> To f̲right the s̲ouls of f̲earful adver̲saries̲,
> He c̲apers ni̲mbly in a l̲ady's c̲hamber
> To the l̲ascivious pl̲easing of a l̲ute.

It is as if the dramatist's aural imagination is an echo chamber: Writing *brows* he hears also *bound* and *bruise, arms* reminds him of *alarums, marches, war;* and *nimbly* accords with *chamber.*

Virtuoso as this is, there is no sense of strain. No word seems to be dragged in for its sound alone. Shakespeare may be showing off, but he does it with discretion. He is not like the writer of the Pyramus and Thisbe drama, which the amateur actors perform in *A Midsummer Night's Dream,* who must have been so proud of writing:

---

[2] W̲ar, in Shakespeare's time, rhymed with far—and so echoed al̲arums and m̲arches.

Whereat with blade, with bloody blameful blade
He bravely broach'd his boiling bloody breast;

What is remarkable about the sound play in the *Richard III*
passage is not how well Shakespeare does it—but that he does it
so seldom. He had battalions of words at his command, he could
easily have set them playing verbal leapfrog, but the more he
writes, the less he does it. There are many example of felicitous
alliteration in his works

Bow, stubborn knees, and heart with strings of steel
Be soft as sinews of the new-born babe.
(Hamlet)

A largess universal like the sun
His liberal eye doth give to every one
(Henry V)

after life's fitful fever he sleeps well...

(Macbeth)

The barge she sat in, like a burnish'd throne.
Burn'd on the water; the poop was beaten gold;
Purple the sails, and so perfumed, that
The winds were love-sick with them, the oars were silver,
Which to the tune of flutes kept stroke, and made
The water which they beat to follow faster...
(Antony and Cleopatra)

But they seem to occur of their own accord, you never feel the
writer drawing attention to himself.

He can, of course, use alliteration to make an onomatopoeic
effect: Listen to the rustling sibilance of sentries' voices in the dark
night before the Battle of Agincourt:

From camp to camp, through the foul womb of night
The hum of either army stilly sounds
That the fix'd sentinels almost receive
The secret whispers of each other's watch.

(Henry V)

But again, as in the preceding quotations, no word is misplaced, no word could be bettered.

Shakespeare was through and through a musical writer. Both in prose and verse, his rhythms are appropriate to the emotions, and the sentences have a shape. Even Bernard Shaw, who despised Shakespeare's "ideas," had to admit that:

> At the great emotional climaxes we find passages which are Rossinian in their reliance on symmetry and impressiveness of march to redeem poverty of meaning. Strip it of that beauty of sound by prosaic paraphrase, and you have nothing left but a platitude that even an American professor of ethics would blush to offer his disciples. Any attempt to deliver such music prosaically would be as absurd as an attempt to speak an oratorio of Handel's, repetitions and all.[3]

Within the sentences he made the vowel sounds chime against each other in a harmonious way. This is what earned him the epithet among university students who hung his portrait on their walls (as students today hang posters of pop stars) of "sweet Mr Shakespeare." But there is no trick, no system; his harmonies elude analysis. Probably that is why he soon abjured the ingenious interplay of vowels and consonants he displayed in the opening of *Richard III*—the mechanism was too obvious. As he matured, he moved on to a subtler verbal music.

---

[3] G. Bernard Shaw, *Our Theatres in the Nineties,* Review of Antony & Cleopatra, 20 March 1897.

He sought, first of all, *le mot juste;* and because his ear was finely attuned to the sound of language, the words he found were also the most harmonious ones. Without trying, he composed phrases whose music takes the breath away—

> What scourge for perjury
> Can this dark monarchy afford false Clarence?

> Good night, sweet Prince,
> And flights of angels sing thee to thy rest.

>           ...Nor poppy, nor mandragora,
> Nor all the drowsy syrups of the world,
> Shall ever medicine thee to that sweet sleep
> Which thou ow'dst yesterday

> I am dying, Egypt, dying...

> The iron tongue of midnight hath told twelve;
> Lovers, to bed, 'tis almost fairy time...

And analyze them how we will, *we cannot see how it is done.*

We have suggested that Shakespeare's text responds to being learned "musically." This has nothing to do with the pitch of the voice; indeed, the learner should try to commit the lines to memory without fixing inflections, without deciding too early what he is going to do with the lines. Inflections have a way of becoming inflexibles. *How* something is spoken can only be suggested after examining *what* is spoken.

While learning, the actor does well to ask himself why Shakespeare uses one particular word rather than another (Why should the swallow "dare?" Why should the tongue of midnight be "iron?"); and why a sentence should be composed in a particular way. (We saw with the opening of *Richard III* how one misplaced word can take away the whole dramatic tension of a line.)

Shakespeare's language is very sensual—it needs to be felt on the tongue and on the lips. The rhythms are all-important, for they reflect the rhythms of the character's thinking and breathing, its dynamism. (Set any speech of Hamlet against one of Othello, and you feel straightaway the difference between the quicksilver fluctuations of a violin and the slow-moving determination of a cello.) To learn to breathe in unison with a character is to know that character physically. To learn a part, in the first place, *musically*, is a step toward knowing the part very intimately indeed.

It is a way of getting to know the character *from the inside, outwards*—knowing his changes of mood and the pulse of his blood. The other way—when the actor thinks "Yes, I know this kind of person," or even tries to analyze him—"I think he's in love with his mother"—is working from the outside, inwards, for this actor's point of view is that of an observer, and he's judging. He is not looking at the character *from the character's point of view*. He's still thinking of the role in the third person.

Anyway, the rhythms are all set down. You cannot go against them, any more than a musician can go against the notes he has to play. So better discover what they are, and let them carry you along. More often than not, especially in mature Shakespeare, the rhythms *embody* the emotions. Leontes (*The Winter's Tale*), certain that his wife is playing him false, is left alone with his child. His head is throbbing:

> Inch-thick, knee-deep, o'er head and ears a fork'd one!
> Go play, boy, play; your mother plays, and I
> Play too, but so disgrac'd a part, whose issue
> Will hiss me to my grave: contempt and clamour
> Shall be my knell. Go play, boy, play...

The throbbing pain can be heard in the rhythm. Jealousy makes his blood beat faster—bang bang bang! "inch thick, knee-deep"— the first line alone has seven stresses—"o'er head and ear a fork'd one!" The pulses continue: "play, boy, play," "be my knell." (We think of Othello's "O bl<u>oo</u>d, bl<u>oo</u>d, bl<u>oo</u>d!") The words sound like hammer blows. And they beat out the word "play," which changes its meaning with every repetition—a child's game, a flirtation, a theatrical performance. All three—Leontes, Mamillus his son, and Hermione his queen—are all "playing" in their different ways. It is immediately after this that Leontes refers to the man in the audience whose "pond has been fish'd" by his neighbor, Sir Smile; acknowledging the fact that while he, King Leontes, plays a part in Sicilia, he is also an actor at the Blackfriars Theater London in a play (called *The Winter's Tale*).

This is rather like those Russian dolls that, when opened, contain smaller dolls, that when opened:

> An actor in a play
> playing a King
> says he is playing a cuckold's part
> because his wife is playing him false
> while his child plays a game...

This is three-dimensional dramatic poetry. The actor who ignores this ("I'm interested in the emotion, not the words") is like a plane flying on one engine too few; but the actor who is aware of this music, and its overtones, is likely to make the audience share his pain.

The writer, as he writes a speech, is *in* the character's mood at the moment of writing. Shakespeare was "being Leontes" when he wrote that speech. To rediscover that mood, the actor needs to feel the music of the speech, and the rhythms will implant the words upon his memory.

## XIII

# SHAKESPEARE AND STANISLAVSKI

~

Not for nothing is the title of this book a nod of respect
toward the first handbook on acting Stanislavski wrote.
Although there are still British actors who, on hearing
the name Stanislavski, reach for their swords, he is a teacher whom
no self-respecting actor can ignore. But when it comes to inter-
preting Shakespeare, is he a help? or is he a hindrance?

If Shakespeare had ever codified his ideas about acting, would
they have had anything in common with Stanislavski's? And if
not, whom should we believe?

Their positions were not dissimilar. Both were managers of
a theater in which they worked also as actor and director. (Only
Shakespeare was also a playwright, while Stanislavski channeled
his creative powers into teaching.) And both were theater reformers: that is, both were out to change a theater that was hidebound
by cliché and artifice, and bring it to resemble "life as we know
it"; or, in simple terms, to replace a prevailing style of "overacting" by a more up-to-date way of "underacting."

English theater had hardly begun when Shakespeare flourished, so it may seem unexpected to think of him—one of its
founders—as a reformer. Yet he was so, as is clear from *Hamlet.*

The Players visiting Elsinore perform for the Prince a scene from their repertoire, in rolling verse full of archaic and *recherché* words about the death of King Priam. Later Hamlet reflects on how:

> this player here,
> But in a fiction, in a dream of passion,
> Could force his Soul so to his own conceit
> That from her working all his visage wann'd,
> Tears in his eyes, distraction in 's aspect,
> A broken voice, and his whole function suiting
> With forms to his conceit? and all for nothing!
> For Hecuba!

Hamlet reflects that if the actor had his—Hamlet's—problems he would:

> drown the stage with tears,
> And cleave the general ear with horrid speech,
> Make mad the guilty, and appal the free,
> Confound the ignorant, and amaze indeed
> The very faculties of eyes and ears...

He contrasts his own behaviour:

> Yet I,
> A dull and muddy-mettled rascal, peak,
> Like John-a-dreams, unpregnant of my cause,
> And can say nothing...

> ...I, the son of a dear father murder'd,
> Prompted to my revenge by heaven and hell,
> Must, like a whore, unpack my heart with words
> And fall a-cursing, like a very drab,
> A scullion!

So conventional acting demanded tears, a broken voice, a whole body wracked with passion, and a deafening delivery; while

Hamlet/Burbage (he is commenting on his own performance) is mooning about, with nothing to say, and occasionally swearing like a kitchen maid.

Hamlet had already advised the Players not to "saw the air too much with your hand, thus," nor to bellow like "the town crier," not to "tear a passion to tatters, to very rags" nor to "out-Herod Herod"; not "to o'erstep the modesty of nature"; to appeal rather to the spectators with taste, than to the masses:

> Now, this overdone, or come tardy off, though it make the unskilful laugh, cannot but make the judicious grieve; the censure of which one must in your allowance o'erweigh a whole theatre of others.
>
> (*Hamlet:* III.2)

The literal reader demands why a Prince should have the audacity to lecture a troupe of professional actors on their job, and who were these actors, these "robustious, periwig-pated fellows" he was attacking. Likewise, he might demand which actor Macbeth refers to:

> a poor player
> That struts and frets his hour upon the stage
> And then is heard no more…

(Did Macbeth go to the theater?) But when we remember that the spectator only *half* believed that the story was set in Denmark (or Scotland, or wherever) and was not troubled by references to contemporary life in London, then we can see that the relevance of these passages about acting is that Shakespeare, through Hamlet's mouth, is commenting on rival theaters.

The play he gives the travelling actors to quote sounds like a parody on Marlowe, and they were presumably directed to act it in the noisy exaggerated style of Edward Alleyn's company, who played at the Rose Theatre, just around the corner. At this time, the rivalries between London theaters came to a head: 1601 is famous for what is known as The War of the Theaters.

While Alleyn as Tamburlaine was roaring and ranting, and all for Zenocrate (see chapter 6), Burbage at the Globe was inaugurating a quieter, more colloquial, more interior kind of acting, his passion prompted by something much nearer home—a father lost and murdered.

We can imagine Shakespeare watching Alleyn's acting, and thinking "But that's not at all how people behave in life!" and instructing his own company to look to nature for their model. We might say that Shakespeare was encouraging a kind of Elizabethan "Method" acting. The message implicit in Hamlet's speech, a kind of apologia for this new acting style, is, "Do you think I'm underacting? Those old barnstorming actors may *do* more—but I *feel* more."

Hamlet's comments on the theater are the nearest we get to Shakespeare's handbook on acting.

((          ((          ((

Most of Stanislavski's encounters with Shakespeare occurred before he formulated what is known as his "system." In his youth (in 1896 and 1897), he had played Othello, a role for which his enormous stature and deep bass voice must have recommended him, and Benedick in *Much Ado About Nothing*. He was not satisfied with either performance. In those days "I thought that the creative road led from outer characterisation to inner emotion," he wrote in *My Life in Art*. This "creative road" was one which Laurence Olivier constantly took—everyone knows how he based his Richard III on a mixture of the martinet Broadway director Jed Harris, and Disney's Big Bad Wolf.

Stanislavski directed both plays himself. The first was like opera, the second like operetta, he was to complain later. He admitted to being inspired by holidays spent in Venice and Turin, and the delights he found in Italian village life. He did a lot of research in museums on period costumes. He admits he chose the plays as a pretext for the spectacle they afforded: "I did not need scenery and costumes for a play, I needed a play for scenery and costumes." He concluded that the stage director Stanislavski hid the actor Stanislavski.

In 1899 he produced *Twelfth Night,* and played Malvolio (another "tall" role). The press complained that his performance drew pity, rather than laughter.

All this was before his historic meeting with Nemirovich-Danchenko in the Slavic Bazaar, where they made plans to reform the Russian stage.

His reforms were well under way when in 1910 he invited the visionary Gordon Craig to direct *Hamlet* at the Moscow Arts, and the result was a mighty clash. Craig at that time was experimenting with monolithic blocks and screens in his stage designs. These were a far cry from the jolly pictures of everyday life in Italy that had been the bases of Stanislavski's own productions of Shakespeare; but the Russian director thought that the Moscow Arts should experiment with new art forms.

The pioneer Craig and the revolutionary Russian director had this is common:

> I could see in Hamlet the history of the theatre. In Hamlet all that is living in the theatre is struggling with all those dead customs that want to crush the theatre.
>
> (Craig)

Which is exactly what Stanislavski was trying to do. In practice, however, it didn't work out. Craig wanted Stanislavski himself to play Hamlet; but this was not to be, so the Russian took over the job of coaching the actors—a necessary measure, since Craig's directions to actors were far from being precise. But where Craig wanted to see huge, super-terrestrial characters to match his monolithic sets, Stanislavski was coaching them in a realistic style, making their behavior as human as possible. While Craig wanted the whole court of Denmark to be seen in a symbolic, nightmare style, presented as seen through Hamlet's eyes, Stanislavski was scaling down their acting and teaching them to behave "such as they actually were." In the end Stanislavski, who was suspicious of abstract ideas, came to the conclusion that Craig was far too ahead of his time. (Craig would have been better understood by Meyerhold!)

One of the problems was the speaking of Shakespeare's verse:

> Stanislavski discovered yet again that while he had managed to devise a style of speaking that would do well enough for con-temporary plays, as soon as verse was attempted the actors fell out of step with him and lapsed into declamation.[1]

Stanislavski had met this problem before, when he played Othello:

> I understood that knowing how to speak verse simply and ele-gantly was itself a science, with its own laws. But I did not know them.

In 1917 Stanislavski took over an ailing production of *Twelfth Night,* and surprised everyone by his "theatricality" and his insis-tence on external effects. What happened to the "System"?, people asked. But it should be remembered that he knew the play well from twenty years before, when he was still in his "spectacular director" days, and also that he was not creating a new produc-tion, but refurbishing one from another director who had lost his way.

As a spectacular director he had still not lost his touch in 1930, when he wrote out his *Othello* production. He was staying in Nice

---

[1] Denis Bablet, *Edward Gordon Craig,* 1962.

for health reasons, and he sat down and penned a production that he sent to Moscow to be realized. Nowadays it seems incredible that a director should write out a production, down to the gestures and pauses and slightest moves—we expect these things to be worked out in rehearsals, with the actors' collaboration. But it is no more strange than a complete film script composed by a director like, say, David Lean, who wanted his films to be planned in advance down to the last detail.

And a film version is what it resembles. All Venice is there, with its canals and bridges—Roderigo and Iago arrive by gondola. The fight sequences in Cyprus are meticulously choreographed, and the noises of clanging bells and clashing swords precisely indicated.

It makes thrilling reading. His notes to the actors are enlightening:

> Already he knows what she is going to say, and he watches her like an examining counsel, trying not to startle his victim…

Othello has thought of a new means to obtain the handkerchief.[2] He reveals to her its magic secret. He even wants to frighten her because, if the handkerchief exists, it may help to produce it. If, however, this last measure fails, all is lost. Stanislavski writes like a novelist, like Tolstoy, minutely tracing the inner thoughts of the characters. His understanding of their psychology is breathtaking. He indicates each look, each look away. He suggests how to pitch the voice, what to do with the hands. He peppers the text with pauses, while the characters gather up their thoughts and decide to say the next line. The production, staged as written, would have lasted several hours.

The players would be doing exactly what Bernard Shaw complained of when he talked of actors who utter half a line, "then stop to act," and utter the other half "and then stop to act again."

---

[2] This handkerchief / Did an Egyptian to my mother give," III.4.

Craig had already warned Stanislavski, Bablet records, that if he treated Shakespeare as he treated Chekhov, "too many superfluous details will crowd in."

Partly this is a question of time. In Chekhov, events *seem* (to the audience) to take the same time as they would in life, whether it's a fire, or an evening party, or people leaving a house. In Shakespeare everything is speeded up—wars are declared and battles won, kings die and are succeeded, young people meet, woo, fight and marry, the "accomplishment of many years" is turned "into a hour glass."

In Chekhov people have the time to drink tea, do their accounts, lose their galoshes, wander to the window and stare at the trees, all these activities being the tenth of the iceberg that is visible—that is the real drama. Shakespeare, on the other hand, shows what is happening above sea level—the storms that toss the boat about, the contrary winds, and the shipwrecks.

And besides, Chekhov's language is grey. He was continually advising young authors to avoid purple descriptions of nature, and to content themselves with simplie phrases like "It was raining." The lines we remember from his plays are quite commonplace: "I want to go to Moscow," "We must work, gentlemen, work!"—"I am a seagull—no, that's not it," "All Russia is our garden." Chekhov's language *conceals,* while Shakespeare's expresses. You cannot treat Shakespeare as if he were Chekhov.

( ( (

Stanislavski's name has come to mean different things to different people. Most people think his name is synonymous with the acting approach taught for many years by Lee Strasberg at the Actors' Studio; others fiercely deny this. Many people know of his ideas only from a book called *An Actor Prepares.*

If we are to understand his ideas, we should perhaps take a little stroll around him first.

To our knowledge he was the first person in the world to set out to write an A to Z of Acting. Until he came, acting was like an unwritten language—it was passed on from father to son, from teacher to pupil, from director to actor. Young actors picked it up, and made it their own. (In Shakespeare's time, boy actors were sent to live with older actors and their families and trained as "apprentices.")

A lot of what was passed on would have been of a technical nature—"Don't drop your voice at the end of a line"; "Before starting to speak, take a breath"; "Keep your head up so that the audience can see your eyes." Shakespeare's youths would have been schooled in elocution, singing, fighting, dancing, projection. They would probably have received instruction in how to play girls' parts, and clowns, and probably ghosts; and if Tom Stoppard is to be believed, in how to die on stage (how many Shakespeare characters do!). However, there is no record of an official "school" being attached to the theater.

As far as pure acting is concerned, what they were taught was probably more in the nature of what we'd call hints, tips, and tricks. Many old actors would have taught by demonstration: "Copy me!" Nobody, until Stanislavski, is known for working out a complete "system."

When we call Stanislavski's ideas "the Method" or "the System," we should bear in mind that Russian has no definite or indefinite articles, no words for *the* or *a*; so what we have come to call "the Method" might mean quite simply, "a Method"— notes on acting methodically set down. "A Method" suggests that there is room for others.

Before he became a teacher, and before he set about defining his ideas, Stanislavski was already a highly successful actor and director. His ideas were rooted in practice and observation. He wanted himself to learn. He watched good actors, and drew his conclusion about why they were convincing (and why lesser actors were not so). He talked to great actors of his time such as the Italian Salvini, and tried to find out what made them tick. He read voraciously in the memoirs of actors of the past, and he immersed himself in books on declamation, oratory, and the new phenomenon—psychology. He set out to find common denominators in all these fields.

He worked on the "unwritten language" of acting as a grammarian does—listening to the way native speakers and writers use a language and categorizing his findings. A grammarian does not dictate the way a language is used—he observes it. So instead of the more rigid words *system* or *method,* we prefer to call his ideas "a grammar of acting."

A knowledge of grammar never made anybody into a good writer—but it can help communication. Likewise, a knowledge of Stanislavski's ideas never made anyone into an actor who hadn't the talent and the temperament in the first place. At best it can only help a talent to express itself. We are minded of Roy Campbell's famous comment "On some South African Novelists":

> You praise the firm restraint with which they write—
> I'm with you there, of course;
> They use the snaffle and the bit all right—
> But where's the bloody horse?

Historically speaking, Stanislavski's system, or grammar, was born of necessity. He wanted to reform the theater of his time, just as Lenin was reforming the economy. What he saw around him appalled him.

He saw plays being under-rehearsed, and actors turning up just before curtain rise. What they did on stage had more to do with showing off than what we could call acting. They used the play to draw attention to their own personalities. They made entrances; once on, they made effects; and then they made exits. There were cliché ways of expressing emotions such as love and jealousy; and he noted, death was always expressed by clutching at the chest or tearing at the collar. Nothing resembled real life.

> They do not walk, they advance across the stage, they do not sit, they ensconce themselves, they do not lie down, they recline, they do not stand, they adopt a pose.

All this had to be changed.

Stanislavski's work should be seen as, at base, a reaction against the prevailing conditions of the time. In the same way, Brecht's famous "alienation effect," the dry, ironic, cool kind of acting that he advocated, was a reaction against the overblown, sentimental romantic kind of acting of people like Fritz Kortner, which was in the mode in Germany. (And Burbage's Hamlet, peaking like John-a-dreams, was a reaction against Alleyn's filling the stage with tears.)

Stories of the excessive means that Stanislavski used to get his results are often used against him.

To achieve a convincing ballroom scene, he once had the antechambers to the ballroom constructed offstage as far as the actors' dressing rooms. The moment they emerged the actors were instructed to start playing their part—greeting people, chatting people up, taking a drink or a *petit four,* and so on, for some ten minutes before they actually appeared on stage. All this ensured that they were in the right frame of mind when the public saw them; it stopped them "making an entrance."

On another occasion, he had been rehearsing *The Cherry Orchard* for some eight months, and continually refusing to let the actors "act" their lines: No, they were just to *say* them. At one point (Orson Welles tells this story[3]) one actor became so exasperated he ran amok. He screamed at his director "I'm going to KILL you!" and chased the great teacher three times round the auditorium of the theater until Stanislavski was forced to lock

---

[3] Preface to *He that Plays the King,* by Kenneth Tynan, 1950.

himself for safety in the ladies' powder room crying for help—"help which was," concludes Welles, "not immediately forthcoming."

Old stagers are amused by such stories. But anyone who has dealt with middle-aged actors set in their ways and who has asked them to reform will know how difficult it is. Reformers always have to go to extremes at first.

Since those days, Stanislavski's ideas and principles have filtered down through the profession, even reaching those who have scarcely heard of him. (Some countries—France, for instance—seem to get on quite well without him.)

It is salutary to remember how old Stanislavski's reforms are. Jean Benedetti, in his excellent biography, reveals that he was already setting out his ideas in 1906. It was 1922 when Richard Boleslavsky left the Moscow Arts and travelled to America, taking Stanislavski's early ideas with him. Central to his teaching at that time was the use of Emotional Memory. Boleslavsky was the teacher of the young Lee Strasberg.

In 1934, Stella Adler went to Paris, where Stanislavski was also staying, and worked with him intensively for five weeks. On her return she told Strasberg that Stanislavski was evolving—he no longer attached so much importance to the idea of Emotional Memory (a matter of thinking), giving precedence to what he called The Method of Physical Action (a matter of doing). Strasberg made the curious reply that he had already formed his "Method" and had no intention of altering it.

Confusion about Stanislavski's ideas was worse confounded by the piecemeal way his writings reached the West. He planned to produce his written System in three parts, the first of which dealt with Experience (i.e., Emotional Memory) and the second with Physical Characterization. A third volume would bear the fearsome title of *Work on a Role, the Creative State and the Unconscious.* His thesis was that the Unconscious is the source for an actor's inspiration. He was anxious that the System be taken as a whole, lest readers of the first part should judge it as being "ultra naturalistic."

His fears were justified. The volume on Experience *(An Actor's Work on Himself)* came out in 1936 as *An Actor Prepares*. For fourteen years this was thought of as the Stanislavski System. Only in 1950 did *Building a Character* (Physical Characterization) appear, and *Creating a Role* had to wait until 1961. By this time most people had made up their minds about Stanislavski.

Besides, there were problems about the American translation, about whose accuracy Dr. Benedetti (whose biography is the source of this information) has grave misgivings. Most foreign translations are based—he tells us—not on the original Russian, but on the version by Norman and Elizabeth Hapgood, to whom Stanislavski had given the world rights, together with permission to cut, edit, and if they thought it necessary, to rewrite, which they did, later claiming to be "co-authors" of the book. Dr Benedetti regrets this, pointing out that neither of the Hapgoods were working professionals, or had seen the System in action, and concludes:

> The omission of key passages and inconsistencies in the translations of basic terms result in a serious distortion of Stanislavski's thinking.[4]

We shall have to wait for a new translation to find out what he really thought. Those who haven't the patience can save time by consulting Dr. Benedetti's pleasantly slim book, *Stanislavski: An Introduction*. The author is himself a distinguished drama teacher; he knows Russian and has waded through all the relevant papers. He sets out clearly and readably what Stanislavski did, and did not say—and when.

((    ((    ((

---

[4] Jean Benedetti, *Stanislavski—A Biography*. Methuen, 1988.

Stanislavski was the first to give names to a number of work-processes in acting that had previously been unnamed—motivations, intentions, units and objectives, obstacles, subtext, circles of concentration, emotional memory, and so on. To his detractors these are jargon words that make the hackles rise: John Gielgud wrote of his experiences in America:

> ...I found a lot of my time was wasted by actors who wanted motivation for Shakespeare's supporting parts. If I said "You're just meant to support Hamlet" they were very hurt and cross.[5]

(We should remember that Stanislavski frequently said, "If my system doesn't help you, don't use it.") These work-process names, however ugly, often denote something quite simple and practical. They are not mere hocus-pocus, they are more in the nature of what instructors in weapon training call the "naming of parts." By looking at some of the principal terms we can see how useful they are in working on Shakespeare.

## EMOTIONAL MEMORY

No wonder this is looked on as Stanislavski's Great Discovery, the cornerstone of his reforms.

I used to possess a manual on acting published in the early 1900s. It was illustrated by photos of a distinguished old thespian demonstrating various facial expressions—rolling his eyes, biting his nether lip, jutting his chin, screwing up his eyes, and even nibbling his thumbnail, and frowning fiercely—he was showing how to play emotions like Scorn, Jealousy, Disdain, Anger, Suspicion.

So it was assumed that to learn to act, you copied other actors, and you imitated the outward forms of emotion. And it was also

---

[5] John Gielgud, *Shakespeare—Hit or Miss*, 1991.

assumed that an emotion (Joy, Sadness, Pity) was a clear-cut thing in itself.

Then along came Stanislavski, and told an actor who had to play Anger not to pretend or copy, but to dig into his memory and recall a time when he himself was angry, and to use that emotion—to investigate his own emotional past, and invoke his own feelings in similar circumstances to express the character's sentiments.

By so doing, he proved that Scorn, Jealousy, Disdain, and so on, did not exist as separate concepts. They were usually mixed: Joy and Sadness often came together; you could be jealous of someone you scorned.

And if you scorned someone, there was a reason for it, in the past—something once happened to ignite that scorn; and that scorn was linked to a *desire* in the present, which might be expressed as "I want that person to feel my scorn."

If the actor has an Emotional Memory then so does the Character. Stanislavski encouraged actors to build up an imaginary past for the roles they played—what sort of childhood they had, how was their early love life, how they earned their living until now.

People mock Stanislavski for this. But we must remember, he was trying to stop actors from playing stereotypes and to encourage them to play individuals, with a past, a present, and a future. Actors in those days often played types, they had what the French call their *emploi* (role-category, speciality)—Heavy Father, Handsome Young Soldier, Comic Servant. Stanislavski wanted them to be more specific—Whose father? and why is he heavy? He wanted actors to feel that his characters came from somewhere, and were going somewhere.

There is no doubt that Shakespeare's company also had their *emplois*. We meet any number of Heavy Fathers, Handsome Young Soldiers, and Comic Servants. But he gave them all touches of individuality. Brabantio is no Baptista; Hotspur is a far cry from Benedick; and Mistress Quickly is a totally different person from

Juliet's Nurse. From their own words we know that they had quite different pasts.

On the other hand I have known students waste a lot of time and energy on inventing pasts for Shakespeare's characters. To fill exercise books with essays on subjects like, Was Ophelia good at school? or What was Feste's love life? does not edge anyone an inch nearer to playing the part well. These questions are superfluous. They do not help to play a more "rounded" character. There's no answer to them in the text, so the questions can only lead to wild surmise. There's no mention in the plays of Mistress Quickly having a husband, so (if he exists) he doesn't take up any of her thoughts. Juliet's nurse, on the other hand, was married, she thinks of him with tenderness (" 'a was a merry man"), so he does merit a thought.

Actors can use their Emotional Memories for Shakespeare only up to a point. They are useful in the more everyday scenes: when the rude mechanicals are indulging in amateur dramatics, for instance, or the Montagues are revelling in the streets on their way to gate-crash a party at the Capulets. But for a lot of the time Shakespeare takes us among the peaks of human experience that have never before been explored, he asks actors to portray experiences that none of them has ever had.

How does it feel to be a deposed king, eighty years of age, and mad to boot, lost in a tempest with only a semi-idiot for company? How does a ghost feel who has spent all day roasting in hell-fire, and has only a few hours free at night? How many of us have ever killed a cat, let alone an old Lord Chancellor who's eavesdropping behind an arras, or a sleeping King of Scotland?

We have all known love—but not love to the degree that Juliet feels it. Some people have had mental troubles—but none to the extent of King Lear's.

Actors who, out of a misjudged respect for "truthfulness," want to bring the plays within the limits of their own personal emotional experiences, will make a sorry job of acting Shakespeare.

Stanislavski, too, recognized the limitations of his exercises on Emotional Memory. He realized that they were useful only in naturalistic situations. He emphasized that they were only part of the preliminary training of an actor. That is why later he went on to develop something that was quite the opposite, and which he called the method of physical action.

## THE METHOD OF PHYSICAL ACTION

Briefly, it consists of this: If an emotion is blocked, the actor must find a physical action to express it.

Imagine, a man comes home from work and his wife has to express her love for him.

She can express this love by taking his shoes off and putting on his slippers or by the way she hands him a cup of coffee or a drink.

Bertold Brecht wrote a whole poem about how Helena Weigel as Volumnia expressed her love for her son, Coriolanus, in the way she prepared him for war, buckling on his uniform and tying his cloak.

As can be seen this has nothing to do with *feeling* on the stage. The actress does not need to feel anything—she expresses the emotion by purely physical means, the way she handles the props, the way she touches her partner. And the audience receives the message far more clearly than if the actress was "emoting."

Indeed, the physical act often induces the emotion. Dancing can make us happy. Smashing something violently can put us in a mood of anger. Pascal pointed out that the act of dipping one's fingers in holy water and making the sign of the cross, on entering a church, was a way of inducing a feeling of reverence.

Those who think that acting is a matter first and foremost of feeling should remember the magic four words of Stanislavski's coeval, Kommissarjevsky:

of feeling should remember the magic four words of Stanislavski's coeval, Kommissarjevsky:

"Acting—not sentimental—physical!"

In Shakespeare, words and rhythms express the characters' feelings: They can also be used to *induce* the actors' feelings. The mere act of speaking physically the long dancing cadences of Rosalind, or the ponderous monosyllabic utterances of Othello, helps us to find the right emotional state.

## UNITS AND OBJECTIVES—ALAS!

Perhaps the most practical discovery Stanislavski made was his way of carving up a scene into what he called "Units" in each of which a character has a clear "Objective." Alas, his choice of basic terms is often ponderous and off-putting. It would be more friendly to say a scene is divided into "stages" and the character has a series of "aims" or "desires."

We can see how this works if we imagine a simple scenario: During a party John goes into the library and finds a dead body slumped over the desk; he goes to ring the police but the telephone's been cut off.

This incident breaks itself down into three "stages"—or "Units":

1) John enters the library. AIM: to look something up in a book. But—

2) John sees the body. AIM: to find out who it is, and if the victim's really dead.

3) John rings the police. AIM: to find the right telephone number, and to dial it calmly.

Any actor can see that each stage has its own rhythm, or mood. John might enter jauntily, or merrily: This would depend on the party he has just abandoned, and on what he needs to look up. The sight of the corpse changes the mood: Unless he's a doctor or a policeman, he will approach the body warily. Hunting for the telephone number (where? in a diary? or a thick telephone book?) will probably have an urgency about it. (Stanislavski was very insistent on the difference of rhythms within a scene.)

The advantage of these separate "aims" is to *clear the actor's mind*. It gives him one thing to do at a time. For instance, every actor knows the difficulty of entering the stage, especially when it is one's first entrance in the play. The mind gets bombarded with irrelevant thoughts—about one's appearance, about the audience, about making an impact. John-the-actor might be thinking, "Oh God, this is the scene where I find the body…I never got this right in rehearsals…I think my mother's in row five…is my tie straight?" Stanislavski had a remedy for all that. He told his actors not to worry about such things, but to give themselves one simple physical action to do when entering (like looking for a book), and to concentrate on that. Instead of "physical action" he often used the word "task."

In the opening scene of *Othello* Iago has the "task" of persuading Roderigo that he (Iago) hates the Moor, and therefore can be trusted; that accomplished, half way through the scene he has another "task"—to get Roderigo to wake up Desdemona's father and make him take action against Othello.

A role, then, is composed of a series of aims, or tasks ("Objectives") that the actor is encouraged to define as in the first person singular:

I want to…convince Roderigo that I hate Othello;
I want to…urge him to upset Brabantio;

and so on. The actor is not asked to "act evil" or to "be bitter" or even "to entertain the audience" but to take the character's point of view, and make the character's "wants" his own.

Of course, this way of thinking drives actors to play together, since "I want…" is usually connected to the person addressed: "I want to make you feel ashamed…," "I want you to kill the King," "I want to take you down a peg," or even, "I want to share a story with you."

Stanislavski also invented something he called "the Super-Objective," which can be defined as the character's Main Aim in Life. This is harder to pin down. Getting it wrong can ruin your performance. He tells how he was playing Molière's comedy *The Imaginary Invalid (Le Malade imaginaire)* and he gave himself the Super-Objective "I want to be ill." The result was a gloomy performance that amused nobody. Suddenly he realized that he had made a mistake. His Super-Objective should have been "I want *people to think* I am ill"—which is more appropriate to a comic hypochondriac. The performance came to life.

Choosing a Super-Objective for your Shakespeare character is a certain way of barking up the wrong tree. Certainly we can attribute to Richard III "I want to be King" or, to Justice Shallow "I want to remember the old days," but these are obvious from the text. A Super-Objective is interesting for an actor when it embodies a *secret* desire that governs his behavior ("I want people to think I am ill" or "I want to be admired by everyone"), and can be useful when an author has not provided all the details.

But the very idea of a Super-Objective suggests defining the character from the outset; it suggests that there is a key to be found that will unlock the character's secrets; it suggests that the actor has a conception of the part and that he knows where he is going. We have tried to show earlier how limiting preconceived ideas can be. A conception can be as confining as a straitjacket.

Shakespeare's major creations are all characters in whom the opposite poles of human behavior co-exist. Hamlet is both philosopher and man of action; King Lear contains both a mighty monarch and a little child; Richard II a vainglorious tyrant and a nowhere-man; Prospero admits that he is a battlefield where his Reason and his Fury fight it out. The interest, and the challenge, for the actor, is to explore these extremes. Their very inconsistency is what makes them worthy of our attention—you cannot clap a simple Super-Objective upon them, they are not the guy next door.

As for the minor roles, as any old actor can tell you, some of them have not enough individuality to be given a Super-Objective. These are the roles whose players irritated Gielgud by asking for their "motivation"—although perhaps the knight had been less touchy if the actor had asked "What's my task in this scene?" or "What's my function?"

The drawback of Stanislavski's basic terms, like Objectives and Super-Objectives, is that they presuppose a self-awareness that the character does not have. A man may go through his life "wanting to be loved" without ever defining it for himself. The hypochondriac certainly "wants other people to think he is ill," but would he ever admit it? So the actor knows things about the character that the character himself does not know. The *actor* may conclude that "Iago is in love with Othello" (a proposition first put forward by an eminent Freudian specialist in the thirties and seized upon by the young Laurence Olivier when he played Iago), but the *character* Iago is certainly not aware of it.

Stanislavski has a tendency to encourage the actor to be the psychologist, and the role his patient. Just as Freud said to a woman who dreamed of a black hat, "You were thinking of funerals, because you want your husband to die," so the actor can say to his role "You do such-and-such a thing *because* your Super Objective is…" and the whole thing is not only explained, but explained away. Yet how many actors have a deep enough knowledge of psychology to be sure they are right?

Even breaking up a scene (or a play) into a series of "aims" can be dangerous. Can we always define our own intentions, or motivations, for all our actions? Don't we do a great number of things on *impulse?*

Harold Pinter is often asked by actors "why" they say a certain line, or behave in a certain way. After all he's the author. His reply is categorical. "I have no idea *why* he says that line, I only know that he says it." We think Shakespeare would have made a similar reply; and if questioned about a character's Main Aim in Life would observe a discreet silence.

Stanislavski, to encourage his actors to behave more naturally, encouraged them to imagine a character's past, and create for them an Emotional Memory; and to give them a future—a Super-Objective (sometimes he used the word "perspective"). Many of his disciples enlarge upon this. The danger is that they push students into spending a lot of time looking backwards and looking forwards and so they neglect what is happening in the present: what is actually happening on stage.

Chekhov's characters sit around in their country houses, in a sort of betwixt-and-between time: Their memories are still alive for them ("It's exactly a year since Father died…"), and they feed on hopes of the future ("…wait, Uncle Vanya, wait. We shall rest…"). It's as though they are sitting in a waiting room. Shakespeare's characters, on the other hand, live in the here and now. If their past life is still important (as with Othello and Henry IV), they talk about it!, but the past is another country. The distant future scarcely concerns them. Even Macbeth sees it as a series of "tomorrows." They live from day to day.

Shakespeare shows them at the actual moment of struggling with great emotions, tempest-tossed by the storms of life—jealousy, madness, love, murder, lust, warfare. In these cases they can only live in the present, grapple with the crises, and hope to survive.

## THE MAGIC "IF"

This was a phrase Stanislavski created to stimulate an actor's imagination. He should ask himself, "What would I do *if* I were in the circumstances that my character is?" That is to say, the actor knows he's in a play, wearing a crown made by the props department, and sitting on a wooden throne painted to look gold, and facing another actor who has a drink problem—in short, it is all artifice; but *what if…?*

Most actors nowadays do this without knowing of the formula, but we must remember that Stanislavski in his youth was working with actors who borrowed emotions rather than use their own, and who probably started with externals rather than with feelings.

The phrase has been misunderstood by many, who think that he suggested that the actor should somehow identify with the role: "What if I were Romeo/Juliet/Mercutio…?" whereas Stanislavski wrote about the "circumstances," the situation. A thorough study of a character's circumstances, the demands made on him, the pressures put upon him, the threats he undergoes, can never be amiss. How many drama teachers have to repeat, time and again, "Don't play the character, play the situation!"

The character reveals itself in the way it reacts to the situation. Acting is chiefly a question of *re*-acting. The stimulus comes from outside. Someone knocks at your door: Do you answer it or not? Yes, if you're at ease; no—if you think that someone threatening is outside.

Hamlet, when visited by his father's ghost and urged to avenge his murder, is presented with a problem—to do the ghost's bidding, or not? How he reacts to this stimulus makes up the play.

The introduction of the concept "I" often blocks an actor. "I would never react like Lady Macbeth," said a student once, "I cannot understand how anyone could urge her husband to commit murder," yet she does, and the role has to be played. The director said, "You would never do such a thing, no, but you might know someone who would. She might be your best friend. Try and find out what pushed her—and show us. Defend her. Be her advocate—her spokeswoman. Of course *you* are not like Lady Macbeth. But forget 'you.' "

The actress, with the pressure taken off, was able to work at her ease. She had shed her self-consciousness.

# DID HE, OR DIDN'T HE?

Since the end of the last century we have learned to distrust what people say on stage. In Chekhov characters frequently aver that they are happy or sad when they are not, that they love and respect their wives when patently this is not so. Eugene O'Neill wrote a play in which people speak their public thoughts behind masks, and their private thoughts when the mask is dropped. Harold Pinter's characters frequently recount their past lives, or even incidents of yesterday, with such inconsistency that we do not know whether to believe them or not—and moreover we shall never know, and it is time-wasting to ask what is true or false. But a lie detector set to monitor their utterances would, we suspect, be bleeping all the time.

In Shakespeare's theater, however, that lie detector would go off only when expected—after a character (Iago, Autolycus, Richard III) had announced to the audience, through an aside, that he was not to be trusted and was about to "dissemble."

> SHYLOCK: *(Aside.)*
> How like a fawning publican he looks!
> I hate him, for he is a Christian ...
> BASSANIO:
> Shylock, do you hear?
> SHYLOCK:
> I am debating of my present store,
> And, by the near guess of my memory
> I cannot instantly raise up the gross
> Of full three thousand ducats...

Did people not lie in those days? Assuredly—Henry V talks of the Agincourt soldier who will "remember *with advantages/* What feats he did that day." But the unspoken contract between the playwright and the public was simpler: Characters are telling the truth unless otherwise stated. When Jacques says "A fool! a fool! I met a fool i' the forest," we can be sure he did; if a Pinter character had said it, we would take it with a pinch of salt.

Before the 1890s, language in the theater was used to express a character's thoughts; afterwards, increasingly, it has become perceived as a smokescreen, to hide them.

In Vienna Freud was making great discoveries in the realm of psychology, and revealed the existence of the Unconscious. In Shakespeare's time Sir Toby Belch could ask "Does not our life consist of the four elements?"—a reference to Empedocles' belief that we are composed of Fire, Air, Earth, and Water; to which Freud would have replied, "No—we are made up of the Id, the Ego and the Superego." Inside man, other hidden beings were determining his conduct.

For writers such as Chekhov, who was also a doctor, the discovery of the Unconscious was like the discovery of the X-ray. It opened up whole new ways of understanding human beings. Instead of stating everything, they could dare to understate. No wonder Chekhov, correcting one of his plays, crossed out a whole long speech wherein a character describes his unhappy marriage, and replaced it by the simple words: "A wife is a wife." He dared to use the banalities of everyday speech in his plays, while giving us to understand that the real drama was happening between the characters on a different level—something unspoken.

Stanislavski too, who was passionately interested in the latest developments of psychology, set the Unconscious as the root of creative art:

> the Subconscious, (he calls it) which constitutes nine-tenths
> of the life of a character, its most valuable part…

Later he compares it to:

...the core of the earth, where you find molten lava and fire, invisible human instincts are raging. That is the realm of the superconscious *[sic]*, that is the lifegiving centre, that is the sacrosanct 'I' of the actor, the artist-human, that is the secret source of inspiration.[6]

He appears to believe that the Conscious and the Unconscious were two separate things. As in the plays of O'Neill, they speak with different voices. As in Chekhov, the Conscious voice says (aloud) "I love and respect my wife," and the Unconscious says (unheard) "I'm bored stiff with her." To the silent voice of thought he gave the name "Subtext." The Subtext often contradicts the text.

Actors were taught to say one thing and convey another; audiences were encouraged to listen for these hidden meanings. And many playwrights have since his time written in full awareness that their dialogue expresses only a tenth of what is really going on—and screenwriters even less.

Shakespeare however worked at a time when explicit dialogue was the mode. He certainly differentiated between a character's public and private utterances—Hamlet in company shows a different aspect of himself from Hamlet in his soliloquies; Iago wears a mask of honesty and bonhomie in public that he drops when he is alone—but if his characters have secret thoughts, they share them with us in asides (as Shylock does).

So text and subtext (if any) are one. The Shakespeare actor is recommended to *act the text*: He who tries to convey a contradictory meaning to it is fighting a losing battle. The character has no thoughts except those expressed in the words (unless he is silent). Just as a good horseman is the one who seems to form an entity with his mount, so the good Shakespearean actor is the one who rides his text like a horse.

---

[6] Konstantin Stanislavski, *Creating a Role*. Theater Arts, 1936.

Stanislavski admitted himself that he never mastered the verse speaking. The superimportance of the words (and not the pauses between them) was evidently something he underestimated.

So, is Stanislavski a help or a hindrance? Practice shows that when he breaks a play or a scene down into "units" or "stages," he clears the actor's mind. We have seen how many a speech yields up its shape and inner tension when divided into parts (argument for—argument against—conclusion).

He is useful when he reminds the actor that he has a *task* on stage in any given scene, and also when he demands that the task should be summed up in an active verb—to persuade, to blame, to accuse, to convince, to change someone's mind, to make a choice, to shock, to challenge, to encourage, to rally an army, to refute an argument, to disturb, to comfort, to discover…

But when he encourages the actor to put his character on the psychoanalyst's couch, and, applying a little imperfectly understood psychology, to pose irrelevant questions about its past or its Main Aim in Life, he only clogs the mind—and is as irritating as the child who interrupts his mother's bedtime story, "Once upon the time there was a King and a Queen…"—"Mummy, were they happy? Where did they live? Did they have any children?"

For Shakespeare's basic concern, to keep his audience's interest, was to tell a story; and what was important was, What happened next? Not what happened twenty years before, or what would happen twenty years later.

Stanislavski may be imperfectly understood, (and no doubt Russians who have been his pupils, or his pupils' pupils, will give a different account of his system from those in the West who know about him only from books, or from acting teachers who have read some of his books), but for most of his adherents he signifies an approach whereby the actor draws on his own personal experience to feed the character's emotional states.

But any attempt to do this in Shakespeare only trivializes the character. I heard a famous actor say on television, "I can understand Hamlet's difficulties with Ophelia, I've had problems with my girlfriend too"; and an actress, who claimed "When my husband was too afraid to go to his boss and ask for a raise, I had to tear a strip off him—oh yes, I know how Lady Macbeth feels"— these artists risk telling us more about their personal life story than about Shakespeare's characters.

Our Emotional Memory is too poor and everyday to take us far into the crises that beset Shakespeare's creations. The most it can do is to help us conjure up *images* connected to single words: night, forest, moon, sun, music, dreams, dagger, blood, sea, storm, mother, son…

Stanislavski, as Mel Goodman said, shifted the center of the play from the author to the actor. The actor became more important than the play, and his own feelings predominant.

This of course leads to excesses of self-indulgence. We get pretty Miss X who excuses herself from doing her Juliet scene today, as she doesn't "feel" it this morning; or Mr. Y who says, no, thank you, he won't rehearse his Macbeth soliloquies beforehand, he'll wait until the performance, when he's "in the mood" and then see where they take him—and, he warns us, they might be different every night according to how he "feels"; and Mr. Z, playing Horatio, who replays his own feelings about a friend who died, and gets so upset by the death of Hamlet that the lines

Good night, sweet prince,
And flights of angels sing thee to thy rest.

are so choked with sobs as to be inaudible.

The idea has come about that if an actor brings out his own "feelings," like a set of old clothes, and makes them fit the character's, he is acting "truthfully"; if not, he's faking it.

Truthful, one might ask, to what? to his own limited experience—or to Shakespeare's vision?

Shakespeare was not primarily writing plays about people's feelings—he was showing how they face up to crises in their lives; he writes down what they DO and THINK and MIGHT HAVE SAID. Their feelings exist only as a spur to further action.

Nor was he writing plays about humdrum everyday life in fourteenth-century Verona or prehistoric Britain, in Illyria or Bohemia (wherever they were), he was writing fables, fairy stories, legends, myths—quite comprehensible on one level, but on another, totally mysterious and evading explanations. His character could be human and down-to-earth one minute, and the next—totally superhuman. It helps to think of his plays as dreams, visions, nightmares. (An actor might draw on the Emotional Memory of his nightmares.)

In dreams, the dead walk again, friends become enemies, strangers become lovers; we can meet our doubles, fly like birds, speak with the tongues of angels; drown—and yet see the bottom of the deep; fall off cliffs, and live; survive shipwreck and hellfire; go blind, or mad.

It is often said that Shakespeare "put himself" into Prospero, the retiring enchanter, in his last play, *The Tempest*—when he said "we are such stuff / As *dreams* are made on." So in his early, lighthearted days, he was Puck, everywhere present, nowhere visible, setting lovers asunder and uniting the grossest of mortals with the gossamer fairy Queen, and finally begging us to consider "this weak and idle theme (as) No more yielding than a *dream*."

And in his middle period, he was the Chorus of *Henry V*, the "bending author…with rough and all unable pen"—urging his audiences to "Suppose…" "Imagine…" "Entertain conjecture…," working on their "imaginary forces," asking them to "Eke out our performance with your mind"—encouraging his public to *dream*.

Stanislavski claimed that his system was based on the fact that the source of an actor's inspiration lay deep down in the human psyche, in "the molten lava beneath the earth's crust"—the Unconscious.

If he had known Shakespeare's "supernatural" works better, he would have seen the embodiment and ocular proof of his idea. But in practice, Stanislavski remained irremediably realistic. And his first English biographer,[7] David Magarshack, was probably right when he said that Shakespeare's plays were "beyond his grasp."

[7] David Magarshack, *Stanislavski—A Life*. MacGibbon and Kee, 1950.

Conclusion
# SHAKESPEARIENCE

In 1936 the Shakespeare Festival Theatre at Stratford-upon-Avon (it wasn't yet the Royal Shakespeare Company) courageously invited a distinguished Russian actress to play Cleopatra. The audience had a confusing evening, largely due to the opacity of Mme. Leontovich's accent. *The Times* next morning titled its review "O Weederdee," because at the moment of Antony's death, at which Cleopatra is understandably heartbroken, the critic heard her say:

> O weederdee degardlano devar;
> Desolderspo lees falln; yong boisenguls
> Alefelnow wimen.

Checking on the play afterwards, he found that Shakespeare had written:

> O wither'd is the garland of the war;
> The soldier's pole is fallen; young boys and girls
> Are level now with men.

(Even in English this needs unravelling: It helps to know that "garland" suggests glory, and that "pole" probably refers to the polestar. So the audience gets three little images of an army in confusion, where no values hold no more.)

Apparently this Cleopatra talked like this the whole evening, so however much emotion she put into her playing, it all *went for nothing*, since her "sound track" was not working properly.

A lot of attention has been given in the preceding chapters to Shakespeare's way of writing and his use of words. This should not give the impression that acting Shakespeare is *only* a matter of speaking and making the sense clear, but it is the key that opens the front door. Not because he is a classic, or that his language is in any way "holy," but because it's the words that do the work, as the notes do the work in music. The language is the cathode-ray tube that brings the actor's emotions home to the viewer, and if there's snow on the screen, the viewer wants to turn his TV off.

Lenin once claimed that the whole of history can be summed up in two words: "Who whom?" meaning "Who did what to whom?" Speaking of Shakespeare's plays we might use the same phrase, adapting it to mean "Who said what to whom?"

He rarely invented plots (Dover Wilson says that only three of his plays have plots invented by the author). He adapted freely from familiar stories and legends, and he adapted from history books. If we want to catch him at work, we can see how he took this, from Plutarch's *Life of Antony:*

> O noble Emperor, how cometh it to pass that you trust these vile brittle ships? What, do you mistrust these wounds of mine and this sword? Let the Egyptians and Phoenicians fight by sea, and set us on the mainland, where we use to conquer, or be slain on our feet.

and, in *Antony and Cleopatra,* turned it into this:

O noble Emperor, do not fight by sea.
Trust not to rotten planks. Do you misdoubt
This sword and these my wounds? Let th'Egyptians
And the Phoenicians go a-ducking; we
Have used to conquer standing on the earth
And fighting foot to foot.

Look how muscled the second one is, and how flabby the first. Would those who wish to "modernize" Shakespeare prefer the Plutarch? Yet the Latin translation was published in 1579, sixteen years before Shakespeare wrote the play—another proof that he was not writing "Elizabethan English," but inventing a theater language of his own. (No wonder that Anthony Burgess advances the theory that Shakespeare was one of a group of poets brought in to polish up the style of the new translation of The Bible, published in 1610—the so-called King James's Version, the one that is still in use.)

Once the actor has mastered the art of speaking Shakespeare *as though it's* his natural way of speaking (he shouldn't play it as if speaking a foreign language; nor should he mumble and hesitate or chop up the sentences as he probably would in daily life), and once he has discovered the arguments that the speaker defends, he has fulfilled the first stage of Shakespearean acting. Then he can go on to the *second* stage—finding the emotions, playing the predicament and bringing the character to life—which are the normal occupations of an actor.

Nothing has been said in these pages about the physical side of acting Shakespeare—stance, movement, gesture—even though he was a very physical playwright. If his Globe Theatre had had an acting school attached, a lot of classes would have been devoted to dancing, fencing, battle fighting, and dying—at all of which his company was obviously adept. (Hamlet, after five acts of playing exhausting emotional situations and dramatic soliloquies, ends with a sword fight—no wonder Gertrude complains that her son is "scant of breath"!) There might also have been extra classes for the youngsters on how to move like a woman, and how to portray aëry spirits (Puck, Ariel), and even lessons, led by Shakespeare himself, on how to play ghosts.

The acting classes proper would have been concentrated on speaking, audibility, and breath control; it is unlikely that any time would have been spent on "reliving childhoods" or on improvization... ("Let those that play your clowns speak no more than is set down for them" warned Hamlet, in his author's voice; just as Donald Wolfit, a Titanic King Lear four centuries later, darkly warned another actor embarking on the same role: "Watch your fool!")

There is nothing hard-and-fast to be said about Shakespearean movement; except to say that I have seen French productions of Shakespeare where they treated him like Racine—immobile, intellectual—conversations between groups of statues. Since Shakespeare's characters are not statues (which idealize their subject), nor even figures in opera (also ennobled, and frequently immobile), but human beings, with their own weaknesses and individualities and appetites, the approach was misguided.

Movement depends on clothes. Luckily the idea is dying out that Shakespeare should of necessity be played in Elizabethan or medieval costumes. (Heavy costumes make for heavy performances, and designers can quite destroy actors' work by weighing them down with heavy velvets and armour, all in the name of some irrelevant "authenticity.") Even the idea of resetting Shakespeare in other specific periods of history—a pre-World War One *Troilus and Cressida,* a French Revolution *Richard II,* or a *Julius Caesar* set in Fascist Italy—is now looking old-fashioned. Directors nowadays feel more free, realizing that the plays have more the nature of myths than chronicles of historical life.

Whatever choice the director makes, it is important to rehearse from the beginning in parts of the costumes, or something like them. Women move differently in blue jeans than in crinolines; men hold themselves otherwise in togas than in blousons. (The English actor, Michael Gambon, when playing a king, insists on rehearsing in a suit.)

Footwear is especially important. If boots are to be worn in performance, they should be worn in rehearsal—you cannot rehearse playing a soldier in sneakers, nor can actresses be fleet of foot in high heels or platform soles. Rehearsing with the right shoes or boots is especially important for the Violas and Rosalinds and Portias, the ladies who disguise themselves as men. The appropriate footwear is essential because it establishes the actor's contact *with the ground,* and it affects the whole dynamism of movement.

For similar reasons, actors should insist on working with sticks, swords, gloves, fans, and hats from an early stage: They are an extension of the actor's body. It's no use the Assistant Stage Manager promising "the props will be there for the dress rehearsal"—this is too late.

Talking about props, Antony Sher made theatrical history when he played Richard III at Stratford-upon-Avon in 1984. He was haunted by the image of the evil king as "that bottled spider,"[1] and examining the kind of deformity that Richard may have suffered from, he decided to play the role on two crutches. Far from being a handicap, these gave him virtually four legs, and enabled him to scuttle about the stage like some horrid insect at double the speed of a normal person. With these extended arms he could grip an opponent by the neck, or lift the skirts of a female prey. In a gripping book about his preparation for the role,[1] he tells how much trial and error went into the fabrication of his crutches. Wooden ones kept breaking, and the only material strong and light enough turned out to be the tubular metal used in the manufacture of bicycles. These "props" opened the way to a surprising new interpretation of the role.

---

[1] Antony Sher, *The Year of the King,* 1985.

It has been impossible for us to generalize about Shakespeare's writing, or his approach to character, or the speaking of his lines, or what constitutes Shakespearean acting; but here, at the last, we may risk a generalization: However Shakespeare is performed, whether traditionally or experimentally, on stage or on screen, he is a writer who demands physical, not sentimental, self-indulgent, actors. The plays are ongoing—they do not stop to bathe in "atmosphere;" the speeches are ongoing—they build to climaxes; the language is outgoing—its object is to work on the imagination of the audience—so audibility and clarity are at a premium; and the ideal Shakespeare actor is one who not only believes in the (theatrical) reality of the situations he or she is enacting, but who uses talent and imagination to *share* that belief with the audience.

《　　《　　《

We have tried to picture Shakespeare in his time, an observant young man with a prodigal gift for juggling words at a time when the English language was a melting pot, arriving in London just as the theater industry was starting to flourish, and taking this affair "at the tide," providing the managers with exactly the dramatic material they needed and thus becoming the major English playwright during the twenty years that bridged the end of the sixteenth and the beginning of the seventeenth centuries.

But were he no more than that, he would be a mere chapter in theater history, a bust in the theater museum, like his contemporaries Marlowe and Jonson, his career over.

> Thou thy worldly task hast done,
> Home art gone and ta'en thy wages.

(Cymbeline)

Only Shakespeare has not gone home and is still earning wages for millions of theater people. As Mike Todd remarked, after a visit to Stratford, "He's been dead for hundreds of years, and he's still making money!"

It's as if there are two Shakespeares—the one, the local hero, who stopped writing when his theater was burned to ashes; and the other who, phoenixlike, survived the fire and is still produced and reinterpreted the world over. This is the writer whom Peter Brook compared to a planet, constantly circling the earth and revealing to every new generation a new face; and the one whom Jan Kott called boldly "our contemporary," the playwright who by looking back at past times discovered a pattern for times to come, who understood so well how the machinery of history and politics worked that his plays about kings and emperors seem like works of prediction. Knowing how men behave when they achieve power, he seemed to forecast the relationships between rulers and their peoples in the centuries to come. And when writing about ordinary people, who have no "power," he knew the currents and eddies that determine the course of love, jealousy, betrayal, ambition, old age, and death, as well as he knew the mysterious movements of the water in his native River Avon.

Furthermore, the busy dramatist knew that his works would live on. Without an ounce of conceit, he could probably lay down his pen after a session of writing with a sigh of "This is good stuff."

> How many ages hence
> Shall this our lofty scene be acted over,
> In states unborn, and accents yet unknown!
>
> (*Julius Caesar:* III.1)

says Cassius. Cleopatra is less optimistic about future productions of the play about her:

> The quick comedians
> Extemporally will stage us, and present

Our Alexandrian revels. Antony
Shall be brought drunken forth, and I shall see
Some squeaking Cleopatra boy my greatness
I'th' posture of a whore.

(Antony and Cleopatra: V.2)

About his Sonnets, Shakespeare had more faith:

Not marble, nor the gilded monuments
Of princes, shall outlive this powerful rhyme…

He was writing both for his current audiences and readers, *and* for posterity. The two Shakespeares co-existed.

The more one looks at him, the more everything about him seems to be twofold. The idea of duality runs through his works. Two is a magic number. Not only did words occur to him in couples (as we have seen)—life/death, day/night, black/white, calm/storm, man/beast; but characters too—the plays are full of pairs: brothers, close friends, fathers, identical twins, identical spies (Rosencrantz and Guildenstern), sisters, girls brought up together "like to a double cherry," murderers, merry wives. There are Two Noble Kinsmen and Two Gentlemen of Verona, besides the pairs of lovers—Romeo and Juliet, Troilus and Cressida, Antony and Cleopatra. In a battle scene of Henry VI Part Three, he balances the lamentations of "a son that hath killed his father" and "a father who has killed his son."

And because one of the Leitmotifs in his plays is "appearances are misleading"—which was probably a new and surprising idea in his time when someone's physiognomy was believed to be a guide to character—he makes great dramatic play with brothers who look alike but are in essence as different as chalk from cheese: Edgar/Edmund, Hamlet's father/Claudius, Duke Frederick/Duke in exile. To seem is not to be: "Seems, madame? Nay, it is; I know not 'seems'.," says Hamlet. Death seems like sleep, but is not so. Hamlet's madness is put on, but Ophelia's is genuine. Iago's "honesty" is fake, but makes Cassio's look like dishonesty, just as the player's acted passion makes Hamlet's real anguish look unconvincing. Pretence often looks more real than truth—no wonder his wooden theater with its painted "Heavens" and "Hell" in the cellarage, pretended to represent the globe.

With all this duality in his writings it is not surprising that his life was full of paradoxes. The solitary playwright-actor, a center point in the hubbub of metropolitan theater could metamorphose into the Warwickshire countryman who enjoyed the company of friends and family in the peace of his garden. Egoless and almost anonymous in his public writings, he could in his private Sonnets share with his readers his most intimate thoughts. Capable in his plays of attaining the highest flights of poetry when writing about death, when his own death was imminent he was content to pen a few lines of doggerel.

His theater too is paradoxical. His plays are as unashamedly theatrical as musical comedies. The action takes place both where the scene is set *and* on the stage of the theater; and the actor is both the character he or she represents, *and* a player in a play.

The last word on Shakespeare can never be said. As long as we look for unity, he will continue to baffle us, for we shall only find a mass of contradictions. Perhaps this is what keeps his plays alive today.

Afterword by Michael York

# STAY ILLUSION:
# SHAKESPEARE ON FILM

*You see, the film studio of today is really the palace of the sixteenth century. There one sees what Shakespeare saw.*

Christopher Isherwood
*Prater Violet,* 1945

How Shakespeare would have loved the cinema! It would have added new, unfettered wings to a soaring imagination that already operated in terms of images, and expanded his Olympian worldview, turning the entire globe into his playhouse. His declamatory Chorus would have metamorphosed into a murmuring voice-over narrator and the "alarums and excursions" of the action scenes would have assumed an exhilarating verisimilitude. No doubt the close-up canine charms of Launce's dog, Crab, would have rivaled those of Lassie, and one can only speculate as to the sensational new value it would have given to that famous stage direction: "Exit pursued by a bear!"

It could be said that, albeit involuntarily and instinctively, Shakespeare wrote screenplays. They are acted without intermission with a "two-hour traffic" that approximates the length of the average feature film. Their ability to swiftly shift from scene to scene, from exterior to interior, from close-up monologue to panning crowd scene, has a cinematic sense. In the films of his plays, little is left to the imagination; such key words as "suppose" and "think," indispensable for his theater, are made thrillingly redundant on screen. Polonius would surely have approved of their charged brevity, of their ability to encompass entire lives from birth to death, "turning many years / Into an hour-glass."

Today, cinema has become the most popular cultural medium and it goes without saying that one of the world's most popular authors is well served by this "brightest heaven of invention." His plays, with their mythic, timeless quality, charismatic heros and forthright heroines, their romance and tragedy, historical sweep and slapstick humour, have adapted well to the screen. Just as the "O" configuration of his theater focused dramatic energy, so the same-shaped lens performs a similar function, but with an added kinetic mobility, for motion pictures primarily create a visual as well as an aural experience.

If, as John Dryden maintained, "The fury of (Shakespeare's) fancy often transported him beyond the bounds of judgement" then the cinema would have provided a perfect means for such aesthetic zooming. Film is the cutting-edge, yet still evolving, arbiter of taste and its appeal and ambition are boundless. It also has the ability to fragment the old unities of time, place, and action. And not just on screen. Orson Welles, for example, could patiently cobble together his *Othello* over the course of years and in many disparate locations, depending on how much money happened to be put currently in his indigent purse.

One of the films that first fired my ambition to become an actor was Laurence Olivier's version of *Henry V.* Amidst the grey gloom of postwar socialist England, its colors and gallantry dazzled and uplifted. The film pays homage to its origins, beginning in the painted, stage-set confines of a packed Globe Theatre and then—"by some illusion see thou bring her here"—cutting into the open, real world of war, where the Muse of Fire is shown in profligate creativity. The thrum of a thousand airborne arrows mixes with the clash of knightly steel on steel as Olivier's warrior king takes on a bold iconic image of chivalry.

He is larger than life at such moments and yet the camera can also quietly dolly in to capture those intimate moments that reveal him as a conflicted, conscience-stricken man. William Walton's majestic score both accompanies and identifies this transition, demonstrating how music, so significant in Shakespeare's plays, is equally important in his films. By harmonizing with, and underscoring, the tempo of the lens changes, it can add immeasurably to the dramatic life of a movie in which, to borrow from Caliban, "Sometimes a thousand twangling instruments / Will hum about my ears, and sometimes voices."

I was fortunate to make my debut as a film actor at a fairly youthful age when there was much to be learned and relatively little to be unlearned. As I have recorded earlier, the occasion was Franco Zeffirelli's film of *The Taming of the Shrew*. As the reigning god and goddess of the silver screen, Richard Burton and Elizabeth Taylor were incarnating Petruchio and Katherine. There was no question of our cinematic lights being hid under modest bushels. All the heavy machinery of the old-fashioned studio system ground into action, ensuring that "the bubble reputation" entirely encapsulated our enterprise. It seemed to involve literally hundreds of people: even in the screenplay, which was credited to three writers other than its "onlie begetter," that scribe with an already respectable Hollywood track record, Will Shakespeare.

It was perhaps no coincidence that in 1929 *The Taming of the Shrew* should serve as a star vehicle for filmdom's first most famous couple, Mary Pickford and Douglas Fairbanks. There was a silent version and then a "talkie" with, in dreadful premonition of Hollywood's multi-authorial penchant, "additional dialogue by Sam Taylor." From its flickering, hand-tinted infancy, the screen had embraced the Bard, his first film apparently being *King John* in 1899 with Herbert Beerbohm Tree as its ill-starred "star."

"Strange to see Beerbohm Tree at last," Adrian recently remarked on viewing the remaining celluloid fragment. "Big Eisenstein-like acting! Silent film was a good medium for him, as he could never remember his lines anyway."

This choice of Shakespeare by the fledgling medium might have suggested that it was attempting to elevate itself with cultural pretensions from a popular craze to serious "art." However, as in the playhouse, so in the movie house, he appealed across all barriers to intellectual and ignoramus alike. Above all he told great stories inhabited by extravagant characters and situations. This explains, perhaps, the success of one of the earliest silent films, a 1912 version of *Richard III,* with its mesmerizingly monstrous hero. It is a measure of Shakespeare's genius in constructing memorable plots and parts that the film succeeds despite its lack of spoken dialogue. It was left to Ian McKellen, in his recent "fascist" updating of the work, with its battle tanks and machine guns, to give the great, final cry "My kingdom for a horse" a startling—and audible—new resonance.

In 1915 there was a melding of traditions, of new world showmanship and old world style, when D.W. Griffith presented Beerbohm Tree in *Macbeth.* Twenty years later, this crossbreeding continued when the great Max Reinhardt, an icon of European respectability with a German *Richard III* already under his belt, directed his only sound film, *A Midsummer Night's Dream,* with those icons of Hollywood popularity, James Cagney, Joe E. Brown, Olivia De Havilland, Dick Powell, and Mickey Rooney. It was a palpable hit, whereas *As You Like It* with another Austrian, Elizabeth Bergner, and a youthful Laurence Olivier, was *not* as most people liked it. Later, in 1953, newfangled American "Method" acting personified by Marlon Brando, and Old School British thespianism in the shape of John Gielgud, met flared nostril to venerable proboscis in Joseph Mankiewicz's cinematic version of *Julius Caesar.*

By then, Shakespeare had inspired the cinema worldwide: *Throne of Blood* could have been his subtitle for *Macbeth* and was indeed Akira Kurosawa's apt choice for his Samurai-style version of the play. Soviet Russia, motherland of the malevolent, manipulative, strong man, made several versions of "Shekspirovski's" *Othello*—a role that Emil Jannings also filmed in Germany. *Forbidden Planet*—a sci-fi, futuristic version of *The Tempest*—featured Ariel as a robot. As for *Hamlet,* there have been over sixty versions, and counting. That old-fashioned dead white male writing with a feather is again hot in Hollywood. A crook-backed Al Pacino has recently been "Looking for Richard" while Kenneth Branagh, planning a series of films from the Canon, is currently brushing up his Shakespeare with a modernized musical version of *Love's Labours Lost.* Even the gory, rarely staged *Titus Andronicus,* its horrors rivalling Tarantino's, has received a cinematic outing. Readiness and ripeness, it seems, is all.

One of my favourite films that features the Bard is Merchant-Ivory's 1965 *Shakespeare Wallah.* It follows the fortunes of a theatrical touring company in India and deals with the looming cultural clash between Bard and "Bollywood." The old Anglo-Indian values of the Raj, and the poet who shaped its language, are under pressure from the mass appeal of the movies, with their glitzy stars and legions of admirers. A staged performance of *Antony and Cleopatra* for a solitary maharajah in his gilded palace while, outside, fans mob a movie star, seems as self-indulgent as the classical lovers themselves—the last polite gasp of a dying culture and aestheticism. At the same time, the notion that Shakespeare on film cannot be simply a recorded stage performance, but has to borrow all the tricks of the cinematic trade, is subtly inferred.

The movie also demonstrates how the portability of the latest equipment has enabled the camera to break free from its studio bondage and become a world tourist. There have been *Tempests* on real desert islands, *Hamlets* in Denmark, *Macbeths* in the Scottish highlands, *Othellos* on the Rialto itself, and *Dreams* bogged down in the mud of authentic Warwickshire woods. Whether this *cinema verité* served the playwright's purpose is open to the same debate as that over the legitimacy of Henry Irving's flying and singing witches and Beerbohm Tree's real forest rabbits—picturesque archaisms that seemed to anticipate the cinema's inherent need to flatter the eye as much as the ear.

The one indisputable bonus is that it ensured that these performances will endure and survive the ravages of "cormorant-devouring time." Shakespeare himself seemed to have predicted the "timeless" quality of his work with his anachronisms—the clock striking in ancient Rome and the bespectacled ancient Britons—that would be quite consistent with future "modernistic" productions. To the question, "How many ages hence/ Shall this our lofty scene be acted over/ In states unborn and accents yet unknown?," the answer is, as long as world cinema and the recorded image endure.

Theater performances are the stuff of unreliable fable: Film provides a more trustworthy "ocular proof." Adrian mentions the experience of seeing Johnston Forbes-Robertson as Hamlet at an age when Polonius or the Player King would have seemed more appropriate casting. Yet the performance is powerfully compelling and makes one regret that the medium came too late to immortalize such other celebrated Hamlets as Henry Irving, John Barrymore, and a whole legion of legendary Shakespearean actors.

It also confirms that the Bard is big box office. Even as long ago as 1623, not long after Shakespeare died, the poet Leonard Digges noted: "So have I seen, when Caesar would appear, and on the stage at half-sword parley were / Brutus and Cassius; oh how the audience / Were ravish'd, with what wonder they went hence." Forbes-Robertson agreed: "When a production of a new play has spelt failure, a revival of *Hamlet* has always set me on my feet again." This mass approbation is important as film, because of its expense, cannot be just caviar to the general, but has to please the million.

It may well be that, in the longer judgment of posterity, Mel Gibson's mad Hamlet rather than his Mad Max will survive the predations of time and taste, and Leonardo Di Caprio's exuberant Romeo will take on a more titanic dimension. Certainly I am constantly delighted as each new generation seems to find pleasure and empathy in Zeffirelli's *Romeo and Juliet,* even though the film is now over twice Juliet's age. I have to confess too, that three decades on, I derive a certain nostalgic, sentimental amusement out of seeing my younger self in *The Taming of the Shrew* going through the exhilarating experience of making a film for the first time.

The first thing one learned was that the usual daily routine was rudely reversed. Whereas the stage performer tried to conserve the creative forces for the evening, the film actor had to come to an energetic boil at an unseemly early hour. Such daybreak dramatics had been dictated by the availability of light when film was in its one-reel infancy. Somehow the *modus operandi* had survived, quite irrationally, into the era of vast studios and lighting that challenged the sun's brightness and yet was still measured in quaint quasi-Elizabethan terms of "foot-candles." Later I was to discover an even ruder reversal when "the bright day is done, and we are for the dark." Night scenes were frequently shot on location—*all* night. The joys of seeing "the dawn in russet mantle clad" were little compensation for the cumulative punitive effect this had on the body and the brain's "distracted globe."

Our *Shrew,* however, was tamed entirely indoors and by "jocund day." Even its extramural landscapes, familiar from a thousand renaissance masterworks, were similarly painted on. Mine was a baptism, if not of fire, then certainly of some heat, occasioned by the "sunshine" radiating from a constellation of studio lamps and by some youthful swaggering in a costume of woollen doublet, cape, leather jerkin, plumed hat, and those inevitable Shakespearean appurtenances, tights. Such costumes, seen in close-up, had to look authentic: The film set was no place for the stage's knitted string armor or gold-painted plastic finery. In this it was closer to the Elizabethan theater's reputed sartorial splendor.

I was in the very first shot on the first day—nay, first hour— of the film schedule. There was simply no time to observe the ways and means of filmmaking from others or, thankfully, to become paralyzingly nervous. Later, I was curiously relieved—and moved—to observe that mastery of the medium seemed ever a mystery, and that experience was no guarantee of success. Our superstar hero and heroine were indulged in the rare luxury of reshooting some of their initial work. Even with camera tests and rehearsals, the correct fusion of all the filmic elements appeared to be mitigated as much by good fortune as by good judgment. That ineffable element that made for triumph in both the theater and cinema, remained elusive. Shakespeare, of course, was fully aware of it: "Oft expectation fails, and most oft there / Where most it promises; and oft it hits, / Where hope is coldest, and despair most fits."

That first shot in the *Shrew* was of myself riding—a real horse, of course, of some few hours acquaintance—through the streets of Padua while reciting a sizeable piece of verse to my servant, Tranio. I was fortunate to be saddled to an old, reliable professional who, perfectly suiting the action to the word, shivered excitedly to life at the command "action" and went patiently and precisely to his marks on the floor, politely ignoring my novice's spurrings and imprecations. The noble beast was an object lesson in unshowy competence—one of the unsung multitude of indispensable supporting players, those lesser luminaries, who make a "starring" role possible.

"That part of philosophy / Will I apply that treats of happiness," I exuberantly intoned, swiftly translating this wish into reality, for the new film medium filled me with the most profound and immediate joy. My rapport with the camera seemed instantaneous and, to my delight and relief, I found it relatively easy to focus my energies on its unwavering, glittering eye. The huge team that serviced the machine was in no way intrusive; on the contrary, their intense concentration seemed to bolster my own.

What did surprise me was the amount of coverage that a scene could require, especially when several actors were involved. Most directors start by filming a "master" shot from one angle, just as if they were recording a play from a fixed point in a theater. This action is then broken down into smaller sections, emphasis being made with close-ups and camera moves. It could all be astonishingly time-consuming. And even offensive. Banqueting scenes, for example—in the case of *Shrew,* filmed over the course of many days—were best finished before the odiferous emanation from the fly-blown feast became unbearable. Lilies that fester do, indeed, smell far worse than weeds!

One quickly realized the importance of learning the optical potential of each lens so that the performance could be adjusted accordingly. Although Duncan in *Macbeth* averred that "there is no art / To find the mind's construction in the face," I discovered the contrary. In extreme close-ups, expecially of the eyes, it was often sufficient merely to think and *relax* the face in order for it to become an instrument of expression—or as the more guilt-concious Lady Macbeth put it, "a book where men may read strange matters." In a scene between one or more characters, where each was filmed individually, it was essential to play "off" camera as intensely as one did "on" in order for the synergy to be maintained. I recently worked with an actress who told me that when filming with the late, now legendary, James Stewart, he had insisted on coming in on his days off, and even putting on his costume for his off-camera scenes.

"A lady in our drama school gives a course on what she describes as 'Acting for the Camera,'" Adrian once wrote. "Hearing about this, another teacher remarked that you might as well teach 'Acting for the Lights'—after all, acting is acting is acting." Film, however, is now an international language with varying regional accents. It would seem that, as with most languages, an instructor would be helpful. But can screen acting be taught?

For the novice, given the lucky chance of working in a movie, the ideal tutor is experience itself, the best "Method" being a certain trial and error. At the end of the day's filming, selected cast and crew would go to view the "dailies" or "rushes"—the record of the previous day's work. (Performing *Henry IV, Part 2* at Oxford with movie-mad students, we noted with amusement that First Groom, obviously a fellow film buff, who enters in Act 5 shouting for "more rushes, more rushes!") These brief sessions—it was generally astonishing how little the long day's toil amounted to—could be alarming experiences. Without the intervention of the editor, and sans music, the untreated portrait could appear to be incurably blemished with warts and all. One learned the hard, Aristotelian way to be objective and to use this ego-pummelling process as a positive, constructive experience.

Adrian visited me on the *Shrew* set in Rome and I was delighted to be able to share my new discoveries and enthusiasms. I mentioned how necessary it was to de-theatricalize one's performance and to resist the temptation to signal intentions. As the great director, George Stevens so succinctly put it: "Film acting is talking soft and thinking loud." The raised eyebrow on camera could have the same emotional impact as the raised arm on stage. Subtleties, often lost in the theater, could be emphasized—like Marlon Brando's cynical screen smile as he turns away from his grief-stricken oration over Caesar's body.

As has been shown, Shakespeare's texts are not ideal material for "naturalistic" acting. His poetry cannot be broken up with pauses like normal speech: It has to trip metrically off the tongue—even in the more "realistic" medium of cinema. It is significant that early films, especially comedies, were mostly played at a fast tempo; when I was directed by the legendary Hollywood maestro, George Cukor, his invariable direction was, "at a clip!" It is only recently that movies have bloated into image-dominant, special effects–driven marathons. "They are as sick that surfeit with too much, as they that starve with nothing."

On film, Shakespeare's words are not as inviolable as they are on stage. Certain cuts are warranted because what can be seen does not have to be described or imagined as in the theater. (This does not quite excuse Olivier's excision of Rosencrantz and Guildenstern from his *Hamlet,* although this did enable Tom Stoppard to redeem and immortalize them in his absurdist *Rosencrantz and Guildenstern Are Dead.*)

Filmed soliloquies worked best when played as on stage, directly to the audience: that is, to the camera. Its lens provides a focus for all those stage speeches that, as Adrian points out, are normally addressed to daggers, suns and moons, and other inanimate objects. This all-seeing, relentless eye makes for a certain truthfulness and literalness, as well as animating the pathetic fallacy. Olivier as Hamlet, for example, could literally immerse himself in a mist of "pale thought" amidst the clouded battlements of Elsinore with the "pitch and moment" of the sea below him giving visible energy to his monologues. Many of these were further internalized with voice-over narration, another distinguishing cinematic feature.

Screen acting involves not just readability, but that temperance and smoothness that Hamlet so admired. Also plausibility. As George Burns observed so brilliantly, "The secret of good acting is sincerity—and, if you can fake that, you've got it made!" The old saw about acting being mostly about *re*-acting is also true. In the 1964 Russian *Hamlet* starring Innokenti Smoktunovsky, Ophelia's madness, for example, is not so much depicted directly on camera but rather reflected in the faces of the appalled and incredulous courtiers.

The technical aspects of film work were, for me, more an

exciting challenge than an irksome discipline. "Hitting" precise marks and "finding" specific lights while at the same time allowing Apollo to sound what stop he pleased, exercised both left and right brain faculties. The imaginary forces were brought into the same play as on stage. Animated conversations were held with nonexistent people, and one used a crossed tape stuck next to the camera lens, both for gazing into the eyes of a beloved, or in horror at what was taking place.

On a purely technical note, the studio rain machine was as important as the theater's thunder sheet, the storm being a central, significant feature of so much Shakespearean drama. Showers drizzled down from overhead spigots with the same damp relentlessness as that which must surely have inundated the Globe's groundlings, while whirling aircraft propellers roared both Bottom-like, "as gently as any sucking dove," as well as blasting out King Lear's "cataracts and hurricanoes." Even those long pauses for technical adjustments, that make a visit to a film set so boring for the uninitiated, were useful, even essential, as they enabled both mental and physical rehearsal, which in the tense, time-is-money atmosphere of the movies, was in ever short supply.

Because film scenes were shot in no particular order, actors tended to progress from location to location and set to set, rather than sequentially from Act One to Finale. I liked this disordered momentum as it mimicked real life, where events and emotions rarely played out in a logical, linear continuity. It brought to mind Shakespeare's cherished image of life being like the ebb and flow of the sea.

Accordingly, a role required the same homework as it did in the theater. The arc of the character had to be thought out so that even if filming began with one's final appearance, that scene would be plausibly consistent with what was going to come before. In *The Shrew,* one shot of me riding into Padua at the beginning of the film was made on my very last day's work. Similarly, the character I played in the movie *Cabaret* left Berlin within moments of arriving there. Hopefully, one had successfully imagined and depicted the wealth of life-changing experience gathered between both sets of entrances and exits.

Audiences, however can interpolate a great deal for themselves if their own imaginary forces are truly engaged. An interesting story is related about Orson Welles' *Chimes at Midnight.* John Gielgud had basically finished filming his role as Henry IV but, before he left for home, Welles requested that he sit for a sequence of simple studio shots. All that he had to do was to look down and then up and to both sides—rather like a police identification photo. In the film's final edit, the shot of Henry IV looking down at his wounded son on the battlefield was infinitely moving as the audience made the connection and interpolated the appropriate emotion.

Orson Welles became the master of the less-is-more school, his expansive imagination, that had once produced a "voodoo" *Macbeth,* perforce constrained by economic realities. The horror of battle is eloquently, yet economically, conveyed in his *Chimes at Midnight* by a few unhorsed, armored knights stumbling agonizingly in the mud. One can only regret projects, such as his *Merchant of Venice* with Peggy Ashcroft, that Welles left unfinished, or which "melted into thin air," like so many cinematic ambitions and endeavors. Minimalism was also the hallmark of such great French actors Jean Gabin and Louis Jouvet in whose unvarying facial expressions each member of the audience could read a whole variety of emotions. There is also the instructive story of an actor who, compelled to do a film he was loath to accept, simply "walked through it" in protest—and won an Oscar for his begrudging efforts!

Fundamentally, one had to accept the uncomfortable reality that, unlike his stage counterpart, the film actor was not totally in control of his performance. In the theater, all the editing was done during rehearsal and, to a certain extent, during performance. On film, the actor provided raw material—however inspired and talented—for someone else to edit. But this incisive process was a double-edged sword. Compensating for the powerlessness and disappointment felt when favorite scenes or takes were consigned to the proverbial cutting-room floor, one had cause to be grateful for the excision of those that were substandard or indifferently played.

Cast in Zeffirelli's *Romeo and Juliet,* as the cocky, libidinous Tybalt, I was originally introduced in the very act of proving my reputation as the King of Cats between the thighs of a Veronese maiden. This was perhaps too obvious an image and it was cut, but I still make my entrance, a trifle more subtly, from the codpiece upwards! Given that we pay homage to Stanislavski with our book's title, I was somewhat bemused to learn from Zeffirelli that when the film was shown in the Soviet Union, I was complimented on playing Tybalt "in the Russian style!"

Another great technical asset at the film actor's command was the A.D.R—additional dialogue replacement or, more commonly, the "looping"—session that preceded the final edit. It provided a rare chance to gild the lily. A performance could be tweaked and modulated at will—the volume could be raised or lowered and the pitch and intensity adjusted to suit the prevailing tenor of the performance or of the assembled film.

This re-voicing was extremely difficult to do in a mouth-moving close-up but relatively easy in a long-shot. For example, extra "walla" could be added to the crowd scenes, with the proviso, of course, that it was all suitably Shakespearean. (It had been amusing to observe our dialogue coach at the beginning of the day's filming handing out Elizabethan oaths and expletives like so much off-color candy!) Zeffirelli maintained a "rep" company of English actors specifically to repair in the recording studio the fractured vowels of the non-English speaking extras, ensuring no further repetition of the "O weederdee" weirdness that Adrian records in his "Shakesperience" chapter.

However, no matter the sophistication of the post-production facilities, a film performance primarily has to be modulated on set, in the very act of execution. There, Welles' rule of Shakespearean filmmaking, that less is usually more, seems to steadfastly apply. A stage role that is not adjusted for the screen can sometimes be hard to take. A case in point is Beerbohm Tree's early histrionics, as well as the much-later film version of Laurence Olivier's legendary 1960s National Theatre triumph as Othello mentioned in the Foreword. On stage, Olivier's thrilling performance could be spoken of in the same terms as those used to describe his 1940s Oedipus, "in which blood and electricity are somehow mixed." To counterbalance this huge figure, Olivier had cast Frank Finlay as Iago. Finlay is a brilliant actor, but was an unequal, or unwilling match for Olivier's virtuoso, attention-grabbing performance. On film, however, the emphasis is curiously reversed. Olivier's dramatics in close-up are too much, whereas Finlay's subtle stage performance is startlingly magnified as he takes both the audience and the Moor into his malign confidence. In the same way, John Gielgud has commented that Vivien Leigh's Lady Macbeth, criticized for being too small in the theater, would have grown enormously on film, had the plans to record her performance, partnered by Olivier, been realized.

Later, when Olivier was older and the wheel had come full circle and the heyday in the blood was tamer, he fortunately did bequeath a moving King Lear to television and to recording posterity. His own physical fragility and wisdom of experience matched that of the old king himself. Art imitated life and vice-versa. It was all infinitely moving. One can only speculate as to the contrast between this majestic performance and his earlier stage incarnations of the role, done at full-throttle, had they been similarly preserved for posterity.

Television's potential as an educational tool, as well as its means of mass entertainment, made it a potent Shakespearean resource. *The Age of Kings* was a celebrated BBC compilation of the history plays, in which Sean Connery gave a memorable, if monochrome, Hotspur, and since then the entire Canon has been recorded. I found playing Benedick for television "better, better'd expection." The lumbering, cable-bound cameras seemed perfect recipients for the lengthy asides that momentarily transformed the principal actors into the kind of "talking head" that normally dominated television. I was also able—oh luxury of luxuries— to eschew the glue and grow my own beard and shave it off at the appropriate moment in the play, as, unlike most films, it was recorded in regular order.

Despite—perhaps because of—its popular appeal, television has always had its denigrators: Even its name, half-Latin, half-Greek, has been a source of suspicion. Olivier's Lear demonstrated that television was not the poor cousin of film, but that its smaller screen could be a positive virtue, especially when dialogue of an intimate, introspective nature was involved. This was re-enforced by his performance as Shylock, similarly adapted from a National Theatre production, for television. It was updated to the nineteenth century so that Olivier, unctuously polite and fastidiously dressed, like Disraeli or a Rothschild, seemed to reflect the popular, costumed dramas that so suited the medium.

Whether on stage, film, or television, Olivier cast a giant shadow. Indeed, Kenneth Branagh performed an invaluable service in presuming to shed new light on the great Shakespearean heroes that Olivier had filmed, when it seemed almost *lèse majesté* to attempt revised interpretations. Sometimes the weight of legend can prove so sclerotically ponderous as to impede progress. Even as long ago as 1785, Sarah Siddons noted this problem with her Lady Macbeth: "In the sleep-walking scene, when I argued the impracticality of washing out that 'damned spot' while holding the candle in my hand, Sheridan insisted that if I put the candle out of my hand it would be thought a presumptuous innovation, as Mrs. Pritchard had always retained it in hers." Undeterred, she invented her own piece of business—licking imaginary blood from her hand and spitting it out—that literally stopped the show.

Branagh's Henry V was a similar revelation. His performance demonstrated how Shakespeare has this uncanny ability to reflect not just his own times, but every changing epoch in which he is performed. In a post-Cold War world, Branagh's troubled warrior King emphasized the price that was paid for waging war. As Adrian remarked: "He did suggest that Henry is twenty-five, inexperienced and nervous, each new step could be fatal. That's the main difference from Olivier, who played a born winner. A play that appears to have no psychological conflict, *does* in fact contain one when put in context: when Henry V is only Prince Hal a few weeks later."

Part of the pleasure of Branagh's next Shakespeare film, *Much Ado,* is due to the fact that it was lensed in sensual color on location, if not in Sicily itself, then in the real Italian countryside. Watching "the golden sun salute the morn" and illuminate ancient buildings and fruitful orchards alike, and seeing torches light up the nighttime revelry with symbolic shadows, reminded me of my own experience of filming *Romeo and Juliet* in Italy for Zeffirelli in the late 1960s, with a cast as equally youthful as Branagh's.

The removal of cars and telephone wires and other modern intrusions instantly transformed Pienza, the Tuscan hill town masquerading as our Verona, back into an authentic renaissance landscape. The dog day heat that so stirred the mad blood was as real as the moon that illuminated the night's dramatic encounters. The extras looked particularly authentic, perhaps because the faces in the crowd were no accidental comingling of characters. Zeffirelli kept a file of physiognomies and would carefully arrange them in his frame like an old master harmonizing his canvas.

And rightly so, because the crowd became an integral part of the action, whether at the dance or the duelling ground. As in the theater, they made their effect *en masse.* However, stage economics often minimized this mass—as Shakespeare knew when he implored his audience: "Into a thousand parts divide one man." On screen, however, whole armies could be involved. Indeed, a

1914 version of *Julius Caesar* was reputed to have a cast of 20,000! Certainly legions of longhaired youths flocked to our film sets from all parts to join the two houses that divided the fair city. Again music, "moody food / Of us that trade in love" played an important role in the film. Nino Rota's wonderful score reflected both the bright romanticism, as well as the darker poignancy, of the story.

The one great advantage of film was that, just as it had enabled the aging Olivier to achieve his Lear, so it allowed our Juliet, Olivia Hussey, to approximate to her specified thirteen years of age. Normally an actress of those immature years does not possess the full vocal and technical equipment to handle the verse. And yet mature actors—like Norma Shearer and Leslie Howard in Cukor's *Romeo and Juliet*—can appear almost too adult in the camera's unsparing close-up.

Once the great poetic passages were broken down into sections, into a sequence of takes, Olivia managed superbly, infusing them with a teenager's zest and impulsiveness, so that each experience, as well as word, seemed delightfully new-minted. In so doing, she—and her equally youthful Romeo, Leonard Whiting—succeeded in seducing worldwide legions of fellow teenagers to Shakespeare's cause. As did Leonardo Di Caprio and Claire Danes with their more recent "punk" version where, perhaps significantly reflecting the *zeitgeist*, the Chorus is transformed into a television commentator.

Film can turn a soliloquy into an intense introspection, but its real forte is action—and the screen has bequeathed a long line of swashbucklers. Even with the divine Sarah Bernhardt, it was only the fight scene of her Hamlet that was immortalized on film. Dueling on stage can be scary—and never more so than in the unlucky, unmentionable "Scottish play!" However, dueling on film can be positively dangerous. "He jests at scars than never felt a wound!"

Although every fight in our *Romeo and Juliet* was carefully choreographed by an experienced coach and rehearsed to keep, as Mercutio excoriates Tybalt, "time, distance and proportion," the experience of filming them was alarmingly realistic. It was a stroke of genius (to give it its more kindly interpretation!) for Zeffirelli to change the location of the duel between Romeo and Tybalt, at the very last moment, from the flat, level ground where it had been painstakingly rehearsed, to a steep graveled slope. This gave an impulsive, mad momentum to the action, throwing up clouds of lung-choking but visually arresting dust, and making us both alarmingly imminent candidates for "worm's meat."

On another occasion, in the middle of a duel with Mercutio, my sword had to be returned so that the action could continue to its fatal conclusion. John McEnery, our Mercutio (whose own screen baptism, incidentally, had been the truly testing "Queen Mab" speech!) had fallen ill. Time and tide wait for no film: Necessity becomes the mother of feverish invention. Unlike in the theater, no understudy could substitute, but, ever resourceful, Zeffirelli devised a shot where he filmed the shadow of himself clad in Mercutio's doublet, hurling the rapier at my feet. Film: *"trompe l'oeil"* at twenty-four frames a second!

Even the warm Tuscan stone was faked, for part of Pienza was duplicated in a scaffold of false facades on the studio backlot at Cinecitta. Thus, a sword thrust made in Tuscany could be parried in Rome! All this screen violence presented few problems for those latter-day Nahum Tates, the film censors. It was rarely gratuitous but frequently graceful, and even symbolic—the turning of word into sword, to use Prince John's apt phrase.

Modern digital technology as much as old-fashioned celluloid will ensure the survival of screen Shakespeare. Indeed, as the broadcast media become more greedy for product as channels and delivery systems multiply, they will both provide a constant kaleidoscopic showcase for his work in all its multifaceted, multilingual manifestations. Shakespeare has long put his own girdle round the earth, one now consolidated electronically by an Internet that lists nearly four hundred productions of his plays that have been filmed or televized. The Complete Works as well as The Complete Trivia can be accessed in innumerable web sites, no doubt keeping other ports, those "of slumber open wide / To many a watchful night." His influence seems permanent and pervasive. Even my humble telephone bill enquired recently, with regard to a new call waiting system, "To click or not to click / That is the question"!

I hope that this book will answer and provoke questions: also awaken, or even reanimate, passion for this unique playwright, who has held the mirror up to our nature in such a beguiling and illuminating way. It may be the start of the journey for some; others may be already familiar with the addictive adventure of scaling the heights and depths of Shakespeare's stupendous imagination.

He was a man, take him for all in all, and yet no one before or since has spoken to us in such high, astounding terms about what it is to be human:

Man, proud man,
Drest in a little brief authority,
Most ignorant of what he's most assured,
Plays such fantastic tricks before high heaven
As make the angels weep.

"The remarkable thing about Shakespeare," Robert Graves affirmed, "is that he really is very good—in spite of the people who say he is very good."

There is an actor of my acquaintance who refers to his periodic returns to the Canon as "getting his acting passport validated." He knows that his fresh-stamped papers will allow him to cross further-flung frontiers and travel safely and more widely in other theatrical realms. For, more than any other dramatist, Shakespeare puts both raw and refined talent—that amalgam of aptitude and application, of sweat and tears—to the ultimate *acting* test.

That is why each succeeding generation avidly embraces his thoughts and feelings, his magnanimity, and, "not only witty in himself, but the cause that wit is in other men," his infectious humor. He shows us, without preaching or polemics, that "The web of our life is of a mingled yarn, good and ill together." The ambiguity of his verse reflects this ambiguity of human nature—that we are both Prospero and Caliban.

Such wisdom has ensured Shakespeare a constant presence, not as an academic discipline, but more as a benign consciousness—as a companion. And never more so than when one is in need of comfort or advice: "But if the while I think on thee, dear friend, all losses are restored and sorrows end." Leigh Hunt asserted, "The birthdays of such men as Shakespeare, ought to be kept in common gratitude and affection, like those of relations whom we love."

For Dr. Johnson, his writings "may be considered a map of life." Goethe, who like Pushkin, Hugo, and so many foreigners, co-opted Shakespeare into his own nationalistic orbit, saw him as the great Nordic Bard and his work "a huge animated fair!" Turgenev was even more possessive, claiming him as "part and parcel of our flesh and blood." For Ben Jonson, he was, above all, a theatrical presence: "The applause! Delight! The wonder of our stage!" Shakespeare's actors may have suffered—like all actors—from typecasting, but he himself avoids this error by resolutely refusing to typecast humanity, recognizing that "There is a history in all men's lives." He writes from everyone's point of view so that his mortals are both the "quintessence of dust" and yet can aspire to the angels.

Certainly, his great philosophy animates the mystical in us, instilling the sense of man being more than the sum of his fallible parts. As it has done so down through the centuries to all peoples, it reminds us that Shakespeare, Milton's "dear son of memory, great heir of fame" was not of the foolish, fleeting moment. "For though his line of life went soon about," a lesser poet, Hugh Holland, paid tribute in 1633, "The life yet of his lines shall never out." He has been nominated, "the Man of the Millennium." This is certainly justified by the astonishing fact that he created close to a thousand characters—enough to individually celebrate "all our yesterdays." As Ben Jonson acknowledged, however, he was more than that: He was "for all time."

So, whether you are amateur or professional, actor or reader, passionate or indifferent, I wish you great joy in your further Shakespearean preparations, both on page and stage. "For now sits expectation in the air…" Nothing can equal that moment of charged anticipation when the house lights dim or the curtain rises or when you open one of his plays and begin to read those pregnant words, "Act One, Scene One." Whether you are peruser or performer I trust that, like Bottom, you will all be rewarded with "a most rare vision." I leave you with this stirring advice from the Bard himself who, justifying his infinite aptness and sheer "quotability," eminently deserves the last word:

> Be great in act, as you have been in thought….
> …So shall inferior eyes
> That borrow their behaviours from the great,
> Grow great by your example.

# Appendix A
# WHO'S WHO

ATKINS, Robert (1886–1972)

> British actor-manager. Established himself at the Old Vic in the 1920s where he produced every play in the Canon except *Cymbeline*. He co-founded the Regent's Park Open Air Theatre and ran it for three decades. As an old actor, growing increasingly deaf, he was known to boom directions to his partners on stage at the same volume as he was booming Shakespearean verse.

BARRYMORE, John (1882–1942)

> American actor celebrated internationally for his Hamlet, for his Mercutio in the 1935 film of *Romeo and Juliet*—also, later, for his inebriation.

BEERBOHM TREE, Sir Herbert (1853–1917)

> British actor-manager. Established his reputation at the Haymarket Theatre and embellished it at Her Majesty's Theatre opposite with many Shakespeare productions famous for their realistic, pictorial decors. Founder of the Royal Academy of Dramatic Art.

BRANAGH, Kenneth (1960– )

> All-around Shakespearean, has directed and produced four successful WS films, with himself in the lead (more than Olivier and Welles), and will probably go on doing more.

BROOK, Peter (1922– )

> Infant prodigy who aged into theatrical philosopher: The one director who's always three years ahead of everybody. At twenty-one directed at

Shakespeare Memorial Theatre; at twenty-two was Director of Productions at Covent Garden Opera—briefly. After showing mastery of all forms of spectacle, from musical comedy and opera to Shakespeare with Olivier and Gielgud, moved to Paris in 1971, took over a gutted theater and founded International Centre for Theatre Research, where he continues gnawing at the question, "What is theater?"

CRAIG, Edward Gordon (1872–1966)
Stage design visionary. Illegitimate son of Irving's leading lady Ellen Terry, he started as an actor in their company but soon revolted against nineteenth-century theater. Set out designing monumental sets too advanced for the twentieth century. In 1903 exiled himself to Europe. His ideas influenced German theater more than British. 1910 directed *Hamlet* for Stanislavski at Moscow Arts. Lover of Isadora Duncan. Died in poverty in the South of France. A lively writer on theater.

GRANVILLE BARKER, Harley (1877–1946)
Preeminent director of W.S. before World War I. His skills as actor and playwright himself enabled him to rescue W.S. the craftsman from nineteenth-century actor-managers' egoism. Retired from the stage at forty to live abroad, where he translated second-rate Spanish plays and wrote his monumental *Prefaces to Shakespeare*—obligatory reading for directors.

FORBES-ROBERTSON, Sir Johnston (1853–1937)
British actor-manager who began as a member of Irving's company at the Lyceum, which he later managed, and where he triumphed as Hamlet and Caesar. He was another Caesar in *Caesar and Cleopatra,* which George Bernard Shaw wrote for him.

GIELGUD, Sir John (1904–2000)
British actor-director and author of several theatrical memoirs and books. Established his early Shakespearean reputation at the Old Vic and consolidated it with his own season at The Queen's Theatre, and at Stratford-on-Avon. His qualities as a verse speaker (impeccable diction, faultless phrasing) are now legendary. He was still working on his ninety-sixth birthday, so his career spanned seventy-nine years. At his death, his English peers hailed him as "the greatest Shakespearean actor of all time."

JONSON, Ben (1572–1637)

English playwright. Apprenticed as a bricklayer, a great quarreler, and survivor of duels, he wrote such plays as *Volpone, The Alchemist, Epicoene, Bartholomew Fair,* and numerous masques. A great friend of Shakespeare whom he famously lauded, he achieved great fame himself, his epitaph being "O Rare Ben Jonson."

GARRICK, David (1717–1779)

British actor-manager, playwright, and theatrical innovator. Schooled by Dr. Samuel Johnson. Managed both Covent Garden and Drury Lane Theatres in London where he was celebrated for his *Richard III.* Organized the Shakespeare Jubilee celebrations at Stratford in 1769.

IRVING, Sir Henry (1838–1905)

King of the London stage in the 1890s; manager, Lyceum Theatre; first English actor to be knighted. Known by his initials, which his followers claimed also stood for "His Immensity." Plundered W.S. for good roles for himself (Shylock, Hamlet, Lear), pruning the plays to his own advantage, earning the ridicule of drama critic George Bernard Shaw.

KEAN, Edmund (c. 1789–1833)

British actor born of strolling players. Established his reputation with Shylock and maintained it through the intensity of his performances. The poet Coleridge observed: "To see him act is like reading Shakespeare by flashes of lightning." A legendary drunkard, he is remembered as well for his off-stage performances. An eyewitness described his final theatrical appearance as Othello as "dying as he went."

LAMB, Charles (1775–1834)

Gentle English belle-lettrist (*The Essays of Elia* 1823) who produced convincing arguments that W.S. was more rewarding when read than when seen in performance, the actors and the staging being "distracting."

MACREADY, William Charles (1793–1873)

British actor-manager. Famous for his hot temper and the telling pause—"The Macready." He established his reputation at London's Covent Garden and Drury Lane Theatres where he instigated many useful reforms, notably increasing rehearsal time and restoring Shakespeare's texts. He also toured the provinces and the United States where his presence caused an infamous riot.

MCKELLEN, Sir Ian (1939–  )

British actor. A Cambridge graduate and cofounder of the Actor's Company, he appeared with both the Royal Shakespeare and The National Theatre companies where he was an admired Coriolanus, Macbeth, and Richard III, which he also filmed. *Acting Shakespeare* was his successful one-man show.

OLIVIER, Sir Laurence (1907–1989)

British actor, director, and manager of stage and screen fame. After alternating Romeo and Mercutio with John Gielgud in 1935 he further established a reputation for Shakespeare at the Old Vic and leading the company at Stratford-on-Avon. Later the director of the Chichester Festival Theatre and the founding director of the National Theatre. He produced, directed, and acted in films of *Henry V, Richard III* and *Hamlet.* He was knighted in 1947 and made a baron in 1970.

QUILLER-COUCH, Sir Arthur (1863–1944)

Cornish adventure story writer who became first Professor of English Literature at Cambridge in 1912. His convivial lectures pursued the question, "How did Shakespeare set to work?" and are still full of robust common sense—published as *Shakespeare's Workmanship.*

RYLANDS, George (1902–1999)

Aesthetic Cambridge academic, "Godfather" and tutor to modern English directors (Peter Hall, John Barton, Trevor Nunn) whom he taught to "read" Shakespearean verse. A pillar of Cambridge student theater, acting and directing, (his delicate personality gave him a preference for roles like Viola, Rosalind, and Volumnia), he was invited by John Gielgud to direct his Hamlet in 1944, but found professional actors "disobedient." Directed recordings of Complete Works by the Marlowe Society.

SHAW, George Bernard (1860–1953)

Irish polemical playwright and publicist, (his *Pygmalion* is the source of *My Fair Lady*). His youthful drama criticism (1895–98) contains much useful guidance about how W.S. should be played (and wasn't). Refused uncritical worship of W.S. (called it "Bardolatry") and impishly claimed to have a superior mind to W.S.'s, though his short puppet play, *Shakes versus Shav,* is far from convincing (but he was over ninety when he wrote it).

SIDDONS, Sarah (1755–1831)

British actress born into a theatrical family—her brother was John Philip Kemble. Famous as much for her beauty as for her tragic acting (Gainsborough painted her as "The Tragic Muse"), she refused to compromise this image by playing comedy.

WANAMAKER, Sam (1919–1993)

American actor-director who made his home and reputation as well in England. He managed Liverpool's New Shakespeare Theatre and starred at Stratford-on-Avon. His legacy includes the rebuilding of Shakespeare's Globe Theatre in London.

WELLES, Orson (1915–1985)

American actor, director, and writer. A cofounder of The Mercury Theatre in 1937 and director of such film classics as *Citizen Kane*. His Shakespeare films include *Othello* (1951), *King Lear* (1956), and also *Chimes At Midnight* (1962), based on *Henry IV* and *Henry V*, in which he played Falstaff.

WILSON, John Dover (1881–1969)

Eminent Scottish scholar and textual editor (Cambridge Shakespeare). Famous for two illuminating books, *What Happens in Hamlet* and *The Fortunes of Falstaff*. Blind in old age (a torment for a man of letters), he dictated a notable edition of *The Sonnets* (Cambridge 1966).

WOLFIT, Sir Donald (1902–1967)

Robust actor-manager who relentlessly upheld nineteenth-century values in twentieth-century theater, touring Shakespeare productions in sets and costumes that were never renewed, directing himself in leading roles with other actors deliberately undercast and underlit. Unsurpassed as Tamburlaine and King Lear. Always referred to W.S. as "our master poet-dramatist."

ZEFFIRELLI, Franco (1923– )

Italian stage designer and director who found early fame with his opera productions. His 1960 Old Vic *Romeo and Juliet* established his Shakespearean reputation, which he consolidated with films of *The Taming of the Shrew, Romeo and Juliet,* and *Hamlet.*

Appendix B

# A BRIEF LIFE OF SHAKESPEARE:
# KEEPING A LOW PROFILE

"Little is known of Shakespeare's life"—so runs the cliché. However some Elizabethan historians (notably the distinguished A.L.Rowse) have expressed their surprise that, (in comparison with other writers of the time) *so much* is known about him.

His life came full circle. He was born in Stratford-upon-Avon, Warwickshire, and spent his childhood there. He retired to Stratford and died there. His baptismal and burial dates are recorded in Holy Trinity Church: They indicate that he died on his birthday, April 23. His middle years were spent in London.

## EARLY YEARS AND FAMILY LIFE

Shakespeare was born to John Shakespeare and Mary Arden in 1564 , the eldest of eight children (four sons, four daughters). His father was a glovemaker, and sometime Bailiff of Stratford, and his mother came from an old Warwickshire family. So William was not a peasant, but rather what we'd call "middle-class." Indeed, in 1568 his father applied for a coat of arms and the title of "Gentleman," but it was not granted. The son did achieve this, when he reapplied in 1596, and the family motto became "Non sanz droict." (Not without right, or deservedly so.)

As the son of a local dignitary he was probably educated at Stratford Grammar School.

In 1582 he married Anne Hathaway, who was eight years his senior, and six months later, in 1583, their first child was born, Susanna. Historians see here evidence of a "shot-gun" wedding.

In 1585, Anne was delivered of twins, Hamnet and Judith. Shakespeare's daughters outlived him, but the son, Hamnet, died in 1596, when he was eleven years old.

As Bailiff of the town, John Shakespeare would have been responsible for receiving, and paying, the theatrical troupes who came from London on tour—and there is evidence of travelling players performing there in 1573, 1576, 1583, and 1587. It would be surprizing if William didn't see them and meet the actors afterwards.

## THE LOST YEARS

From 1585 we lose sight of him for seven years, the period known as "The Lost Years."

A century later memoirists were claiming that he worked as a schoolmaster, or served as a soldier under Sir Philip Sidney at the Battle of Zutphen (1586), or that he worked as a lawyer's clerk. Nobody knows.

These were his formative years—the age when an author gathers experiences and impressions that will serve him in his later work. We can only guess at how the Stratford lad became the poet-playwright.

In 1587, a theatrical troupe called The Queen's Men arrived on tour in Stratford, and there was a vacancy. One of their actors, William Knell, had just been killed in a fight. The actor's widow was later to marry John Heminges, one of the actors who would later collect all Shakespeare's plays together after his death.

Perhaps young William filled the vacancy. His father was by now in financial straits, and William was the eldest son. It would be possible that he went off with the actors to make his fortune in London.

There again, this is pure guesswork—an activity that his biographers call "joining up the dots."

## THE LONDON YEARS, 1590–1611

He spent twenty years in London, writing, acting—and making money. Few realize what a shrewd businessman he was. Within seven years he had earned enough to buy the second biggest house in Stratford, called New Place.

His earliest plays, *Henry VI* and *Titus Andronicus,* though little appreciated nowadays, were box-office successes. When the embittered playwright Robert Greene attacked him in a pamphlet as "Shake-scene" and parodied a line from *Henry VI,* Shakespeare must have been well-known enough for readers to recognize the reference.

He became the "house writer" to the Lord Chamberlain's Men, and a shareholder in the company. Other playwrights sold their works on a freelance basis, but Shakespeare had a regular job. He became, as it were, the first professional playwright.

When in 1592–93 all London theaters were closed down because of an outbreak of the plague, he had no outlet for playwriting, and turned to poetry. Two long narrative poems, *Venus and Adonis* and *The Rape of Lucrece,* were published, dedicated to the Earl of Southampton. In 1594 the Earl is recorded as giving Shakespeare a gift of £1000 "to enable him to go through with a Purchase"—what, we do not know, perhaps it was a share in the company.

In 1595 he was named (together with Richard Burbage and Will Kempe, the famous clown) as one of three payees for performances given before the Queen. This indicates that he is already one of the heads of the company.

The Lord Chamberlain's Men were going from strength to strength. While playing The Theatre, they hired a second playhouse, The Curtain, in 1583, and played both houses for some fourteen years. In 1599 they built the Globe. When Queen Elizabeth died in 1603, her successor King James I appointed them to be called the King's Men and demanded far more royal command performances than Elizabeth ever had. In 1608 they acquired an indoor theater, the Blackfriars, where they could give winter seasons—and Shakespeare's plays, after that date, became more difficult to understand.

In 1613 he bought a house in Blackfriars, near the theater—his first London property. Until then he had lived in lodgings (part of the time staying with the family of a French wig-maker called Mountjoy, to the east of St. Paul's Cathedral), which suggests that he never really settled in London. He must have kept contact with his family in Stratford, since he had bought a house there. After the age of forty he probably spent more time in the country, for some of the later plays contain more elaborate stage directions, which suggests that he was not always on hand to arrange the staging himself.

Writers' lives are often disappointingly uneventful for their biographers, since they spend a lot of their time just sitting at a table, writing. In those twenty years, he wrote some thirty-seven plays, and maybe more—an average of two a year—as well as a good deal of poetry, which is a good output for any writer. Besides this, he was actively involved with the running of the company, and that company produced about fifteen plays a year, as well as acting in his own and other men's plays. We see that he had a full life. No wonder he was said to be rather unsociable, "not a company man" who seldom went out—according to John Aubrey—"and if invited to, writ: he was in pain."

A public figure as a writer, as a private man he kept a low profile.

## SHAKESPEARE IN LOVE

Yet he also left behind a work so personal and self-revealing that some have called it his autobiography: a cycle of 154 Sonnets.

Herein, said Wordsworth, "Shakespeare unlocked his heart." And Bernard Shaw claimed that with the Sonnets in our hands we know more about Shakespeare than we know about Dickens or Thackeray.

They tell us no facts about his life, but everything about his feelings. They are an autobiography with the prose bits left out. The order they are published in is probably not the right one, and the publication may not have been authorized by Shakespeare since some of them are unfinished.

Writing sonnets was a popular game among lettered men, and they circulated privately, an Elizabethan form of *samizdat*. Perhaps Shakespeare's were gathered up by an admirer, and sold to the printer.

They are a series of poems about love, and when read through, a story emerges. The poet, "I," has a young friend of androgynous beauty, and it is to this youth that the earliest Sonnets are addressed. Knowing that Time will eventually destroy that beauty, as it devours all living things, he begs him to marry and produce an heir so that his beauty may be reproduced. The young man is constantly in his thoughts: Even when Shakespeare is feeling depressed and outcast, he only has to think of him and his "sweet love." "That then I scorn to change my state with kings."

The young friend is not always faithful to the author: There is talk of a "rival poet" who claims the youth's affections.

The "I" figure also has a mistress—black-haired, black-eyed, and maybe even dark-skinned. She has come down to history as "the Dark Lady"—Was she Italianate, or black, or simply raven-haired? His affection for her is purely carnal, more like lust than love, and she comes across as very demanding and very changeable, rather like the Cleopatra he was later to create. He refuses to be romantic about her, as poets do—she is no goddess, and he has no illusions about her love for him—he knows she's lying half the time.

"Two loves have I, of comfort and despair" he writes, and his despair increases when the young friend, instead of producing an heir, forms an alliance with the Dark Lady, and both grow apart from him. He shows no jealousy, but the pain is evident.

Finally the young friend seems to disappear from the story, and the poet is left alone with the mistress.

> Him have I lost; thou hast both him and me:
> He pays the whole, and yet I am not free.

It is a story of "the eternal triangle," but the characters are not the cliché figures of The Man, His Wife, and Her Lover, but a more unusual combination of the man, his bisexual friend, and his mistress. On the one hand there is the Platonic love between the two men; on the other, the sexual love of both for the same woman. It is a situation that Harold Pinter could have made a play about.

Was Shakespeare homosexual? The question is a clumsy one, for he abhors labels. Certainly he calls the youth "my lovely boy" and "the master-mistress of my passion," but Elizabethan English was more colored than our own, and there is no talk of a sexual relationship between them. On the contrary: He blames Nature, when she created the young man, of falling in love herself and "adding one thing to my purpose nothing," and that one thing is made clear in the next line:

> But since she prick'd thee out for woman's pleasure,
> Mine be thy love, and thy love's use their treasure.

The poet's love for him was constant and unchanging, not sullied with jealousy or bitterness or deceit, as sexual love is. It is a quite different emotion from that which he feels for his mistress, which he likens to a fever, or madness—ecstasy followed by bouts of self-disgust.

Historians have long tried to discover who the Dark Lady is, and who the Friend. Perhaps it is nobody's business but Shakespeare's. It is the poems themselves that count, and not the gossip surrounding them. On his tomb stone he warned off future generations from trying to "digg the dust." And anyway, the Sonnets are works of art, not historical documents. A certain amount of poetic license may be involved. Perhaps "the mistress" stood for several mistresses.

It may seem strange that Shakespeare, usually so careful about guarding his privacy, here "unlocks his heart." For once he is writing in the "I" form, not hiding behind a mask, as he does when he writes roles for actors. He is going through a deep emotional crisis, and he records things as they occur, not in recollection. Just as statesmen in times of crisis confide in their diaries, so he turns his worries into sonnets. Yet they were not private papers, for he frequently claims that his "rhymes" (a modest appraisal) will outlive not only the Friend, but more long-standing objects such as marble and "the gilded monuments of princes." So he was not just doodling, or writing to himself, he was writing to be read. (The person who gathered these poems together and rushed them off to the printer, some half-finished, may have jumped the gun.)

In these 154 Sonnets he allows us to see him face-to-face. As a chapter of autobiography, they tell us everything about his feelings—that part of him that is common to all men—and nothing of his history. It's as if he wants to be, in Ben Jonson's phrase, "not of an age, but for all time." Anyone who wants to know "what Shakespeare was like" has only to read them and try to solve their enigmas.

The Sonnets show that the story of Shakespeare's love life is far more complex than the film of *Shakespeare in Love*.


## STRATFORD—THE LAST YEARS

In 1613 the Globe Theatre burned down. Prospero's words (written two years before) sound like a premonition:

> the great globe itself.
> Yea, all which it inherit, shall dissolve
> And, like this insubstantial pageant faded,
> Leave not a wrack behind.

A new, even more splendid theater was erected within a year, the second Globe, but Shakespeare wrote no more.

In Stratford he passed his last years (says Rowe) "in Ease, Retirement, and the Conversation of his Friends." He was occupied with business deals and litigation—buying land, selling malt, and chasing up debtors. He was always a good business man.

He died in 1616, as the result of what a later Vicar of Stratford called "a merrie meetynge" with his friends Ben Jonson and the poet-laureate-to-be, Michael Drayton. No doubt it was a birthday party.

Seven years later, Heminges and Condell published the First Folio.

# Appendix C
# CHRONOLOGY OF
# SHAKESPEARE'S PLAYS

Most Collected Works follow the order of the First Folio, and begin with *The Tempest*, which was in fact his last complete play. (*Henry VIII,* which followed it, is thought to be a work of collaboration.) If an edition were brought out following the order in which he wrote the plays, it would indicate how he developed as a playwright.

1590–1592
    *Henry VI, Parts 1, 2, and 3*
    *Richard III*
    *Titus Andronicus*
    *The Comedy of Errors*
    *The Taming of the Shrew*
    *The Two Gentlemen of Verona*

1592–1596
    *Love's Labours Lost*
    *Romeo and Juliet*
    *A Midsummer Night's Dream*
    *The Merchant of Venice*

1596–1599
    *King John*
    *Richard II*
    *Henry IV, Parts 1 and 2*
    *Henry V*

| 1599–1601 | *The Merry Wives of Windsor* |
| | *Much Ado About Nothing* |
| | *Twelfth Night* |
| | *As You Like It* |
| | |
| 1601–1603 | *All's Well that Ends Well* |
| | *Troilus and Cressida* |
| | *Measure for Measure* |
| | *Julius Caesar* |
| | *Hamlet* |
| | *Macbeth* |
| | *Othello* |
| | |
| 1606–1608 | *King Lear* |
| | *Timon of Athens* |
| | *Coriolanus* |
| | *Antony and Cleopatra* |
| | |
| 1608–1613 | *Pericles* |
| | *Cymbeline* |
| | *The Winter's Tale* |
| | *The Tempest* |
| | *The Two Noble Kinsmen (co-author)* |
| | *Henry VIII (co-author)* |

Appendix D

# READING LIST

~

## ON SHAKESPEARE'S LIFE

Brown, Ivor. *Shakespeare*. Collins, 1949.

Burgess, Anthony. *Shakespeare*. Jonathan Cape, 1970.

Quennell, Peter. *Shakespeare*. Avon Books, 1963.

Rowse, A.L. *William Shakespeare: A Life*. Macmillan, 1963.

Rowse, A.L. *Shakespeare the Man*. Macmillan, 1973.

Schoenbaum, S. *William Shakespeare—a Compact Documentary Life*. Oxford, 1977.

Speaight, Robert. *Shakespeare, the Man and his Achievement*. Dent, 1970.

Wilson, Ian. *Shakespeare—the Evidence*. Headline, 1993.

## ON HIS PLAYS

Bradley, A.C. *Shakespearean Tragedy*

Coghill, Nevill. *Shakespeare's Professional Skills*

Granville Barker, Harley. Prefaces to Shakespeare (*Hamlet, King Lear, Cymbeline, Julius Caesar, Antony and Cleopatra, Coriolanus, Love's Labours Lost, Romeo and Juliet, The Merchant of Venice, Othello*). Princeton University Press, 1946.

Kott, Jan *Shakespeare—Our Contemporary*. Methuen, 1965.

Quiller-Couch, Arthur. *Shakespeare's Workmanship*. Cambridge, 1931.

Wilson, J. Dover. *What Happens in Hamlet*. Cambridge, 1964.

Wilson, J. Dover. *The Fortunes of Falstaff*. Cambridge, 1964.

## ON HIS THEATER

Adams, John Cranford. *The Globe Theatre—its Design and Equipment.* Barnes and Noble, 1961.

Gurr, Andrew. *The Shakespearean Stage.* Cambridge, 1970.

Hodges, C. Walter. *The Globe Restored.* Bonn. 1953.

Speaight, Robert. *Shakespeare on the Stage.* Collins, 1973.

Yates, Francis A. *Theatre of the World,* Routledge and Kegan Paul, 1969.

## ON HIS WRITING

Barton, John. *Playing Shakespeare.* Methuen, 1984.

Bate, Jonathan. *The Genuis of Shakespeare.* Picador, 1997.

Granville Barker, Harley. *On Dramatic Method.* Hill and Wang, 1956.

Hughes, Ted. Preface to *A Choice of Shakespeare's Verse.* Faber, 1971.

Hughes, Ted. *Shakespeare and the Goddess of Complete Being.* Faber, 1992.

Rylands, George. *Words and Music.* Hogarth Press, 1928.

Speaight, Robert. *William Poel and the Elizabethan Revival.*

Spurgeon, Caroline. *Shakespeare's Imagery—and What it Tells Us.* Cambridge, 1935.

## ON HIS TIMES

Brown, Ivor. *How Shakespeare Spent the Day.* Bodley Head, 1973.

Chute, Marchetta. *Shakespeare of London.* Dutton, 1949.

Halliday, F.E. *Shakespeare in his Age.* Duckworth, 1956.

Rowse, A.L. *The Elizabethan Renaissance* (three volumes). Macmillan, 1971–72

Wilson, J. Dover. *Life in Shakespeare's England* (anthology). Cambridge, 1911.

## AND

Wells, Stanley. *Shakespeare—An Illustrated Dictionary.* Oxford, 1976.

Wilson, Edwin, ed. *Shaw on Shakespeare—*An anthology of Bernard Shaw's writings on Shakespeare. Cassell, 1962.

ADRIAN BRINE was born in London, England in 1936, and made his first professional stage appearances as a boy actor in 1949 in Bromley, Kent (the hometown of Michael York). Graduating from Oxford University in 1960, he became a member of the BBC-TV repertory company that was assembled to record the cycle of Shakespeare's history plays under the title An Age of Kings. Later he was appointed staff producer at Dundee Repertory Theatre, Scotland, and was for three years a teacher at L.A.M.D.A. (London Academy of Music and Dramatic Art).

In 1965 he was invited to direct in Brussels and became permanent guest director at the Rideau de Bruxelles, a post he still holds thirty-five years later. After he moved to Europe, he was co-artistic director of the Globe Theatre Company in Amsterdam 1970–77; and from 1980–86 worked as artistic consultant to the Belgian National Theatre.

In 1995 his first production in Paris, Oscar Wilde's *An Ideal Husband* (in a new version by Pierre Laville), won ten nominations for the Prix Molière (the French Tony Award) and was awarded two prizes, one for Best Production.

In 1998 he directed in Paris Dion Boucicault's *London Assurance,* and in 1999 *The Prisoner of Second Avenue* (retitled *Comedie Privee*). He has also directed at the Dormen Theatre in Istanbul and at the Shaw Festival Theatre, Ontario.

He has taught at the Theaterschool in Amsterdam, the Institut National Supérieur des Arts et Spectacles in Brussels, and at the Conservatoire of Geneva.

In 1992 Adrian Brine was decorated by the Belgian government as Chevalier dans l'Ordre de la Couronne, and in 1998 was awarded a Lifetime Achievement Award for his services to the Belgian theater.

He has directed some ten plays of Shakespeare and appeared as an actor in ten others.

MICHAEL YORK was born in England in 1942 and is an alumnus of the National Youth Theatre and of Oxford University. As a professional actor, he performed with Laurence Olivier's new National Theatre company and made his film debut in 1966 in *The Taming of the Shrew*, directed by Franco Zeffirelli for whom he subsequently performed in *Romeo and Juliet* and as John the Baptist in *Jesus of Nazareth*.

York has since expressed his versatility in over fifty films including *Accident, Something for Everyone, Cabaret, The Three Musketeers, Logan's Run, The Island of Dr. Moreau, Fedora,* and more recently in the two *Austin Powers* movies and in *The Omega Code*.

His television work has been equally varied and international and includes *The Forsyte Saga, Great Expectations, Space, The Heat of the Day, Fall from Grace,* and *The Far Country*.

In 1973, York made his American stage debut in the world premiere of Tennessee Williams' *Outcry* on Broadway where he later starred in *Bent, The Crucible,* and *Someone Who'll Watch Over Me*.

He has recorded over fifty audio books including *The Book of Psalms, The Berlin Stories, The English Patient,* and *Brave New World*. His recording of *Treasure Island* was nominated for a Grammy, and he has also made an audio version of his autobiography, *Accidentally on Purpose*.

Recently he has lectured internationally on Shakespeare, Kipling, and the history of acting. He lives in Los Angeles where he serves as Chairman of the California Youth Theatre and on the Western Region Board of the Shakespeare Globe Centre. His services to the arts were recognized with the award of the French Ordre National des Arts et Lettres and the Order of the British Empire.

Adrian Brine and Michael York
*photo by Pat York*